THE
LIMITS OF
CORPORATE
RESPONSIBILITY

THE
LIMITS OF
CORPORATE
RESPONSIBILITY

NEIL W. CHAMBERLAIN

BASIC BOOKS, INC., *PUBLISHERS*

NEW YORK

[PREFACE]

What contributions can business be expected to make to the amelioration of contemporary social problems, for the existence of some of which it must itself assume some responsibility? What are the contours of the relationships between business and society that emerge as business responds to changing social circumstances and pressures? These are the questions to which this book is addressed.

The answers are sought not in a general analysis but by reference to a series of quite specific issues that the large corporation now confronts. I have tried to avoid moralizing and prescribing and to restrict myself to dispassionate analysis, though I suspect I have not been totally successful in that effort.

I acknowledge the financial assistance of the Faculty Research Fund of the Graduate School of Business, Columbia University, and the unflagging and cheerful cooperation of Wilda Hayes and Mercy Garcia in the preparation of the manuscript.

NEIL W. CHAMBERLAIN

1973

[CONTENTS]

THE
LIMITS OF
CORPORATE
RESPONSIBILITY

[1]

THE CORPORATE

SYSTEM

WHAT can the large corporations do about the social problems of our times? The thesis of this book is that they can do remarkably little.

Large numbers of frustrated and impatient citizens are unwilling to accept this conclusion. They view big corporations as virtual empires, their power resting on economic rather than on military might. They feel that with proper use of that power, these large institutions could—if they would—go far toward meeting the clash of races over jobs, housing, and educational opportunities; they could help to restore our cities and to rehabilitate our transportation networks; they could reverse environmental deterioration, restoring to the public clean air and clean water and conserving irreplaceable natural resources.

Many who believe in the potential goodness of our major corporations are convinced that only their present selfishness prevents them from making the desired social contribution. The corporations' drive for profits is unrestrained by any conception of social responsibility. Some exceptional corporations have provided evidence—meager though it is—of what can be done: Xerox, Polaroid, Cummins Engine, and a few others might be cited for their socially oriented behavior. If all major corporations would only recognize the consequences of their present social failures and the social benefits latent in more responsible uses of their power, we could experience a veritable social revolution without bloodshed.

This demand, plea, or hope for corporate responsibility emanates from critics outside the business system. There is, however, a counterpart philosophy on the inside. A few corporate executives, particularly in companies based on high technology, are convinced that they could help to

3

remedy society's ills if only they were given the initiative to apply their scientific techniques—in particular, by approaching society's problems as interrelated issues that require a systems solution, rather than by treating each problem and each locality in a piecemeal, ad hoc, uncoordinated fashion. These are the social technicians—experts in operations research and the application of management science. They know that everything is related to everything else—crime is related to education, just as education is related to housing, and housing is related to employment, and so on in an intricate web of relationships. Their creed is that the system of yesterday is the subsystem of today. What people viewed in the simpler past as a discrete social institution—a "system" in its own right, to be developed and nourished by its own set of functionaries— can effectively perform its role in today's complex society only if it is recognized to be a smaller part of a much larger whole. If we are to get the results we seek, the several parts of which a whole society is composed must be consciously joined together, complementing each other like the pieces of a jigsaw puzzle. The managers of complex business organizations are best equipped to carry out this designing of social systems, responding to the broad objectives that government sets and operating within the familiar and proved framework of the profit incentive. We can call this the Social Engineering Thesis.

The argument of this book is that neither of these approaches has any prospect of implementation and that the only initiatives that can be expected even from our largest and financially strongest corporations will be necessarily limited in scope and substance, barely touching the most grievous social problems. We cannot rely on big business for social reform.

The basis for this view is not a low opinion of business, either in terms of motivation or of efficiency, but a recognition that every business, whatever its size, is in effect "trapped" in the business system that it has helped to create. It is incapable, as an individual unit, of transcending that system and metamorphosing into something else. Hence the dream of the socially responsible corporation that, replicated over and over again, can transform our society is illusory. Moreover, the corporate system of which it is an integral part is not a hierarchically structured and unified whole that can collectively transform itself into a different kind of efficient, productive network capable of re-engineering society to more utopian specifications. The Social Engineering Thesis, if it could materialize at all (itself a dubious proposition), would have to be founded on something other than our present system of more or less "autonomous" corporations.

4

Powerlessness of the Individual Corporation

It is difficult to conceive of our giant corporations, dominant as they are in American society, as being "trapped," or as powerless to effect significant social change. The idea requires some elaboration.

We visualize General Motors and General Electric as empires in themselves, and an empire implies an emperor, and an emperor connotes vast independent authority. But the analogy is imperfect. For all their size, GM and GE are only parts of the network of relationships that binds American society together. Such discretion as they can exercise must be exercised within the limits of that network. Obviously they enjoy considerable independence—they can determine where they will locate their plants, when those plants will operate or shut down, what products they will produce, and what technologies they will employ. We could extend at length the list of discretionary decisions open to them, but such a list would be revealing in its omission of many, if not most, of the matters included under the rubric of social responsibility. To a degree, these might be omitted simply because they have only recently played on our consciousness, so that we do not associate them with matters on which corporate managements normally reflect. But to a larger degree, they are omitted because the management of any single corporation can do relatively little about them, within the framework of the corporate system of which that corporation is an *integral* part.

The prospering corporation can, of course, exercise its social consciousness in various ways. It can lend some of its personnel to serve on community projects on company time, finance the training of the unskilled beyond its own needs, and contract with minority businesses ("black capitalists") even when its needs could be more cheaply met elsewhere. It can even do something about pollution, on a modest scale if its action involves additional out-of-pocket expense, on more substantial lines if (now alerted) it discovers that antipollution investment can actually provide some return.

Even in these limited exercises in social responsibility the individual corporation must recognize two constraints. First, it must show a profit that compares favorably with the profit positions of other major corporations. This is necessary for several reasons. The legal framework vests ultimate corporate authority in a board of directors nominally elected by the stockholders, and incumbent managements must perform well enough to forestall a challenge to their position. The threat of a proxy

5

fight is not an idle one.[1] Further, although internally generated funds provide much of the capital needed by large corporations, it is occasionally necessary to resort to the capital markets for new financing. Whether in the form of equity issues or long-term loans, the terms on which that capital can be secured depend on the price at which the corporation's stock is selling, which in turn reflects its present and prospective profit position. Moreover, a strong profit position is necessary to discourage an attempted takeover by a less socially conscious corporate raider who sees a return on assets that is not being fully realized by a management that may have followed its "corporate conscience" with excessive zeal.

Second, a corporation must maintain a size (preferably a rate of growth) that permits it to continue those facilitating activities—advertising, research and development, personnel policies, public relations—on at least the scale that has brought it to its present position. A decline in size, even a declining rate of growth, creates problems of holding onto and recruiting high-quality talent and of finding places for or dismissing older employees who are then becoming an increasing proportion of the corporation's population, with all the ensuing morale problems that such actions provoke.

Such a fixation on profit and size does not arise because these are necessarily the most desirable objectives that can be imagined, even by a group of corporate executives, but because the company is driven to them by the requirements of its position.

T. V. Learson, former president of IBM, has made the point effectively: "Business usually profits best when it serves the public interest within its ability to do so. But we can never loosen ourselves from the iron law of profit which necessarily limits our freedom of action and puts bounds on what we can do. . . . If a corporation so diverts its energies and resources as to go broke, there is nothing it can do—nothing at all—even if it claims to have a heart and conscience as big as the world."[2]

Sherman Adams, as senior vice president of the First National City Bank of New York, underscores the same point: "In a competitive, market economy, profit-oriented companies simply cannot devote a really sizeable portion of their resources to unprofitable, or even relatively low-profit, activities."[3]

These comments are especially noteworthy because they come from executives of corporations that have sought to show that they are socially responsible. Learson, indeed, is concerned to avoid unduly discouraging young people who "expect our business corporations to become conscious architects of social improvements." There are, he says, a great many things that a corporation can do at its own discretion, even within the constraints of the system. He mentions charitable contributions, support for higher education, and "equal opportunity" policies that seek to remove discrimination. But even in listing these possible fronts for corporate social activity, he unconsciously emphasizes their limitation. Without demeaning the desirability of such corporate actions, we can recognize that they scarcely touch, either substantively or quantitatively, the social needs of our times.

Limited Responsibility

Thus, every corporation and its managers must experience a sense of relative powerlessness to cope with social problems, even though, in the aggregate, large corporations constitute the dominant force in our society. Because their aggregate power is not unified, not truly collective, not organized, they have no way, even if they wished, of redirecting that power to meet the most pressing needs of society or of channeling their enormous aggregate influence in support of new programs designed to cope with the malignant problems arising out of changes in economic and social conditions. Such redirection could occur only through the intermediate agency of government, rewriting the rules (constraints) under which all corporations would operate.

But that approach has very limited appeal to corporations. There is no consensus among them as to how the rules might or should be changed in a way that would permit them to assist in meeting the needs of the times without undermining their present positions, nor is there any instrument available to them for achieving consensus. There is no organizational hierarchy stretching across individual corporate boundaries that can impose its decision on all. Moreover, there is an understandable reluctance to assent to any change except the unavoidable, because changes in the prevailing framework connote concession and retreat—and who knows where that may end unless checked. Perhaps most important, there remains a fear in many corporate headquarters that to build up the instrument of government is to make it less amenable to the restraints to which the corporate community can now subject it. The government stork may become the king of the corporate frogs and wind up swallowing them. Hence the preference of business executives for incremental changes to meet current needs, modest step-by-step

7

actions on the pollution, racial, consumer, and urban fronts, rather than more sweeping institutional reform.

The modest, incremental changes to which the large corporations lend themselves are generally initiated as responses to pressures from outside the system. Those aggrieved by what the corporate system does to them or fails to do for them from time to time give vent to public protest, violent or political. At this point "authorities"—from government, universities, or professional associations—propose remedial measures that usually involve some constraint on the discretion of the individual corporation. But even if these proposals are adopted, the network of relationships is likely to be only slightly modified.

Even when dissatisfactions are concentrated enough, exacerbated enough, or widespread enough to elicit political initiatives seemingly inimical to corporate interests, as notably in the catalog of regulatory actions under the New Deal, the implementation and effectuation of those actions eventually results in changes much more modest and minor than appeared likely to proponents and opponents alike at the time of their adoption. As long as the large corporations remain the focal points of the network of social and economic relations, the innovations are assimilated into the system.

Nor is this so offensive to the public at large. Given the hold that any established order has on so many people and the stake (however little it may seem to some) that they have in its perpetuation, it is a safe conclusion that most people prefer to avoid major institutional change, involving vast unknowns, if there is any prospect that minor program changes will make the system work a little better.

This process of slow, cautious, and modest reform is reinforced by the increased sophistication of the large corporations. In the face of criticism from vocal minorities that they have ignored the impact of their manufacturing operations on the environment, companies like GM and Dow Chemical have established board committees or staff vice presidents charged with evaluating corporate policy in this area. Others have stepped up training programs for blacks (especially in cities, where blacks have become a large proportion of the labor pool from which companies must draw) and have eased a few blacks and women upwards in the organization, in a few instances as far as the boardroom.

Some companies have experimented with a "social audit" designed to measure their social performance and to take its place alongside their financial statements. So far, this rather heady thinking has not produced an operational result, which is not surprising given the difficulty of quantifying the components (just as economists have found it difficult to quantify the "human" factors in cost-benefit analysis applied to public policy). What is apparent, however, is that all such efforts take place within the framework of existing practice.[4]

Other companies have responded to government-subsidized programs in such areas as skill training for the hard-to-employ (both on the job and in the classroom) and large-scale urban redevelopment. They have contracted with local schoolboards to provide "programmed" education where traditional methods were not succeeding and with the federal Department of Housing and Urban Development for experimental programs to increase the supply of low-income housing. These programs are small-scale supplements to the companies' principal operations and usually entail no loss, though sometimes a foregone profit.

The most common corporate response to criticism of a deficient sense of social responsibility has been an augmented program of public relations. Standard Oil of New Jersey, for example, takes an eight-page advertisement in leading magazines to justify offshore drilling and to minimize consequent danger of pollution. Ford Motor Company repeats its message in many media that it is "listening" sympathetically to people's criticisms and will do its best to meet them. Atlantic Richfield Company, in a peculiarly neutral *mea culpa*, sponsors a series of ads with a flavor of conversion on the road to Damascus, which reassures Man that he (and the corporate system) can do better. (One reads: "The real: Man has created a technology that distorts his humanity. The ideal: We can shape a new technology that moves us toward a future which honors the human dimension.")

These varied responses of individual corporations to public criticism serve to reinforce the corporate system and the policy of limited, incremental change in the face of unmet social needs. There is little else that the individual corporation can do. In distinction to the Social Responsibility Thesis and the Social Engineering Thesis, let us label this approach of modest, incremental, assuaging actions the Limited Responsibility Thesis.

In sum, those who ascribe no special power or dominant role to corporations are clearly in error with respect to corporations *in the aggregate;* the American social system is oriented around their operations, giving them an enormous influence that individual corporate managements may indeed be unaware of because they take it so much for granted. The source of that dominance lies not in any coercive power, but in the fact that so many other members of American society identify their interests with the interests of the large corporations. This is not because of any crude sense of loyalty or feeling of affinity: indeed, big business has been a whipping boy for populist causes ever since its emergence, and corporate managers have become accustomed to the pillory. Nevertheless, in contemporary America no other institution does so much for so many. National prosperity depends on corporate prosperity. The welfare of jobholders, stockholders, consumers, and local communities rises and falls with the fortunes of the large corporations. The national identity, from which each citizen derives an important part of his personal identity, is bound up with corporate initiative and enterprise that have given the United States the strongest materialistic base in the world and projected it to a peak position of international influence.

The values that business professes have come to be accepted as national values: material abundance and a pecuniary measure of welfare, voluntaristic activity inhibited by government as little as possible, competitive opportunity for all with a distribution of rewards in accordance with individual achievement. If these values have been subjected to some questioning in recent years, there is little doubt they still remain for most Americans the American creed. As such, they continue to reinforce and protect the position of the large corporation.

But each corporation, while a beneficiary of the power of the corporate system, is likewise constrained by it and has little independent discretion outside the areas which the system specifically allows it. This constraint applies to social initiatives on any significant scale. Hence the basic unreality to corporate managements of the social responsibility with which they are forever being burdened, except for token expressions to show their good intentions. Hence the understandable sense of powerlessness on the part of a dominant class when each member of that class thinks of itself as one, as operationally it must.

But if the Limited Responsibility Thesis is most clearly accurate with respect to the individual corporation, absolving it from the assumption of more sweeping social responsibilities, that thesis overlooks the potential effect on the survival of corporations in their present form (that is, within a corporate system) if responsibility for the solution of expanding social problems is then shunted to other shoulders or ignored.

In the chapters that follow, the abstract propositions of this chapter are given empirical content by an examination of specific problem areas where social reforms have been called for or where prevailing social values have been called into question. In each instance the question is raised: How much initiative for reform can be expected from the "powerful" corporations that dominate our economic landscape? The question is raised, not to invite a predetermined conclusion, but to gain perspective on a plague of social problems that afflict our times.

[2]

CORPORATIONS AND CONSUMERS

AMONG the ways in which business has been called on to be socially responsible, perhaps none is more important than in its treatment of consumers. This involves more than good faith between a corporation and those who buy its products, though this relationship is indeed a significant one, and we shall examine it first. In addition, the interaction between corporation and consumer also involves the promotion of the consumption ethic itself, an ethic on which the prosperity and dominant influence of the large corporations rest.

Corporations can expect to confront new laws protecting consumers. But however restrictive these appear, *within a consumption-oriented society* the mass of consumers will itself ensure that the flow of material gratifications is not curtailed by "excessive" regulation.

Consumer Protection

The ultimate rationale for the existence of business firms, both large and small, lies in their service to consumers. One might suppose, as business spokesmen have often stressed, that management would for that reason assiduously cultivate their customers and avoid any practice that might offend those on whom it depends for its existence. But economic relations, like all human relations, involve many more variables than any simple formulation would indicate. Government regulation of business activity for the protection of consumers goes back for a hundred years. Among the historic landmarks are the Pure Food and Drug Act of

1906 and the Federal Trade Commission Act of 1914. The latter is especially noteworthy because it established the Federal Trade Commission (FTC), which has been made the enforcement agent for a number of subsequent pieces of consumer legislation, including the following: the Wheeler-Lea Act of 1938, which authorized curbs on false advertising; the Wool Labeling Act of 1939 and the Fur Products Act of 1951, which required informative labeling; the Flammable Fabrics Act of 1953, which authorized promulgation and enforcement of standards of flammability of clothing fabrics; and the Textile Fiber Products Identification Act of 1958, which added a requirement of informative advertising on top of the informative labeling which had previously been exacted of wool and fur product manufacturers. More recent legislation, as we shall see, has still further extended the powers and duties of the FTC.

Consumer Protests

During the 1960s, increasing consumer protests gave birth to a movement that quickly acquired the name "consumerism." This movement has no high command or central organization. It is composed of a number of associations, some with interests extending beyond consumption, that are loosely linked at best. It includes some long-standing organizations, for example, labor unions, and others more recently founded, such as student public-interest crusaders. In general, these allied but largely uncoordinated groups have focused on three demands:

1. *The campaign against fraudulent and deceptive practices.* This has for the most part centered on misleading advertising practices. The FTC has responded with citations against Campbell Soup for using marbles to push up the solids in its soups in televised commercials, against Coca-Cola for false implications of nutrient values in its "Hi-C" beverage, against Standard Oil of California for unsubstantiated claims concerning its "F310" additive and for deception in televised demonstrations. The Fair Packaging and Labeling Act of 1966, sponsored by Senator Philip Hart of Michigan, is another aspect of this phase of consumerism.

2. *Demands for safeguards against hazardous or unreliable products.* This campaign has aroused perhaps the greatest interest. Ralph Nader's single-handed attack on the major automobile companies for allegedly

turning out products whose defects annually resulted in thousands of human casualties was given sudden national prominence when GM was exposed in the shabby behavior of shadowing Nader, inferentially to silence him by "getting something on him." Subsequent congressional hearings resulted in the Federal Traffic Safety Act of 1966, which established the Highway Safety Bureau and made it responsible for identifying defects whose correction warranted the recall of cars and for specifying standards of safety for car performance.

That product unreliability was a problem by no means confined to the automobile industry was underscored when Senator Warren Magnuson's Senate Commerce Committee, with the assistance of the Consumers Union, compiled a list of several hundred hazardous products, including numerous electrical appliances, kitchen and garden implements, sprays and cleansers, children's toys, and clothing. Threats to health were found in meats, fish, and poultry (in some instances because production was confined to a single state and hence escaped federal control), as well as in drugs.

Aside from such hazards to health and safety, the poor quality of some manufactured goods has also come under scrutiny. One common complaint has been that both manufacturing companies and their retailers fail to provide adequately for the servicing of products once sold. Product warranties have also come under attack. This device, originally "written by lawyers for the express purpose of protecting the manufacturer against unreasonable product claims from the consumer," [1] has within the last ten years been steadily shorn of this restrictive intent by judicial decisions. The old common-law doctrines of contributory negligence and "privity of contract" (the latter denying a direct contractual relationship between buyer and manufacturer because of the intervening position of the dealer or dealers) have been increasingly eroded. An implied warranty or contract has been found when the manufacturer's advertising claims could reasonably be said to have induced an attitude of trust on the part of the consumer. We shall return to this matter.

3. *Consumer demands for the fuller disclosure of product information.* These have encompassed standard quality grading, clearer identification of the quantity contained in packaged items (sometimes going beyond this to require "unit pricing" by retailers—so many cents per ounce, for example—for ease of price comparison), and special information relevant to particular products. As an example of this last category, the FTC has since 1967 required tire manufacturers to provide information relating weight of car and tire performance.

13

In addition to these three areas of consumer protest-action, a fourth complaint has been voiced, though less frequently and insistently, against the exclusion of foreign products. Tariffs, quotas, or arbitrary standards (such as a minimum size for "mature green" tomatoes) have sometimes deprived consumers of "better buys."

Business Reaction

The business response to such consumer complaints in the past (and frequently still today) has generally been to minimize their significance on the grounds that they originate with a small minority of ideologues and malcontents, that in fact the American public enjoys the highest consumption standards in the world, that such criticisms as have validity relate to the behavior of a small minority of unscrupulous and irresponsible business operators (a phenomenon characteristic of any social group, whether academic, trade unionist, or political), and that competition could be relied on to drive such undesirables from the marketplace.

No one can doubt the vigor of the competitive drive of American business, whatever its occasional lapses in this respect, but what can be doubted is that it will necessarily have the effect that business spokesmen say it will. Certainly the large corporations do not mean to exempt themselves from the discipline of competition. Yet their names appear in the FTC citations along with the small fry, and the consequence is not to drive them from the field.

Indeed, intensive competition among business firms may lead to the very conduct complained of. Exaggerated claims for products, for example, become so widespread that they become an accepted and ethically acceptable method of doing business. After all, what is so sinful about putting marbles in a bowl of soup to make it more appealing on television? Is it any worse than adding artificial color to vegetables and fruits?

But in addition to these more elusive effects, competition may drive firms to cut costs in order to meet rival prices or to achieve profit targets, with some consequent impact on quality. The efficiency experts and corporate budgeters have long emphasized that in mass production minute savings per item can cumulate into a handsome total saving. "Cost pressures often cause manufacturers and suppliers to try to cut corners," the *Wall Street Journal* editorially remarked in looking for an explanation of why "many consumers feel there has been some recent deterioration in what they are offered on the market." [2]

Competition may also lead producers to release new products prematurely. Otherwise, rivals may beat them to the market or in any event reduce their lead time. Moreover, once an innovation is in the field and proves popular, the pressure is on competing companies to reproduce it. Paul Brodeur's account of the detergent industry's rapid movement into enzyme detergents, despite lack of knowledge about their effects and subsequent indications that these might be serious, concludes:

What appears most likely is that speculation about the effects of proteo- lytic-enzyme detergents and their accompanying protein impurities will go on for some time to come. In the meantime, new techniques of encapsulating en- zyme dust in detergent granules may or may not take care of any future health problems in the factory and in the home. Whatever happens, the fact remains that the major enzyme-detergent manufacturers are still revising their enzyme products even as they continue to sell them by the millions of boxes to millions of consumers all over the world. If no problem develops in the coming months or years, it seems safe to conclude that it will not be because any intelligent decision has been made by anyone in a position of responsibility for the public welfare. It will be luck. And even if the public should be lucky on this occa- sion, the question remains whether it will be similarly fortunate the next time a substance with unknown biological effects finds its way into practically every home across the land within a few months. [3]

If competition cannot be relied on to protect the consumer, business associations have sometimes suggested self-regulation. In the matter of product reliability, for example, the board of directors of the U.S. Chamber of Commerce adopted a statement on warranties setting forth "basic elements to be recognized in every warranty and guarantee and emphasizing the importance of clarity and nontechnical language in product warranties and guarantees." [4] Codes of appropriate behavior have been proposed or adopted by industry and trade associations in a variety of fields for a number of years. A major difficulty with such ventures is that they are seldom enforceable. [5]

Underlying Conditions

Yet the defensive attitude that business has commonly adopted is not wholly unwarranted. If the consumer has a problem, it is not solely because the conscienceless corporation is interested only in his pocketbook. There has been a proliferation of new products that most consumers find desirable, but this makes the job of informing oneself on

15

their respective merits all the more difficult. Many products have increased in complexity, so that operating instructions are not easily mastered. Perhaps consumption can no longer be regarded, in Benthamite fashion, as an effortless pleasure. After questioning business firms with respect to the servicing of their products, the FTC reported:

> The consumers themselves are said to be a major source of difficulties. While they insist on elaborate design and selective operational characteristics, they are unwilling to read and to follow the instructions which outline procedures requisite to the proper functioning of the product. Sometimes this results in damage or malfunctioning for which they blame the manufacturer. Frequently a serviceman is summoned and finds that he need only explain to the consumer how to operate the product.[6]

Furthermore, though mass production techniques have brought more and more goods within the financial reach of more and more families, mass production has its own deficiencies. Quality control becomes institutionalized on the basis of statistical probability. Repetitive, fractionalized operations dry up workers' interest in their jobs and sap any sense of personal responsibility for the product. The consequence is an almost predictable increase in the proportion of defective items, many of which will be caught and rejected, but some of which will get into marketing channels. To tighten up on quality controls would increase the cost and the price. It seems preferable to risk complaints from the few in order to price lower for the many.

As to limitation of foreign competition, businessmen are joined in this effort by their own labor unions, which are seeking to protect the jobs of their members.

Consumer complaints are, of course, not peculiar to the American private-enterprise economy. Socialist countries are scarcely noted for the quality or design of their products. That comparison, however, evades rather than meets the problem under scrutiny.

Opposition to Regulation

We have already noted some government responses to consumerism, and others could be added. Thus we now have "truth-in-packaging," "truth-in-advertising," and "truth-in-lending" laws; approximately twenty-five million cars were recalled by auto manufacturers in the first five years since passage of the Highway Safety Act; cigarette advertising has been banned from television, and printed advertising for cigarettes is required to carry warnings of health hazard, made "clear and conspicuous" by FTC specification of the type size. These are only recent highlights in what could be an extensive catalog of legislation and administrative regulation intended to protect consumer interests.

The effect of this substantial intervention by the federal government has been to induce a sense of paranoia on the part of a number of businessmen, who feel victimized by politicians seeking easy popularity with the mass consuming public. Automobile manufacturers fear that consumer and antipollution legislation will increase the costs of production beyond the customer's ability to pay.[7] The paint industry warns that sanctions against the use of lead in paint would increase paint prices, reduce sales, and force many small retailers and manufacturers out of business.[8] Representatives of the advertising industry argue that an FTC proposal requiring that deceptive ads be offset by "corrective ads" would result in "product suicide." [9] More generally, it is argued that however limited the impact of any single regulatory action may be, the cumulative result will be to put producers in an economic straitjacket, sacrificing the corporate goose that lays the consumers' golden eggs. Some have gone so far as to hint at a "conspiracy" against business, or an open attack on the American system by antagonists who use consumerism as a weapon.[10]

Opposition by business to regulation has taken a number of familiar forms. It has lobbied in Congress for defeat or modification of proposed measures.[11] It has sometimes brought economic pressure to bear on media to induce them to oppose, or to punish them for favoring, unwanted legislation.[12] It has organized sympathetic groups on its behalf. It has sometimes engaged in delaying or obfuscating tactics.[13] It has sought to rally public support by warning of the adverse effects which would follow from regulation. And when regulatory action has been taken, despite these efforts, it has sometimes fought its validity in the courts.

Limits to Regulatory Effectiveness

The expressed fears on which such opposition has often been based (whether actually believed by those who voice them or exaggerated for effect) have almost always proved excessive and occasionally groundless. The reason lies in the built-in limits to effective governmental regulation. One is the limitation of resources—principally staff—to carry out the regulation provided for. Another is a possible lack of zeal on the part of the administrator to use the powers given him, perhaps out of caution, perhaps because of the need to establish priorities within the framework of his limited budget, perhaps because he is lukewarm to some of the provisions of the legislation he is charged with administering.

An example of the interaction of these budgetary and personal considerations is provided by the decision of the FTC to require producers to justify their advertising claims. Such authority had been provided by the Wheeler-Lea Act of 1938, but it was not until 1971 that it was actually used. In the years since its founding, the FTC had acquired a reputation as a do-nothing agency, a label applied to it by a recent study group of the American Bar Association that had recommended that it be activated or abolished. When the chairman of that study group, Miles Kirkpatrick, was appointed chairman of the FTC in 1970, he was in effect given a mandate to act on his own recommendation. There followed a marked increase in zealousness in consumer protection. Among other things, the authority to require the substantiation of advertising claims was put to use. Here the personal element was involved. The consequence of this stepped-up activity was in part what the FTC hoped for. Both producers and their advertising agencies combed out of their advertising copy some of the more dubious language, which might have fallen under FTC condemnation. But the campaign was not wholly successful, as staff inadequacies had their effect.

In a number of product categories, beginning with automobiles and continuing through tires, TV sets, cold remedies, electric shavers, air conditioners, and toothpastes (with more to come), the FTC has ordered advertisers to document their claims. The commission's idea is that, by putting the documentation before a skeptical public, the press and consumerists will point accusing fingers at perpetrators of fraudulent claims.

In practice, however, the idea has not worked out very well. Automobile advertisers, for example, flooded the overworked FTC staff with a mass of technical material that has taken many months to evaluate. It concluded that 13 of 75 claims were not supported by empirical data, 21 had incomplete data, and 32 could not be evaluated at all because the terminology was too technical.[14]

When one considers the lengthy list of products manufactured, the frequency of product innovations and modifications, and the possible variations in advertised claims, the burden of discharging the task that the FTC has assumed seems beyond the capacities of even a zealous chairman. One can readily imagine that a few chairmen down the road the FTC will come under a leadership which will moderate the present campaign. Industry need only curb its worst advertising excesses, which is scarcely a hardship and may be all to its own good, and be patient.

Another limitation on effective regulatory action in the consumer field is the number of sometimes overlapping laws and agencies involved. In the matter of enzyme detergents, for example, the FTC first questioned the possible hazardous nature of the product, but the Food and Drug Administration (FDA), which some considered to be the appropriate authority to carry out the necessary research, preferred not to be involved. Detergents did not, it believed, come under the Federal Food, Drug, and Cosmetic Act (which would have required FDA approval of the test data submitted to it by the manufacturer), but rather under the Federal Hazardous Substances Labeling Act (which makes the manufacturer responsible for determining the safety of a product under criteria set forth in the act). ". . . the FDA people were playing it safe by staying strictly within the terms of what they took to be their given legal authority." [15]

The same cautious approach was shown by the FDA in connection with intravenous feeding solutions manufactured by Abbott Laboratories. Although the agency knew in January 1971 that these solutions were somehow related to an outbreak of blood poisoning that had resulted in several deaths, and in early March had found that "a large percentage of the Abbott solutions were contaminated with the infectious bacteria responsible for the blood poisoning," it did not recommend against their use until March 22. In explaining why action had not been taken more promptly, the FDA commissioner said: "You've got to understand that all we had at that time was very preliminary data. We believe that the precautions [recommended to hospitals in using the solutions] could allow the solutions to be used safely." [16]

Apart from limitations inherent in the bureaucratic process, there are also difficulties in enforcing compliance with administrative orders. Sometimes this is built into the legislation itself. The Fair Packaging and Labeling Act, for example, provides that the Secretary of Commerce must first determine that an "undue proliferation" of weights or measures of packages handicaps consumers in making value comparisons and then request the producers and distributors involved to participate in drawing up a set of voluntary standards. If for a year after the Secretary has requested such participation the industry gives no evidence of intention to move, or if it has participated in drafting standards but is not observing them, then the Secretary is to report to Congress "promptly" and recommend whether Congress should impose its own standards on the recalcitrant industry. This is hardly a recipe for effective enforcement of the presumed intent of the act. (It was, however, a "compromise" formula that was necessary to secure passage of the act.) [17]

In those cases where the regulatory agency must go to court to secure compliance, the action complained of may continue for several years before a final court decision. "Experience has shown that cases in which the FTC charges deceit take years to wend their way through the commission and subsequent court tests. . . . Admen know, too, that in practice, most controversial ad campaigns are ended long before a final decision is reached and a consent order signed." [18]

Just as budgetary and staff limitations prevent effective administration, they likewise prevent effective enforcement. The government is put in the position of choosing which cases are important enough to warrant the necessary costs in staff time in prosecuting them.[19] It is scarcely surprising, then, that Betty Furness, President Johnson's special assistant for consumer affairs, should conclude:

> Some of the laws which have been enacted under promising consumer protection titles right up to this session of Congress come close to being name-only bills. Or the limited appropriation, limited administrative or enforcement staff provided tends to make them "name only. . . ."
> Such laws deceive consumers into believing they have been given more protection than they actually have. The industry intended for regulation may have gained more protection than the consumer. With a law on the books, there will be less public pressure on the Congress, and it will be quite some time before Congress can get up the steam to amend and strengthen the law.[20]

Strict Liability

One other limitation on the effectiveness of consumer protection we have already noted—the inability to judge, in the absence of any experience, the effects of some new products, particularly drugs and chemicals. The unpredictability of what is not known or even guessed at, or if suspected is not testable or ascertainable with present knowledge, may allow products to go unregulated for some time. Should such a product be banned until it is "cleared"? And what constitutes clearance—when can we know for sure that no adverse side effects may result? If the product is permitted to be marketed and subsequent experience or new knowledge confirms a hazard, are those users who have been injured entitled to compensation from the producer because he marketed something concerning whose injurious effects he *could* have had no knowledge? Should he be held culpable for trading on lack of knowledge, or should he be excused for that reason? This is the case of thalidomide, of lung cancer from cigarettes before the relationship between the two was known, and of enzyme detergents.[21]

Extend the issue further. Assume a product that is normally safe but is rendered hazardous through faulty production or processing—a new car with a defective steering column, canned foods that have developed botulism. To what extent is the producer responsible if he has exercised every reasonable precaution? Can he be held liable for the safe quality of every item he produces for sale, no matter under what conditions of *mass* production?

Push the matter still further. Is a manufacturer responsible for injuries resulting from his product even if it is safe under "normal" use? Is a clothing manufacturer liable for injuries sustained by someone wearing clothing made of artificial fibers who sustains burns when another person accidentally touches him with a cigarette that ignites that clothing? What of the child who suffocates by drawing a plastic bag over his head; is the maker of the plastic bag at fault? We could extend at length hypothetical cases of injuries from products that under some conditions become hazardous. How establish an equitable principle of producer responsibility in the interests of consumer protection?

Actual—not hypothetical—situations such as these have given rise to a movement to hold producers to a strict liability for the effects of their products. Until recently common-law precedents protected the manufacturer from responsibility to the ultimate consumer even for products that are defective due to negligence in their production. This was under the "privity of contracts" doctrine, which held that any warranty, expressed or implied, did not "run with the goods," in the phrase often used. The consumer could seek satisfaction only from the retailer who had sold him the defective product. The retailer, in turn, could recover if at all only from the wholesaler, and so on back up the marketing chain. Only at the final step of the complaint process (the first step of the marketing process) was the manufacturer called to account.

In recent years, court decisions have steadily eroded this doctrine and have held the manufacturer of defective products directly accountable to the customer by virtue of the direct relationship between the two through the media of advertising. Television, in particular, effected this change of view. As one attorney explains this development: "Television put the manufacturers themselves—of everything from toothpaste to automobiles and office copying machines—right in the customer's living room—and even his bedroom. Express representations as to product superiority, safety, and other such benefits were made directly to the consumer. In the eyes of the law, such direct contact constituted a promise by the manufacturer of what we term the 'merchantability' of his product." [22]

Thus came a shift from the traditional view of consumer purchases as private, contractual relationships with the immediate seller, and a shift, too, away from the traditional supplementary defense of the producer that "contributory negligence" on the part of consumers absolved him from responsibility. The law came to recognize a more general imputed relationship between the producing firm and its consumer constituency. In the words of the U.S. Chamber of Commerce's Council on Trends and Perspective on Business and the Consumer:

> There has been a fundamental shift from the principle that all business is essentially private and accountable only to stockholders and the free marketplace to legal doctrines that make large enterprises, in particular, "quasi-public," and thus more and more accountable to the general public. This change is further reflected in the shift from laws which impose minimal liabilities on enterprising activities toward laws which impose *strict liabilities* on industry even for unintentional and non-negligent harm inflicted on consumers and other groups in society.[23]

Professor Friedrich Kessler has pointed out that the movement toward strict liability was accompanied by an enlargement of the concept of defective product. Not only the unit made hazardous by faulty or negligent manufacturing processes but products whose design made them hazardous became the basis for consumer action. "Furthermore, a product not inherently defective will be treated as defective if its use has caused harm because of improper directions or inadequate warning. Even unforeseeability of harm, given the state of available knowledge, has, occasionally, not afforded an excuse from liability. And assemblers have not been excused simply because they bought from otherwise reliable suppliers and were not negligent in inspecting. Strict liability is therefore far more than negligence liability in disguise." [24]

The public policy basis for strict liability has been grounded on a series of propositions embodied in judicial decisions: that simply by marketing a product, a company assumes a responsibility to anyone who may be injured by it; that the public has a right to expect that reputable sellers will stand behind their goods; that as a matter of public policy, the burden of accidental injuries caused by a product should be borne by those who distribute it and should be treated as a cost of production against which liability insurance can be obtained.[25]

The doctrine of the equitable placement of the burden of injuries sustained in the course of using a product was nicely set forth in a California case:

Corporations and Consumers

Even if there is no negligence, public policy demands that responsibility be fixed wherever it will most effectively reduce the hazards to life and health inherent in defective products that reach the market. It is evident that the manufacturer can anticipate some hazards and guard against the recurrence of others, as the public cannot. Those who suffer injury from defective products are unprepared to meet its consequences. The cost of an injury and the loss of time or health may be an overwhelming misfortune to the person injured, and a needless one, for the risk of injury can be insured by the manufacturer and distributed among the public as a cost of doing business. It is to the public interest to discourage the marketing of products having defects that are a menace to the public. If such products nevertheless find their way into the market it is to the public interest to place the responsibility for whatever injury they may cause upon the manufacturer, who, even if he is not negligent in the manufacture of the product, is responsible for its reaching the market. However intermittently such injuries may occur and however haphazardly they may strike, the risk of their occurrence is a constant risk and a general one. Against such a risk there should be general and constant protection and the manufacturer is best situated to afford such protection.[26]

Such a public policy, if adopted, would carry the possibility of broadening into a general "consumer protection" system comparable to workmen's compensation, where fault is not at issue but the hazard is assumed to be inescapable in the functioning of the economy. In a high consumption economy, where products have become sufficiently complex and the processes by which they are produced sufficiently specialized, can it not likewise be expected that consumers will from time to time be subjected to hazard through no particular fault of their own or of anyone else, but simply as a by-product of the economic system?

Limits on Strict Liability

Predictably businessmen have reacted with despair and frustration; the paranoid effect asserts itself. Against the consumer activist who dins into the public ear that if we can go to the moon, surely we can guarantee the quality of our simpler consumer goods, how can the businessman get across his defensive position that a journey to the moon is a monumentally specialized custom effort sparing little expense and financed by government, while guaranteeing product quality involves a maze of mass-production operations governed by the principle of least-cost enforced by competitive conditions? He reacts as he has typically reacted in the past in the face of restrictive legislation or judicial action: he protests that the result will be to drive many businesses to the wall, spread unemployment, leave many communities without a tax base—in short, economic catastrophe.

But his despair is premature. Strict liability, like all regulatory legislation, carries its own limitations. If the strictness is excessive, it will be moderated in its application. If enforcement proves impossible, the standards will go by default. If producers are held more broadly responsible for any adverse effects of their products, even in the face of no negligence on their part and negligence on the part of the consumer, then at some point rising costs will force the public itself, or its representatives, to set "reasonable" limits to such no-fault consumer protection. The many who would be disadvantaged by higher prices would grumble enough to override the many fewer who would be seriously affected by product failures. Or if innovation is slowed because producers have been made wary of unforeseeable consumer hazards in the use of new products, the consequent slowing down of new job creation and income growth can be counted on to elicit a reaction limiting producer liability in one way or another.

One effect of the movement towards stricter product liability seems predictable: it will focus attention on the large corporations, those that are the most visible. They are responsible for the mass-produced goods that are most likely to give rise to product hazards and failures, partly as a matter of statistical probability and partly because of the difficulty of adequately controlling the innumerable specialized links in the manufacturing-marketing chain. At the same time, by spreading risk, by relying on specialized and sophisticated managerial and legal talent, and by concentrating so many allied interests in their orbit, they are also the firms that are best able to weather the costs first of challenging the new standards or regulations and then of accommodating to them. Whatever system of consumer protection evolves is thus likely to be more compatible with their modes of operation than with those of small-scale enterprise, a fact that emphasizes still further their central role in the economic system. This is not to imply that they will obtain a favored position for themselves—indeed, they are more likely to feel discriminated against *because* they are large—but that stricter liability for consumer protection can be made workable only if it takes cognizance of its close causal relationship to mass production. In doing so, a consumer-protection system will largely gear its criteria and procedures to the large corporations responsible for production for the masses.[27]

Impact of Consumerism on the Corporate System

Whatever regulatory controls may be forthcoming, of one thing we can be certain: business will be able to cope with them. That is indeed the working premise of the regulators.

We can reasonably expect an amelioration of problems relating to effective warranties, improved product service, curbs on misleading advertising and trickster marketing methods. It would be foolish, however, to expect any change in the cultivation by business of continued growth in consumer demand or any loss of enthusiasm for a GNP whose basic characteristic is that it continue to expand on the part of a society depending on that result for job and income security and a rising standard of living.

It would also be excessively optimistic to expect any marked improvement in product quality or the elimination of health and safety hazards in the use of products. Here amelioration will take the form of compensation—the movement toward stricter liability that we noted. Producers can develop ever more refined techniques of quality control, but complex products, fragmented production processes, continuing innovation, and the inability to remove the human factor altogether all guarantee that faulty products will escape into the marketing network.

The anonymity of the individual employee in large-scale production and far-flung marketing processes eliminates the sense of personal responsibility for any end result. Historically, an artisan was responsible for a whole product, and customarily he produced for a local market where social pressures reinforced whatever pride he took in his performance. All this changed once Western society had embarked on the path of specialization. With the rise of the entrepreneur, whose contribution was that he coordinated the labor of others for a profit without himself laboring, with the extension of the market through the growth and dispersion of population and improved forms of transportation, and with a continuing search for technological innovations to lower costs of production, the days of the independent artisan were over. He became an employee of an enterprise, assigned to certain repetitive tasks—a status to which the skilled worker did not easily adjust, as attested to throughout the nineteenth century by the recurrent protests against the "wages system" and by the persistence of the illusory dream that economic independence could be regained if workers could establish their own cooperative workshops.

25

The profit drive stimulated growth in the size of corporations, both for the economies of large-scale production and the absorption of actual competitors or the inhibition of potential competitors. The gap widened between the independent artisan and the employee who sold himself by the hour and was assigned to ever more fragmented tasks that he was required to perform at specified speeds, sometimes in prescribed ways. Galsworthy's story of the old bootmaker who continued at his trade until age and the slow loss of his old clientele finally closed his shop— an anachronism who survived briefly in an age taken over by a new breed—is symbolic of the passing of a way of life. The focus of society gradually shifted from the learning of a trade, a production orientation, to the earning of an income, a consumption orientation. Nowhere was this shift more marked than in the United States.

This displacement of small-scale producer interests with consumption interests in a society founded on an egalitarian ideology gave a distinctly non-Marxian flavor to economic development in the United States. Once the shift in focus had been adjusted to, everyone could look forward to increasing satisfaction—quite in contrast to Marx's immiserization of the proletariat. Only the nature of the satisfaction had changed. The movement was away from individualism, with its high component of control over one's *activity,* toward organization, which allowed little control over activity, but compensated everyone with new and increasing rewards; this was perhaps a more lopsided form of existence, but one that all the members of a growing society could share. The dominant group came to consist of those who control and manage the economic organizations that make the consumer satisfactions possible, but their position of dominance is maintained only if they continue to satisfy the mass-consumption appetite.

In the resulting corporate system there is a built-in concern with innovation, which captures the consumer's fancy and therefore can be said to satisfy his needs better, and a fundamental unconcern with the quality considerations that had been important in the artisan's life. Quality is now important only if it provides a competitive advantage, and not for any psychological reward it provides to those who make the product. To build something extra into a product—in terms of quality and aesthetics —which does not give a cost-compensating competitive advantage would simply be inefficient, adversely affecting the return on investment, the standard by which the desirability of any discretionary business decision is now judged. The very nature of competitive, private-enterprise, consumptionist society is precisely to proliferate products, to seek aggressively to sell them to a mass market, emphasizing differences (however trivial) with rival products and underplaying weaknesses, cutting costs of production to realize as large a rate of return as possible.

No society can dispense with some concept of profit as a gauge of efficiency, in view of the inescapable scarcity condition. Profit, in the efficiency sense, is basically an expression of opportunity cost—if more labor or material is used in producing certain goods, less is available for producing others. But when this efficiency aspect of the profit concept is tied to a distributive aspect—that the "something" that is left over as a result of more efficient operations accrues to a particular class of people (the stockholders) who differ from the producers, then the stage is set for unconcern with quality except as it produces a profit. In an egalitarian, consumption-oriented society, the objective of bringing an ever larger array of goods to the masses goes hand in hand with the objective of shaving costs by whatever means does *not* sacrifice customer appeal. The product itself is made more acceptable at the same time that it is devalued. The advertising linkage between sex appeal and product appeal is easily understandable.

Each person will make his own judgment as to whether this is for good or for ill; the result pleases some and displeases others. The choice is one of values. It is inconceivable that any mass-consumption society could be based on a quality standard. The latter requires that the producer receive part of his reward from the pleasure of creating, which reduces the output and directs a larger proportion of it to privileged classes who can command it. The artist (who was originally viewed as an artisan) illustrates the point nicely. Mass consumption, on the other hand, relies on mass production, which necessarily thwarts the pleasure of creation but substitutes, for all, pleasures of consumption once reserved for the privileged. A mass-consumption society is likely to produce proportionately fewer Beethovens and many more Beatles. It will also produce Chevrolets that look like Cadillacs. Sumptuary differences are eroded. Egalitarianism removes the finer distinctions of quality and distributes the resulting "leveled" output more widely.

This impact of mass consumption on quality has been observed, fittingly enough, by Henry Ford II, though he attributes the result to consumers' lack of perception rather than to the corporate system itself:

> The most effective discipline over product quality is the long-range impact of reputation on a company's sales and profits. . . . When a company offers a really bad product or service, the word gets around, and the company suffers long after the product has been corrected.
> The discipline of the market is limited, however, by the customer's tastes and judgment. Improvements in reliability and service may add more to costs

and prices than they add to the customer's perception of value at the point of sale. The average customer will often pass up the product that offers reliability and good service at a higher price, in favor of the product that is cheaper, or looks better or offers more new features.[28]

Ford's conclusion that "the sooner customers learn to buy on the basis of reliability and service, the faster manufacturers will improve reliability and service," substitutes these two considerations (on which incremental improvements *can* be made) for quality in its historic and more fundamental meaning, involving the substance of the product itself, which depends on an individual's investment of himself in the product he produces, something the system of mass production and mass consumption cannot allow.

The same basic limitation applies to the regulation of advertising. Whatever the FTC may do to curb the excesses of particular advertising appeals, the role of advertising as an institution remains intact: it continues to reinforce the consumer orientation on which the existing economic system is based. The late David M. Potter underscored this insightfully by identifying advertising in its modern usage as an American invention and classifying it as "one of the very limited group of institutions which can properly be called 'instruments of social control,'" such as church and school. "What is basic is that advertising, as such, with all its vast power to influence values and conduct, cannot ever lose sight of the fact that it ultimately regards man as a consumer and defines its own mission as one of stimulating him to consume or to desire to consume." [29]

The pervasive influence of this institution on culture is best illustrated by its impact on the forms of communication, which address themselves to mass audiences as carriers of the advertising on which their revenues largely depend. To Potter, a fixed cycle was virtually inescapable: circulation is necessary to win advertising revenue, and advertising revenue is necessary to price newspapers and magazines within the reach of the consuming masses, with the result that their content is designed (like any mass-produced product) to appeal to large numbers. This effect is even more pronounced in the case of radio and television, which depend exclusively on advertising revenue. "The program or the article becomes a kind of advertisement in itself. . . . Its function is to induce people to accept the commercial, just as the commercial's function is to induce them to accept the product." [30] This institutional role which has devolved on advertising and its relation to the means of communication remain even when marginal modifications are required in specific advertising content; such regulation need not significantly disturb the underlying social function.

One other cultural effect of advertising should be briefly noted now, though we shall have occasion to examine later the more general problem it raises. Printed materials, with their appeals to buy, bypassed the nonreading public, which was heavily concentrated in the poverty sectors. Radio made a greater impact on this group, but television, more than any other medium, has dramatized and glamorized the gospel of consumption, raising expectations even among the poor. If this was the American way of life, why were they being left out? It is an unprovable but reasonable hypothesis that television, more than any other single factor, created the welfare movement of the 1960s, which—merging with the civil rights movement—caused all the major cities to assume partial support of millions of individuals, especially blacks, who had previously been more willing to accept their meager lot.

To sustain a consumer-oriented, egalitarian society requires cutting the disadvantaged in on the televised goodies for the masses.[31] Hence the movement towards expansion of the welfare system. Hence the extension of product lines to cheaper (shoddier but eye-catching) merchandise. Hence the development of methods of extending credit to the poor in ways that distribute the risk. As David Caplovitz concludes in his perceptive study of the low-income consumer: "A fairly intricate system of sales-and-credit has evolved in response to the distinctive situation of the low-income consumer and the local merchant. . . . Almost no one—however great a risk—is turned away. Various mechanisms sift and sort customers according to their credit risk and match them with merchants ready to sell them the goods they want. Even the family on welfare is permitted to maintain its self-respect by consuming in much the same way as its social peers who happen not to be on welfare." [32] Hence also the increasing "hidden" redistribution of income through pilferage and theft, which become accepted as a "normal" cost of doing business and get built into insurance premiums and passed along to paying customers.

In the light of so pervasive a consumption orientation, the ascetic recommendations of Nicholas Johnson, a crusading member of the Federal Communications Commission during his term, have an otherworldly quality:

If you start looking around for simplification, for ways to make you less possession-bound and give you more chance to participate in your life, the opportunities are endless. Start by searching your house or apartment for things you can throw away. Ask yourself, "If I were living in the woods, would I spend a day going to town to buy this aerosol can?" Look for simple substitutes.

Take bicarbonate of soda, for example. You can substitute it for the following products: toothpaste, gargle and mouthwash, burn ointment, stomach settlers, room fresheners, fire extinguisher, icebox cleaner, children's clay, baking powder, and so forth. And it costs only 12 cents a box! [33]

Such a style of living takes its place as a lesser version of Thoreau's *Walden* existence—touching in its idealism but out of touch with reality. It may win a few converts but—like the modest incremental changes made for consumer protection—it will not shake the corporate system. The roots of that system are sunk deep in a generalized consumption orientation.

[3]

CORPORATIONS
AND THE PHYSICAL
ENVIRONMENT

THE centrality of consumption as a social value is splendidly displayed in the matter of environmental quality. Public alarms over pollution and resource exhaustion lead to legislative controls and regulatory actions. These can be modulated, "within reason," with incremental effects on the environment. But if they begin to bite, in the sense of threatening consumption through higher prices and taxes, industry can count on a reduction in the alarm level. Not only industry's ox but society's own horsepower is being gored. Industry's responsibility to the environment is thus limited by society's conception of the good life—a conception that, as we observed in the preceding chapter, can be traced back ultimately to values inculcated by the corporate system itself.

No single corporation—whatever its size or however socially sensitive its management—can break out of this institutionalized constraint.

The Dark Underside of Economic Growth

Concern for the conservation of natural resources has a long history. Originating in aesthetic revulsion at the commercial despoliation of natural resources such as timberlands, scenic areas, and animal life, it eventually extended also to outcries against the unrestricted and wasteful exploitation of land and fossil fuels. Concern with pollution also has a long history. It early expressed itself in abhorrence of the concentration of smoke in Europe's growing cities and the fetid atmosphere of the "Satanic mills" of the industrial revolution. This latter, however, was viewed as a matter of entrepreneurial greed, a kind of class conflict rather than a general social disaster.

Present fears concerning depletion and pollution are more widespread, embracing imminent dangers both to life as we know it and to life itself. They are expressed in picturesque concepts such as "spaceship earth," which views the planet as a vessel in space, whose stock of provisions are all there is to sustain whatever the number of passengers, and so both provisions and number of passengers must be managed carefully. Others have described ours as a "throughput economy," which mines the earth for the materials out of which it fashions articles of consumption for temporary enjoyment; these, once used, are thrown back on the earth as though it were a dumpheap. The "mines" become exhausted and the dumpheap grows.

Let us agree at the outset that the problems of depletion and pollution are basically the same in that both involve the using up of natural resources. Pollution uses up air and water, just as extraction uses up minerals. Pollution reduces people to using air and water of inferior quality, just as mineral extraction drives producers to lower-grade ores. Presumably the producer bears the cost in the latter case but not in the former, but in both cases it is the consumer who ultimately pays, either a money cost or a real cost, and in any event this distinction is one that could conceivably be erased by appropriate forms of taxation on the producer, a subject with which we shall deal later. Production that takes place without pollution may nevertheless involve depletion, by dispersing scarce natural resources, but that distinction too, if important, could presumably be met by some form of "recovery" tax or regulation. The antipollution movement is founded on the "discovery" that air and water are natural resources that should not be squandered as though they were unlimited in quantity. They are now appreciated as scarce resources requiring economic use like any other resource. Thus, whether our discussion deals with one or the other, it relates to both.

In the face of smoke and smog, fishkills from oil spills, and beaches unfit for bathing, pollution control has become, in the enduring phrase of Oliver Wendell Holmes, Jr., a "felt necessity" of the times. Our economic system, with its expanding production and consequent increased use of resources and discard of wastes, has come to be viewed by many as responsible for both depletion and pollution of the environment. But this raises an intriguing question. Until just a few years ago, economic growth was viewed as the preeminent national objective. Countries vied with one another to attain comparatively higher rates of increase of GNP. The United Nations proclaimed the 1960s to be the development decade, with a general target for each country of a doubling of its national income. If such growth-mindedness is now regarded skeptically, even negatively, we may justifiably wonder why, within the space of only a few years, economic growth has changed from being a gleam in the eye of many intelligent observers and has become instead a mote. How has it come about that industrial dynamics, until recently viewed as a multiplier of the earth's riches, can now be regarded by some as a despoiler of man's real wealth?

There is no agreed-upon answer to those questions, but three possible causes are most commonly seized on, singly or collectively. These are: (1) the increase in population, (2) the spread of affluence, and (3) the greater impact of technology. Let us examine these briefly.

POPULATION

As the numbers of people multiply, they tend to deteriorate the physical environment, both because they require greater absolute quantities of limited resources and because it is more difficult to maintain the quality of the environment in which they live. The population of the United States alone has increased from 123 million in 1930 to 205 million in 1970. The added millions obviously can be sustained only by using more resources. Some of these are replenishable, at least within present population levels; food production can still be expanded without "using up" the land. But richer deposits of minerals are depleted that much faster and are not replaceable; inferior sources have to be developed. And at some level of continued population increase, one can anticipate competition for alternative uses of land—whether it must be held for additional food production or whether it can be used for highways to carry the larger number of automobiles, or for more housing for the larger number of families, or for expanded recreational areas. Technological improvement in the use of natural resources may delay the day of forced choice; methods of food production (improved fertilizers or seeds or methods of insect control) may provide greater yields; better methods of extraction and reclamation may do the same for minerals and fossil fuels; the automobile may give way to improved forms of transportation, and new forms of housing may be developed. Nevertheless, if the number of people continues to increase, at some point in the future more intense pressure on resources can be confidently predicted. The Malthusian trap cannot forever be avoided *if* population continues

33

to grow. Optimists simply have faith that population growth will level off soon enough to forestall major disaster, as seems to have happened in the United States.

It is not only the growth in absolute numbers that is important, however. It is also their distribution. The increasing concentration of people in the cities leads to the interrelated problems of water and air pollution. "Over half of the population is crowded into only one percent of the nation's land space, and two-thirds occupy 9% of the land. Manufacturing, power plants, wasteburning units and transportation facilities are also highly concentrated in this small area."[1] Cities also give rise to "noise pollution," perhaps the most recently discovered of our forms of environmental degradation.

AFFLUENCE

"Rising affluence is at least as important as a growing population in creating additional demands on the supply of natural resources," the Council of Economic Advisers reports,[2] and it documents this conclusion by pointing out that per capita consumption expenditures, in constant (1958) prices, have risen from $1,145 in 1929 to $2,323 in 1970.

Professor Jean Mayer of the Harvard Center for Population Studies has strongly emphasized this impact of affluence on the reduction in physical amenities and the quality of social life in the developed economies:

> Malthus was concerned with the steadily more widespread poverty that indefinite population growth would inevitably create. I am concerned about the areas of the globe where people are rapidly becoming richer. For rich people occupy much more space, consume more of each natural resource, disturb the ecology more, and create more land, air, water, chemical, thermal, and radioactive pollution than poor people. So it can be argued that from many viewpoints it is even more urgent to control the numbers of the rich than it is to control the numbers of the poor.[3]

Professor Mayer profiles the deteriorating style of American life by pointing to the vast increase in rubbish disposal disfiguring the landscape, including the abandonment of nine million motor vehicles every year; he also notes that the shortage of water in many cities is attributable not to more people drinking and bathing, but to the increased numbers of air conditioners and private swimming pools, and to industrial uses that cater to consumers' wants. The same phenomena degrade the quality of the air and water, as automobile exhaust and power plant discharges fill the atmosphere, and throwaway litter and manufacturing

34

wastes are emptied into water systems, which, to be made usable again, must be further treated chemically.

TECHNOLOGY

Industrialization itself is a product of technological change. To the extent that industrial activity is responsible for pollution, then, we are in effect holding our technologically oriented society, and its support in scientific knowledge, as the basic source of pollution. And industry is in fact a major contributor to our environmental problems.

Economists of the Chase Manhattan Bank have calculated that industry is responsible for one-fifth of the nation's tonnage of the five most important air pollutants. It contributes more to water pollution than do all the country's households, with the chemical industry alone defiling our water supply to a greater extent than does the entire population served by sewers.[4] Cyril M. Harris, professor of acoustics at Columbia University, has added noise pollution to this indictment of industry. "Lots of people in the city work in such noisy places, mostly factories, that in time the workers will become deaf, and the chances are they do not know it." [5]

Like the rise in incomes, and indeed related to it partly as cause, partly as effect, industrial activity in the United States has been increasing in absolute volume over the years. Goods production has gone up from a value of $104 billion in 1929 to $389 billion in 1970, in constant (1958) prices. Pollution has increased right along with it. Nevertheless, a quite different slant on the relation of technology to pollution has been advanced by Professor Barry Commoner. In his view it is not so much the *volume* of industrial production but the change in its *composition*, largely since World War II, which has been the responsible cause.

Within what Commoner calls the categories of "basic life necessities" —food, fiber, and clothing, freight haulage, household necessities— "there has been a pronounced displacement of natural products by synthetic ones, of power-conserving products by relatively power-consuming ones, of reusable containers by 'disposable' ones." [6] Food producers —"agribusinesses"—have been among the worst ecological offenders by their increased use of inorganic fertilizers (draining off into waterways) and of synthetic pesticides such as DDT and by their reliance on feed-lots for the fattening of cattle (having the same effect as the concentration of people in cities so far as disposal of wastes is concerned).

The increased consumption of energy, Commoner points out, is attributable, not just to more production, but to the substitution of new

35

materials and products for old—of highway for rails, of aluminum for steel. The displacement of soaps by detergents has fouled the environment and made us no cleaner. Synthetic polymers, which have increasingly replaced natural fibers, are ecologically indestructible and can be disposed of only by burning (with consequent pollution of the air) or dumping. In short: "Productive activities with intense environmental impacts have displaced activities with less serious environmental impacts: the growth pattern has been counter-ecological." [7]

Commoner comes close to absolving population increase and concentration as well as growing affluence of baneful influence on the environment. Their contribution is at best marginal. And on the technological front, according to him, if one digs deeper to explore what has given rise to this sudden flourishing of new products and processes, he is driven to the conclusion that it lies in the fragmentation of knowledge that has given rise to specialized sciences, each with its specific applications and its general disinterest in "whole effects" or total relationships. The new technology "was like a two-legged stool: well founded in physics and chemistry but missing its essential third leg—the biology of the environment." [8]

Commoner is at pains to affirm that he does not belong to the anti-industrial school of thought. He does not believe that technology by itself is faulty, but that there can be (and has been) faulty technology. He believes that we can overcome present environmental problems, not by abandoning technology, but by devising ecologically appropriate technology.

There are thus two views of the culprit role of technology (or industrial production). One sees our expanded and advanced industrial activity as generically the cause of environmental despoliation, whatever might be done to change that in the future. The other views a shift in the forms of industry as being the root cause, not industry itself.

The Sudden Emergence of Environmental Problems

Thus, we have three principal explanations for the emergence of environmental problems—population, affluence, and technology. None of these necessarily excludes the others: they could be cumulatively and jointly responsible. But we have not yet satisfactorily come to grips with the question of why, assuming *any* of these causes, except for Commoner's version of the technology impact, society became aware of the consequences only so recently. (Commoner's thesis does quite explicitly deal with the sudden, precipitous development of the new technology following World War II.) The question is all the more perplexing because economists have generally recognized since Pigou's *Economics of Welfare,* first published in 1920, that marginal private cost was not the same as marginal social cost. The dirtying of the housewife's washday laundry (a social cost) by the neighboring factory's smoking chimney was not incorporated into the factory's estimate of its cost of production. This long familiar classroom example of the cost of pollution is simply a homely case of the way that industry's books of account fail to measure the costs of pollution imposed on society because they treat air and water as "free goods," there for anyone's discretionary use. But it has taken almost half a century for economists to move from the housewife's washday frustrations to society's concern for its general environmental health and safety. It has required some time, that is to say, for them to realize the extent of the problem. And we ask why.

The most plausible reason is that the problem has only recently taken on serious proportions. A hundred years ago the United States was still largely a wilderness. By means of steady and unspectacular growth in productivity and population, its national output rose steadily, doubling roughly every twenty years. In a young and developing country that was to be expected. But a hundred or so years down the historical road the United States, now highly industrialized, with a base GNP measured in the billions, was still growing at about the same rate—not year by year, because depressions and wars intervened, but secularly, averaging the years. But while the *rate* of growth remained relatively stable, the *absolute* growth had become stupendous. Thus when GNP doubled during the 1950s and 1960s, the *absolute* increase was on the order of $350 billion, in constant (1958) prices. With no change in the rate of increase in productivity and labor force—and no significant change can be anticipated—GNP will double again in the 1970s and 1980s. Only this time the *absolute* increase will run to $700 billion, still in constant prices. The compound interest or exponential principle is at work here. Within a given period, the percentage change remains constant but the absolute growth is by leaps and bounds.

This growth may not yet have created Malthusian problems of a general scarcity of resources, but at some stage of doubling and redoubling of industrial output we are likely to encounter a scarcity of specific natural resources. It seems a reasonable surmise that it has been only within the last doubling stage that the vastly expanded industrial output began pressing on the limited resources of clean air and water. In the words of the Chase Manhattan economists: "If, as seems a reasonable judgment, the nation was close to the absorptive capacity of the air and the water ten years ago, the addition of 24 million more people and 50% more real GNP in the past decade pushed us well over the edge." [9]

Thus we have two possible and plausible explanations for our seemingly sudden concern with the environment: the phenomenal absolute increase in GNP that has been taking place in all industrialized countries and the recent shift in the composition of that output toward more synthetic and energy-consuming products. These explanations suggest that concern for the environment is not, as some cynics have suggested, this year's passing political fad but something rooted in genuine economic and ecological phenomena that will not simply go away when we stop worrying about them.

Government Response to Environmental Concerns

As concern for the environment spread from a handful of conservationists to a more general public, the federal government reacted with legislation to curb pollution. But how does a government go about such a task, when "the problem" has scarcely been defined and means of combating it are in a trial-and-error stage? The consumer-protection movement offers something of a model. Modest legislation takes a few hesitant steps forward. Thus in 1955 the Public Health Service was authorized to conduct limited research on air pollution and to offer technical assistance to state and local governments. The Clean Air Act of 1963 moved a little further by providing grants to the states to establish and maintain air-pollution control agencies and by authorizing federal authorities to initiate proceedings against interstate polluters. A 1965 amendment to this act for the first time recognized automobile exhaust as a contributor to unclean air and empowered the Secretary of Health, Education, and Welfare to set emission standards. This was followed by the Air Quality Act of 1967, which retained the provisions of the preceding legislation, but also called for collaboration of federal and state governments and major industrial corporations in setting standards for the most seriously polluted regions. Beset with seemingly insoluble problems of determining meaningful criteria to apply to a particular region and susceptible of application to individual sources of pollution (that is to say how to measure the whole effect and allocate the partial responsibility), little headway was made under the new legislation.

Corporations and the Physical Environment

In response to growing public sentiment, the Clean Air Act of 1970 was designed to meet the most serious of these weaknesses. It made state pollution-control legislation mandatory and required that enforcement procedures be approved by federal authorities. If state plans are unacceptable, the federal government may intervene to impose its own procedures. The 1970 act also provides for *national* ambient air quality standards as well as emissions standards for particular (stationary) pollutants. Automobile emissions were subjected to federally determined standards, and by statutory provision were to be reduced to specified and rigorous levels by given target dates.

Federal control of water pollution was technically inaugurated by congressional actions in 1948 and 1956, but these were largely of a token nature. These acts were amended in 1961, the Water Pollution Control Act was passed in 1965 and was further upgraded by the Water and Environmental Quality Enforcement Act of 1970. The latter was triggered largely by public repugnance at a few spectacular oil spills, the widely publicized "death" of Lake Erie, and the fouling of underground water by chemical components of detergents, which had virtually displaced soap cleansers. The new law imposed stricter liability and preventive measures in the water transport of oil, gave the federal government authority to regulate discharges of waste into bodies of water, and required state certification that any new industrial facilities would not adversely affect water quality.

In 1970 the Environmental Protection Agency (EPA) was established under administrative reorganization procedure, bringing together the water-quality office lodged in the Department of the Interior, the air-pollution control group in the Department of Health, Education, and Welfare, the pesticide control function then in the Department of Agriculture, and nuclear-radiation control previously under the jurisdiction of the Atomic Energy Commission. The new agency was mandated to conduct research, and to set and enforce standards with respect to air, water, and solid-waste pollution.

In addition to this action agency, a Council on Environmental Quality had been established under the National Environmental Protection Act of 1969. Congressional intent was that this office should develop and coordinate all policy in the extensive and amorphous "environmental field," ranging, as one journalist put it, "from protection of wildlife to the preservation of historic buildings." [10] But perhaps the most significant portion of that act, Section 102, requires all government agencies to file with the newly created council a statement of the environmental impact of any major project in which they are involved. Because such projects extend to subcontracts to private business and authorizations for private initiatives (the Alaska pipeline, for example), these "impact statements" have assumed critical importance in opening to public scrutiny and possible court challenge both public and corporate actions viewed as environmentally deleterious. The consequence, at least in the early years of this new procedure, has been to delay a number of governmentally sponsored or approved projects, to elicit changes in construction plans, and occasionally to cause their abandonment.

Federal efforts at pollution control have been supplemented by state and municipal provisions. In some jurisdictions, detergents containing phosphates have been banned, automobiles have been prohibited from certain sections of cities during hours when these are most populated, and use of incinerators in apartment buildings has been controlled. Nor does this brief summary take into account numerous other related provisions of federal acts ranging from subsidies and tax credits for industrial investment in pollution-control equipment to noise-level control under a 1969 amendment to the Walsh-Healey Public Contracts Act.

If public awareness of environmental decay is recent, government response has been relatively quick and extensive. Indeed, the Nixon Administration by 1972 had moved to the position that Congress was overreacting and that such measures as the Water Pollution Control bill (enacted later that same year), which required total elimination of all effluent discharges into the nation's waterways by 1985, are wasteful, if not capricious. The Chairman of the Council on Environmental Quality has pointed out that the cost of pollution control, too, has an exponential aspect, so that removal of the last 1 percent of contaminant may cost as much as the removal of the first 99 percent.[11] "Zero discharge" may thus be a goal that diverts substantial resources away from other more badly needed public works to an unnecessarily finicky scrubbing of air and water. In any event, we are safe in concluding that once the public had recognized pollution as a problem, the political authorities vied with one another in doing "something," piling laws on administrative agencies and legislative amendments on regulatory orders.

Business Reaction

Could anything be more predictable than the response of business to this flurry of political activity? We have already encountered the pattern in the case of consumerism. The first reaction is defensive and bitter: business is being made a scapegoat for society's own failings; politicians are pandering to a panicky public; the cleanup demanded will bankrupt many companies and increase the public's cost of living more than it realizes. After this initial irritation, business professionalism reasserts itself: the public-relations offices take over with the soothing message that industry is busily coping with an admittedly serious problem. Millions of dollars are being spent on the research needed to take effective action, even as billions are being spent to improve old equipment and develop new equipment in line with what is already known. This is the period when resistance to remedial action shades over into acceptance of the inevitability of some action, but this is accompanied by pressures for making standards "practical" and the time period for their enforcement "reasonable."

This reaction pattern is wholly understandable. It suggests that at least in some respects the Supreme Court was not too far afield in picturing the corporation as human. When, within the space of a decade, a cause takes on the dimensions of a crusade, with industry assuming the role of the infidels, what else but a defensive reaction can be expected? With pollution controls entailing costs running into literally unknown but clearly massive sums loosely spoken of as the "ransom" that would be legislatively demanded of business to permit it freedom to operate, how else could business feel but victimized, at least in the first fresh shock of recognition that the contest was "for real"?

The instinct to fight back, with whatever arguments come to hand, is surely understandable. Thus one leading businessman informed—mistakenly—a college audience that "U.S. Department of Commerce figures show that 219 plants last year were forced to shut down because of environmental pressures." [12] As a House-Senate conference committee pondered legislation to set strict limits on automobile pollution emissions in 1975, the executive vice president of Ford Motor Company, urging a specially called meeting of principal Ford suppliers and dealers to initiate a telegram campaign to their Washington representatives, "went so far as to claim that the bill 'could prevent continued production of automobiles after January 1, 1975.'" [13] The president of a steel company, speaking before a group of university economists, emphasized the adverse effects of ill-advised pollution control legislation: "The thrust for an improved environment has caused many of us in the steel industry to close and/or drastically alter plant operations; . . . shifted vital funds away from essential revenue producing activities, including research

41

and development; increased the competitive advantage of foreign competitors; placed an additional annual operating cost burden on our industry of about $412 million." [14]

A sanitation engineering consultant, speaking of Detroit's costly and largely "wasted" efforts to control discharges into Lake Erie, drew more lurid conclusions: "This excessive expenditure diverts funds from other environmental blights in Detroit such as crime on the streets, ghettos, malnutrition, and the needs of education. Can Detroit afford to have such a warped concept of environmental priorities? Why can't a child be as important as a fish?" [15] Such costly public ventures into pollution control obviously increase business taxes and provide undesirable examples of what might be expected of business itself. A suspicious business partisan might conclude and feel justified in suggesting to others that there are "efforts afoot, avowedly to control the quality of the environment but more accurately to control industrial operations and the American way of life." [16]

Business's counterattack has included undercover efforts to "defuse" the public. A "news" item describing the movement against leaded gasoline as "misleading and irrelevant" asserted that no evidence existed that lead in the atmosphere poses a health hazard. *Natural History,* a magazine published by New York's American Museum of Natural History, traced the story to *Editor's Digest,* a division of Planned Communications Services, Inc., "a company that writes and distributes stories to small-circulation newspapers on behalf of corporate and industrial clients. This story, it turns out, originated with the Lead Industries Association. . . ." [17]

Corporate leadership is, on the whole, too sophisticated to rely solely on opposition when a problem has been shown to be real and demand for its solution has generated a popular following, however misguided. One time-tested device is to join the opposition in calling for a "common" effort. "We" have erred, but "we" can make up for our folly. Again Atlantic Richfield Company, employing reproductions of contemporary art to illustrate its "cultural" concern, offers what might paradoxically be referred to as a "good" example:

The ideal: Seas that are permanently protected from man's abuse.
The real: Thoughtlessly, man spews waste into the world's oceans. From the air, from the stream, from ships, all of it from ourselves.
We must find new and better ways to guard our waters from ourselves. Our solutions must be swift. They must be creative and mature. For tomorrow the waters of the world will inherit what we do today.
Throughout the world, man must learn to function without fouling the

oceans—and the air and earth that adjoin them. Until then, we cannot protect the environment in which life began—and on which our lives still depend.[18]

In place of such soothing syrup, the steel industry prefers the language of hard cash: "Our industry has put its money where its mouth is. Companies producing about 98% of the nation's iron and steel spent slightly over $735 million between '66 and '71. In '71, they spent $161.5 million, equal to 10.3% of our total capital expenditures . . . the largest of any industry and twice the average for all manufacturing. Last year, environmental control spending accounted for about 20% of net profits. An additional 12% of initial construction costs, or $142,000,000 a year, must be spent annually to keep equipment working." [19]

But communicating with the public is not enough in a situation where the stakes are so high. The real objective is to help mold the legislation which cannot be avoided. Industry finds itself, willy-nilly, engaged in a bargaining process with politicians over the shape of pollution-control laws that will satisfy the public. The politicians can ignore neither the interests of large-scale industry, which after all exercises enormous, if not dominant, influence over the very structure and functioning of the American society,[20] nor the wishes and interests of their popular constituencies, whose votes must return them to office. Bargaining is something at which both politicians and industrialists have long been adept.

The passage of the Air Quality Act of 1967 nicely illustrates this process. Although the whole story of such an event can never be reassembled, it appears that the White House was more interested in the political than the pollution effect of endorsing *national* emission standards and actually offered little support for its own bill when introduced into the Senate. Industry lobbyists, at first alarmed over the bill's stringent provisions, became reassured during the course of informal meetings with staff members of the Air and Water Pollution Subcommittee of the Public Works Committee. In these discussions details were hashed out over such issues as how *regional* criteria would work, timetables for coordinating state standards, whether the federal government should be given powers to subpoena company records and monitor industry emissions.

Thus a new bill was taking shape. . . . When the [public] hearings began, practically all industry testimony was identical. Each made passing remarks about the desirability of regional flexibility, the criteria standards approach, and the need for more federal research to determine effects on health. But the great bulk of industry testimony was spent blasting a concept it knew was not even being considered—national emission standards. Thus there was a lively public debate over what all knew privately to be a dead letter. The effect was to set up a straw man for industry to demolish publicly, while the real hearings were going on behind closed doors.[21]

Bargaining occurs not only with respect to the terms of legislation, but also its application. The case of Union Carbide's Marietta, Ohio, ferroalloy plant is instructive in this respect. Its soot and sulfur dioxide fell abundantly on the town of Vienna, West Virginia, just across the Ohio River. Acting under the Clean Air Act of 1963, the National Air Pollution Control Administration (NAPCA) convened a conference in Vienna that found the Marietta plant to be the region's major polluter, inferentially responsible for a marked regional increase in respiratory diseases. "For the next two years, Carbide refused to supply complete data on emissions, and, at one point, barred federal inspectors from the Marietta plant." It failed even to attend a second abatement conference, which recommended legal action by the Department of Health, Education, and Welfare (HEW), NAPCA's parent. The enforcement action permitted under the 1963 act was involved and time-consuming, but it did induce Union Carbide management to begin "serious negotiations." The company "first proposed that the government should pay half the cost of installing the scrubbing equipment, arguing that it was breaking new technical ground. HEW rejected the proposal as not sufficiently 'unique.'" Carbide then submitted another proposal. Whereas HEW had prescribed a 40 percent reduction in sulfur dioxide emissions by the end of 1970, and 70 percent by April 1972, Carbide management offered a 12.5 percent reduction by the end of 1971, 28 percent by 1972, and 70 percent by September 1974. Meanwhile EPA had been created and was administering the more forceful Clean Air Act of 1970. It rejected the company's counterproposal and insisted on the schedule laid down by HEW. The company thereupon moved to comply, but not without warning government authorities that it would probably have to curtail production in the process, laying off 500 employees. The bargaining relationship was thereby kept alive, at the same time now involving the unions representing the company's employees. The president of District 50, Allied and Technical Workers, fearing joblessness for his members, argued that the government ought to give the company more time. The president of the Oil, Chemical and Atomic Workers local union, taking a less tractable stand, said: "We resent the fact that Union Carbide is using our members as pawns in its resistance to clean up the air around Marietta." [22]

One common ploy in the bargaining contest between polluters and antipolluters is for each side to discredit the other's "facts." "For example, one recent EPA study put the cost of suppressing sulphur oxides from copper smelters at $87 million. The copper industry says that much larger outlays will be required—$345 million if new control technology works out, $1.2 billion if it doesn't." [23] A steel representative testifies that to comply with existing federal ambient-air standards and proposed water-pollution controls would require the industry to invest $3.5 billion, with annual maintenance charges of $400 million. "This burden represents eight times the total earnings of our industry during 1970, and more than we've made in the last five years." [24] But federal authorities point out that such projections, however reliable, do not take into account the existing costs that pollution imposes on the company, and the fact that capital expenses, though spread over twenty years, can be depreciated in five years, and are sometimes given beneficial financing terms. The Chase Manhattan Bank's Economic Research Division comments that while the costs for pollution control are certainly large, "they do not support many of the scare headlines which say that necessary expenditures to deal with pollution will cost hundreds of billions of dollars, and stunt progress in other fields." [25]

Disputation over cost data is simply one special case of a general bargaining tactic—the argument that more information is needed on which realistic and reasonable standards can be based. Because the collection of information is time-consuming and subject to methodological hassles before, while, and after it takes place, the more that industry insists it is "necessary" to know, the longer delayed is regulatory action. "So facts are needed, facts not conjecture, and by impartial scientists on such a plane that a real and time analysis is possible. These *prerequisites* are essential to anticipating effects of changes and this is vital to our future, not the hysteria and prohibitory legislation in vogue." [26] The rebuttal is again supplied by the Chase Manhattan economists: "Evidence on what air pollution does to human health is far from complete, but major illnesses linked to air pollution include emphysema, bronchitis, asthma and lung cancer." [27] Presumably such linkages warrant action even before *all* the facts are in.

But while such bargaining between industry and government continues, the major corporations are not standing still. The Conference Board reports that a survey of 174 firms in "pollution-prone" industries in North America shows that 89 companies (77 in the United States, 12 in Canada) have set up special units to deal with the problem or have made it a major responsibility of an existing corporate department.[28] This does not, of course, necessarily connote maximum feasible effort; it does, however, suggest some forward movement.

The variant reactions of industry to the challenge of environmental protection were given sharp focus by the original Senate bill to achieve zero discharge of waste into the nation's waterways by 1985. Some corporate groups "weighed in with dire predictions. The American Paper Institute says that zero discharge would cause plant closings, create unemployment, and drive paper prices up by 50%." On the other hand, "several companies, including Dow Chemical and Hercules, are already operating plants that have achieved zero discharge through recycling." [29]

In short, despite the lamentations of corporate spokesmen over the cataclysmic effects that pollution control could be expected to have on their operations and on the economy, legislation so far enacted has been largely taken in stride. A detailed study of the prospective impact of controls on fourteen major industries over the period 1972–1976, undertaken by eleven private consulting firms for the federal government, suggested that of 12,000 firms surveyed, "about 800 would close in the normal course of business." An additional 200 to 300 might be pushed over the brink by pollution-control costs, but these would be so economically weak that they would probably go under in another few years anyway.[30]

Limitations of Environmental Controls

If the environmental crisis that erupted in the 1960s has had only a limited impact on corporate economics, is it equally true that corporate actions that have been compelled so far have had only a limited impact on the environment? Is there any reason to expect more sweeping legislative and administrative measures in the future, which will more seriously disturb the corporate sector? And if there is not, does this imply that the environmental job is being done, that pollution and depletion of natural resources will have been brought under control—or, on the contrary, that this can be done only through more sweeping changes, rather than through incremental adjustments? It is to these issues that we now turn.

As in the case of consumer protection, so with pollution control is it true that there are basic limitations built into the legislative and administrative processes that diminish their effectiveness. A number of measures which are still pending are intended to tighten or extend the regulation of industrial activity adverse to the environment. We may confidently expect that scarcely a session of Congress will go by when additional bills will not be introduced. Some of these are likely to be passed. Nevertheless, it is a safe prediction that neither present nor future legislation will have the impact on environmental protection that their language seems to promise. There are a number of reasons for this, which we need touch on only lightly because we have already encountered them in discussing consumer protection.

Despite the coordinating efforts of the Council on Environmental Quality and EPA (the relationship between the two agencies is itself ambiguous), overlapping and uncertain jurisdictions of numerous government authorities, inevitable in a federal system of government and virtually guaranteed in one operating on the scale of the United States, will frustrate administrative efficiency. The Army Corps of Engineers retains certain authority with respect to use of waterways for waste disposal, going back to a law of 1899. Its jurisdiction at times overlaps with EPA and also at times with state water-control agencies. Instances have arisen when a company obtains state approval for waste discharge, under state water-quality standards, only to have its plans (or construction) contested by the Corps of Engineers or EPA. The Federal Power Commission has charged EPA with interfering in matters reserved to it.

Questions over whether a waterway is intrastate or interstate further confuse the placement of regulatory authority. In some instances state agencies have set stricter standards than federal ones, thus inviting corporate maneuvering to bring itself under the more lenient jurisdiction. The courts as well have sometimes been involved in these intramural contests. A company, ready to comply with state standards, seeks to secure assurance of the sufficiency of its compliance by means of a state court order, but is confronted by federal attorneys moving in a federal court to obtain a decree enforcing other requirements. The impact statements required by the Council on Environmental Quality provide information on the basis of which citizen action suits may be initiated to set aside governmental authorizations.

Professor Harris has pointed out the same jurisdictional difficulty with regard to noise abatement. A city must obviously take the initiative, but its powers are limited by federal authority over air traffic, state control of trucking standards, and sometimes regional administration (as, for example, the Port of New York Authority) of other forms of traffic.[31]

Among the problems besetting regulatory agencies, perhaps none is so universal as the inadequacy of budget and staff to do the job that the legislation calls for. Limiting the size of their appropriations is one sure way of diluting their effectiveness, a relatively safe ploy that might be engaged in by some congressmen who vote for pollution-control legislation in a show of public spirit, but who also are subject to special-interest pressures to render the legislation harmless. Even with the best of intentions, appropriations for one purpose must compete with appropriations for other purposes, and honest judgment may sacrifice pollution control to another cause. The Executive Office, through its budgeting authority, is subject to the same pressures. Thus the Clean Air Act of 1970 authorized expenditures of $350 million for the following fiscal year, but the amount was cut back to $150 million by the Office of Management and Budget. For solid-waste disposal, congressional authorization of $150 million was reduced by executive budget officials to $25 million. Congressional appropriation for the Water Pollution Control Act of 1972 was reduced $6 billion by order of the president.

One example of the way in which limitations of administrative staff and resources can undercut legislative intent is provided by the impact statements called for by the National Environmental Protection Act of 1969. Permission to discharge industrial waste into national waterways must be granted by the Army Corps of Engineers. Because this constitutes a governmental action, the 1969 act requires a statement spelling out the environmental impact of granting the permit. Under a ruling of a U.S. Circuit Court of Appeals, that statement must be prepared by either the Corps of Engineers or EPA. In the first six months of 1972, following that ruling, some 20,000 permits were backlogged, because neither agency had the manpower to comply with the court's interpretation of legislative intent. In such a situation, obviously something has to give. It is an easy prediction that it will be the method of issuing impact statements or of granting discharge permits, rather than the closed federal purse strings that would have to open in order to hire the army of permit analysts that would be called for.

Still another halter on the effectiveness of federal pollution-control agencies lies in the division of opinion within government itself as to the agencies' appropriate objectives. Legislation, however clear it may appear in mandating certain actions, has no means of self-enforcement. Inevitably, discretion remains within the enforcement agencies themselves as to which sections of a law will be given priority, which will be downplayed. From both Congress and the Executive Office emanate pressures to move in one way rather than another. An overzealous administrator will find himself cut off from the financial, moral, and political support that is essential for him to be effective.

The administrator of a sensitive agency finds it necessary to attend to, and often to placate, the views of numbers of officials whose influence can aid or thwart his program. The head of EPA has said that he must keep in constant touch with fifteen congressional committees. One of these is the House appropriations subcommittee that must pass on EPA's budget, whose chairman, it was reported, "takes a dim view of EPA's moves to restrict the use of pesticides and has threatened a searching investigation of how well EPA is handling its $2.48 billion budget." [32]

On the executive side, Maurice H. Stans, a former Secretary of Commerce, characterized by *The New York Times* as "industry's foremost exponent of the 'go slow' attitude on pollution control," criticized EPA's administrator for a "negative" attitude toward business. He charged that by ignoring the economic impact of pollution-control actions, the jobs of thousands of workers were endangered, and asserted that business "on its own" was moving toward national antipollution objectives. At the Secretary's urging, the guidelines that EPA had prepared for state implementation of the Clean Air Act of 1970 were modified by executive authority to include a clause advising the states to consider the economic impact, which some considered an open invitation to moderate pollution standards.[33]

The conflict of objectives even within the government is nicely displayed in its actions with respect to the automobile industry. With automobile exhaust considered a major source of air pollution, and with EPA contemplating the need to reduce the number of automobiles concentrated in a number of principal cities, the president in 1971 ordered the removal of the federal 10 percent excise tax on automobiles to spur their sales and give an economic fillip to a sluggish economy. A year later, the executive Office of Science and Technology released a report prepared by a sixteen-man panel appointed by the president to investigate the costs and benefits of safety and pollution-control devices that have been required for 1976 model automobiles by EPA and the National Highway Traffic Safety Administration.

As *Business Week* reported:

The apparent aim was to weaken the regulatory power that permits these two agencies to set standards for automotive safety and pollution.

The report concludes that, over-all, safety and pollution control equipment now required for 1976 models will not be worth the price—an estimated $873 over the cost of 1971 models ($350 for emission control and $523 for safety). . . .

In effect, Nixon is chastising his own agencies for their zeal in enforcing legislative action. "There is need," warns the report, "for a coordinated approach for both the legislative and executive branches." [34]

Aside from understandable and inevitable differences in political judgment as to how vigorously legislation should be enforced, a further limitation on bureaucratic effectiveness rests in the ambiguity of what it is that should be enforced. This is the question of adopting standards to which those regulated shall be held, of determining the criteria by which their compliance with the law will be judged. This is a particularly thorny issue in the matter of pollution control. It is closely related to differences in objectives, just discussed, but is not the same. Even people with the same environmental philosophy and administrative objectives may find it difficult to agree on defensible standards.

Ascertaining the effect of a particular pollutant at different levels of concentration, in different combinations with other pollutants, and in different environmental settings calls for knowledge and understanding that even the experts now lack. Nevertheless, the Clean Air Act of 1970 required EPA to propose air-quality standards for six major air pollutants within thirty days after passage of the act. Understandably its findings have been subjected to challenge by interested corporations, but independent experts have also expressed doubts. A former New York City pollution-control official and a university professor of chemistry have suggested that a proposed nationwide standard for nitrogen oxides could prove to be either too rigorous or too lenient, and have advised against enforcing it on industry until more is known.[35]

Although the establishment of standards is distinguishable from the setting of objectives, inevitably the two become entangled, confusing even to those charged with enforcing pollution legislation. The former head of EPA has said: "In the Clean Air Act I'm mandated by Congress to set a standard that will protect public health. It doesn't say protect public health if we can afford it or if the costs are not exorbitant—it says protect public health. So to that extent there is built into the law the factor of ignoring cost." This position identified the standards with a single objective. No additional political judgment seems called for. But the same official found it impossible to maintain so absolute a stand, and as the economic factor inevitably began to creep into EPA calculations, he commented: "We could make highways safer by enclosing them in rubber tubes. The reason we don't is that it costs too much. The question of what cost for what benefit is at the heart of the controversy swirling around us today, and essentially these are political questions."[36] This position distinguishes standards and objectives, by admitting other objectives that are affected by the standards set. The standards in fact determine what other objectives must be given up in pursuing this one more vigorously, a political decision.

The cost-benefit equation is one that has fascinated economists over the years, and we shall return to it later. Despite its impeccable logic it involves measurement problems that lie in the realm of moral or political judgment. The consequence is that standard setting in such matters as pollution control becomes a quagmire compounded both of lack of knowledge and lack of agreement on the significance of knowledge known, thereby limiting the effectiveness of regulatory action.

Finally, we come to administrative weakness in enforcing whatever standards may be set. In the case of pollution, this takes on several dimensions. Aside from the enormousness of the inspection problem, because virtually all industry is involved and in more than one way, the problems dealt with are relatively technical and require special knowledge. The stakes to industry are high enough to warrant their hiring the best of talent. Thus government agencies with limited budgets and a vast field of technical enforcement to cover are in effect pitted against a large number of corporations, each highly motivated to limit its financial responsibility and financially capable of employing experts to make its case. The situation is roughly comparable to a company's seeking to hold down its tax obligations by whatever procedures are recommended by its legal and accounting experts. The prime difference lies in a potential for adverse public relations.

Given this situation, the pollution-control agencies must rely to a very large extent on the cooperation of those whom they regulate, and on implementation by state control boards. Such dependence was dramatically demonstrated in mid-1972 when the Ford Motor Company, on its own volition, reported to EPA that emission tests required to be made on new model cars before being shipped to dealers had been improperly conducted. Contrary to regulation, maintenance repairs had been made on test cars during their running. At the time that this occurrence was reported to top management, and it in turn had reported to EPA, the 1973 model run was scheduled to begin within a month. To rerun the 50,000-mile pollution test might consume as much as four months. Faced with the fact that strict compliance with the law would require a possible three-month shutdown, with a layoff of as many as 170,000 employees, an arrangement was worked out under which cars could be made and shipped to dealers, but could not be sold, prior to certification.

The *Wall Street Journal* caught the significance of what it called the "Ford imbroglio":

The cries from Detroit have created the specter of a growing regulatory monster in the nation's capital that seems more powerful than the auto industry itself.

But if there is one thing that has become clear so far from the current mess over engine certification at Ford Motor Co., it is this: The monster is in truth a toothless tiger. Indeed, the Ford situation has, in the minds of government and auto men alike, raised some fundamental questions about the ability of the government to enforce the mounds of antipollution regulations it has heaped on the industry in recent years. . . .

. . . As it stands now, the auto makers themselves, at great cost in time and money, are ultimately the chief enforcers of the standards they are supposed to meet, and federal regulators, hopelessly outgunned, can do little more than monitor the industry's self-regulation.[37]

In the Ford case, as the *Wall Street Journal* points out, the unauthorized adjustments came to light only as the result of an internal company squabble, after a computer analyst noticed a discrepancy between company records and records submitted to the government. Management officials themselves informed EPA of the unsanctioned noncompliance. The company was subsequently fined $7 million by a federal district court, but the reliance on corporate self-regulation (and beyond that the reliance by the corporation itself on the good-faith cooperation of the employees responsible for testing) was revealed in the court's decision. Ford was required, for ten years, to keep written records of its testing procedures and to warn in writing all employees involved in those procedures of the penalties for delinquency. The company's general counsel observed that the suit had served to demonstrate "how complex, expensive, and difficult" it is for both company and government to comply with the law.[38]

In the more general controls over air and water pollution, federal agencies must commonly collaborate with state boards. But in a survey conducted in 1970 by *The New York Times*, it was found that "most of the state boards responsible for cleaning up the nation's air and water are markedly weighted with representatives of the principal sources of pollution." This practice has been defended on the grounds that such representatives supply technical expertise that would otherwise be difficult to come by, and that the importance of their role in the economic life of the state justifies their involvement. The result is that "the roster of big corporations with employees on such boards reads like an abbreviated blue book of American industry, particularly the most pollution-troubled segments of industry."

Under the circumstances, some conflict of interest is scarcely avoidable. A federal official commented: "As far as we know these are all upright people. Many undoubtedly strive to be objective. But if you were trying a case against the X.Y.Z. Paper Clip Company, would you want an official of the company on the jury?"[39]

The Water Pollution Act passed by Congress in 1972 strikes at such conflicts of interest insofar as they involve representation by any member of an industry seeking a discharge permit on the control board that issues it. Air-pollution control boards are not affected, however, nor does such exclusion of industry representatives from the decision-making bodies preclude the latter's reliance on the former for information on which decisions are based.

To some degree, federal environmental agencies also depend on citizen initiatives in the form of civil suits brought to enforce pollution legislation. Public-spirited citizen actions are not, however, always locally welcome. In Blackwell, Oklahoma, a suit brought by thirty-five people, mostly farmers, against a zinc smelting operation of American Metal Climax Company led to the closing of the obsolete smelter. What might appear to the outsider as a victory for the community, freeing it from the "thick cloud of acrid smoke" that has sat in its vicinity for decades and has saturated the surrounding soil with zinc, in fact engendered a local vendetta. The smelter had accounted for more than half the manufacturing jobs in town. Company employees, as well as local merchants, expressed their bitterness against the pollution plaintiffs through threats, boycotts, loss of employment, and ostracism.[40] Such episodes are not likely to encourage citizen suits elsewhere.

One other enforcement problem deserves notice. In view of that lack of scientific information on the effects of pollutants that we have already noted and the relative recency of attention to pollution problems, corrective technology is not always available. Nevertheless, legislation and administrative regulations have sometimes called for controls that would require the development of needed technology by specific dates, on the assumption that with this spur industry could produce the needed devices. The analogy of setting a target date for a journey to the moon when the means for achieving it were still unknown is frequently referred to. Nevertheless, if such technology-inducing provisions do not eventuate in the needed instruments, there is really no effective sanction possible. If devices for a specified reduction of automobile exhaust pollution are not forthcoming by a specified date, does anyone really believe that the manufacture of automobiles in the United States will cease?

In short, controls over industry there are, and there will be more, but any which pose a threat to continuity of the corporate system as we know it are likely to be curbed not by the government's "knuckling under" to blatant industry demands, but simply by tempering the regulatory process. This can be done through jurisdictional ambiguities, budgetary curtailment, concessions to other competing political objectives, uncertainties in standard setting, and weakness in enforcement.

Acceptability of Limited Progress

These limitations on the legislative and administrative protection of the environment do not mean that public interest will be slighted and the public's will thwarted. On the contrary, such incremental measures as are forthcoming to alleviate, in whatever degree, the discomforts of pollution will probably be sufficient to satisfy public pressures. This is because any more effective environmental controls would require a larger sacrifice of immediate pleasures and preferences than the public is willing to make.

When the costs of achieving more stringent standards of air and water purity drastically affect the prices of consumer goods, we can expect public resistance to the higher standards. We have already noted the contribution made by divided political objectives to less effective pollution control. In the kind of consumption-oriented society that we encountered in the preceding chapter, consumer goods and clean environment become seriously competing objectives. If, as has been estimated, the standards for automobile emissions now set for 1976 will add between $390 and $425 to the price of a car, we may confidently anticipate an outcry by the automobile-buying public. I concur with René Dubos when he says: "We would like to improve our polluted and cluttered environments, but we like gadgets and economic prosperity even more. In fact, values such as political power and gross national income so dominate our collective lives that we shall undertake the social and technological reforms essential for environmental control only if we are forced into action by some disaster." [41]

This consumption-mindedness of the American public goes beyond a desire for more goods. It is linked to a way or style of life that those goods make possible. It is thus not only the price increase that irritates car buyers, but the fact that even present emission controls increase fuel consumption and reduce engine performance. One consequence has been that some car owners have had emission controls disconnected. The manager of the auto-diagnostic clinic of the Missouri Automobile Club reported that one-fourth of the late-model cars going through his clinic had their emission controls tampered with. A Detroit automobile mechanic says that thirty of the forty automobile tune-ups he does every month involve modifications of the control system. [42]

The former head of EPA had no illusions about the unpopularity of actions necessary for effective pollution control if these begin to affect people's private lives. It has been popular to talk about "changing life styles," he observed, "but when someone finds out that means bicycling or carpooling to work, or going home at a different time, he may not be for it." [43] Nor do the politicians have any illusions on this score. When the iconoclast Admiral Hyman G. Rickover testified at House hearings on the prospects of a national energy shortage, he suggested the desirability of banning "nonessential" air conditioners and putting a high tax on such "luxuries" as clothes driers. A congressman thereupon "observed with undisguised disdain that the admiral had never run for office. 'What do you think we can do and still stay in office?'" he asked. John B. Connally, then Secretary of the Treasury and a former governor of Texas, advised the House committee that he too "was too much of a pragmatist" to embrace the Rickover program. He could live without air conditioning but would "hate to give it up." People can "save a tremendous amount of energy just by going around and turning off a few lights," Mr. Connally counseled reassuringly. [44]

Ambivalence over priorities in establishing political objectives ripens into profound disagreement between the disadvantaged minorities and the more advantaged majority within the general public. Blacks and Latins, large numbers of whom have suffered from lack of social amenities in matters of housing, health, education, and employment, often believe that the billions of dollars of expenditures that they hear advocated for clean air and water should be redirected into improving their general way of life. Appeals of the conservationists to save the marshlands near urban areas or the Everglades of Florida sound like an almost callous disregard for more fundamental reforms needed in the ghettos. It is not that the ghetto residents do not suffer from bad air and bad water; if anything, they are more the victims than the suburban whites. The polluted beaches characteristic of most large cities deprive black children of desirable recreation far more than they adversely affect white children who have access to less polluted waters of remoter areas, not to mention backyard swimming pools. Nevertheless, to blacks fighting against what often appears as a hopeless existence, pollution control emerges as a political objective rather far down the list. Consumption is more important than environment.

As one black leader put the matter: "We suffer from pollution as much as anyone, but we're not the beneficiaries of the affluence that produced the pollution." [45] For the government to institute stricter controls over industry, an action that causes the latter to pass along higher costs in the form of higher prices, thus appears to shut the blacks off from any opportunity of achieving the material advancement that they seek. It would be as though the government had capriciously increased the cost of the goods they buy by 10 or 20 percent at the very time it professed to be seeking to improve their standard of living.

Blacks and Latins are not the only groups who see their economic interests jeopardized by the campaign to clean up the environment. Workers whose jobs appear threatened by new pollution standards have often joined in opposition. The previously cited example of community persecution of a citizen group that secured a court order against the Blackwell, Oklahoma, zinc smelter of American Metal Climax has numerous counterparts. The 1972 National Conference on Strip Mining, meeting in Kentucky to pass a resolution urging abolition of this form of coal extraction, was harassed by some hundred strip miners from neighboring counties, wearing their work clothes and hard hats decorated with stickers proclaiming "I Dig Coal" and "Coal Puts Bread on My Table." "'I think you can understand the feelings of the men,' said Paul Patton, the young president of the Kentucky Elkhorn Company, who is a leading spokesman for the smaller operations. 'These people [the conferees] have the emotions of idealism, but my men have the emotions of their livelihood, which is a lot stronger.' "[46]

Although a number of national unions have adopted positions favorable to environmental protection, local union leaders often find themselves placed in an ambiguous position when the employment of their members seems to be the price of a cleaner environment.

A United Steelworkers local in El Paso lobbied hard and successfully in the city council recently to help an American Smelting & Refining Co. plant to obtain more time in which to bring its air-cleanup equipment up to par; many of the plant's 1,000 employes faced possible layoffs.

Representatives of the Teamsters Union, Glass Bottle Blowers Association and Steelworkers helped in September to stymie efforts by New Jersey legislators to impose restrictions on nonreturnable containers; there were warnings that up to 30,000 jobs were threatened.

Local 1 of the United Papermakers and Paperworkers in Holyoke, Mass., has replaced its customary fall job-safety campaign with a drive "to save jobs by halting the ecology steamroller." Union officials contend a local paper company had to abolish more than 150 jobs this year because of the "excessive cost of a pollution-control system. . . ."

A Maine labor representative arguing for a new oil refinery along the state's picturesque coast maintains, "We can't trade off the welfare of human beings for the sake of scenery. . . ."

United Auto Workers President Leonard Woodcock recently told a congressional subcommittee that "their economic circumstances require them to think first of jobs, paychecks and bread on the table. . . ."

Even A. F. Grospiron, president of the Oil, Chemical and Atomic Workers, which has taken a tougher antipollution stand than most unions, warns: "We will oppose those theoretical environmentalists who would make air and water pure without regard to whether or not people have food on their tables." [47]

Nor has management failed to perceive the advantage of encouraging closer collaboration with organized labor in opposition to more stringent environmental legislation or administrative regulation. "One of the things industry and labor have to do is get together to protect ourselves from these ecology groups that have one-track minds," one manager comments.[48] Corporate officials have also played on labor's fears and self-interest by pointing out that costly pollution standards required by the U.S. government, but not matched by foreign governments, would put American industry at a competitive disadvantage and thus would cause further loss of employment. The same argument has been used in support of federal assistance to industrial research and development and to such industry projects as the supersonic transport plane, which has been condemned by numerous scientists for both known and potential adverse environmental effects. The president's special consultant on technology asserted that the United States "needed" the program to stay competitive in technology with foreign countries.[49]

The consumer culture is too closely allied with corporate interests to subordinate the latter to ecological considerations. The dominant role of the corporation in American society derives from its ability to satisfy a mass-consumption appetite, not from its contribution to an unpolluted environment. Thus, when the Bay Area Rapid Transit was proposed for the San Francisco area, it was hailed as the answer to air pollution and traffic congestion, by substituting mass transit for the rising tide of private automobiles, and as the means for opening up a wider geographical range of jobs for blacks confined to the ghettos. "But in spite of such possible advantages, it was not ecology or job access, but the potential profits from land development and the rejuvenation of downtown San Francisco that prompted a group of influential businessmen to provide the push necessary to bring a transit system to the Bay Area. . . . Nurtured more by vested interests than by a desire of Bay Area residents to find an alternative to the automobile, BART was built without a long-range commitment to shift the emphasis to public transportation in the Bay Area. Thus highway construction continues. And the region could end up with the harmful side effects of both mass transit and the automobile." [50]

Corporate profit-mindedness is of course directly related to the nation's consumption. By hallowed tradition, the former is identified as the reward for superior performance in the service of the latter, in the supply of public needs and wants. As we noted in examining the consumer-protection movement, manufactured products—especially, but not only, drugs—are often put on the market before their long-run effects on people or on the environment can be established. The purpose may be profit, but the justification lies in not keeping from a waiting public products that produce immediate gratification.

Within the prevalent American culture there is thus a coalescing of interest in improving environmental quality only within bounds that do not basically threaten the more basic consumption objective. Corporation executives who have been most responsible for nurturing that focal value; workers—organized and unorganized—whose position in the consumer culture depends on the continuity of their employment and the buying power of their wages; disadvantaged minorities who aspire to catch up with the material success that they have so far been denied; and government officials who depend for their office on performing satisfactorily a brokerage function between dominant interests and a mass electorate—all these unite in insisting that the admitted problem of protecting the environment be met by incremental measures that do not rock the economic boat. The result may be modest improvement over time, or it may be simply to slow the rate of deterioration.

Technological Solutions to Environmental Problems

Perhaps the ameliorative approach that has won the greatest following is the one that comes most naturally to a technologically based civilization—that the problems that have largely been attributable to our industrial technology can be solved by industrial technology. If automobiles pollute, they can be re-engineered not to pollute. If it is argued that this will increase their cost and raise their price to unacceptable levels, that is a conclusion premised on present knowledge: research will provide cheaper solutions. History offers reassuring parallels. "In 1863 [Britain's] Parliament passed the Alkali Act, which called for a 95 percent reduction in hydrogen chloride emissions. Almost immediately technologists developed better gas absorbers and commercial processes for converting hydrogen chloride into chlorine gas. Half a century ago the dairy industry opposed legislation for pasteurization of milk on the grounds that it was impractical and would be too costly. But once the law was enacted scientific technology developed a safe, efficient, and inexpensive method of pasteurization. Instead of pricing milk out of the market, as had been predicted by the dairy industry, pasteurization decreased its price by increasing its shelf life." [51] In our own time there have been similar instances. The Dow Chemical Company allocated $8.5 million to control air and waste discharges at its Midland, Michigan, facilities. Though normally this would be viewed as a nonproductive expense, the general manager has said: "From an operating man's standpoint, the emphasis on waste control is one of the better things that has happened to us. It sharpened up our whole operation. We will not accept a plant that doesn't have its pollution control in hand before it's built." "Sharpening up" the company's operations has improved the yield from its raw materials, by reducing leakages and losses, in the amount of $6 million in three years.[52]

Urbanist Jane Jacobs foresees that cities will become huge, rich, and diverse mines of raw materials. As "natural" mining enters the stage of rapidly diminishing returns, city wastes will, by contrast, become the richest source of industry's raw materials. Waste recyclers will at first derive their income along the lines of the present St. Petersburg trash and garbage processing plant, which receives a flat payment by the ton for handling the city's wastes and the rest of its income from the sale of any materials it recovers from them. But soon, Mrs. Jacobs predicts, the proportion of unrecovered wastes will decline and the income from sales of processed waste to industry, as raw material, will increase. The waste collectors will eventually wind up bidding against one another for the privilege of hauling away municipal refuse.[53]

Even Barry Commoner, who has often been cited as a prophet of ecological doom, denies that his strictures against the forms that technology has taken in the past mean that he construes technology as being necessarily harmful to the environment. Quite the contrary:

Suppose that sewage, instead of being introduced into surface waters as it is now, whether directly or following treatment, is instead transported from urban collection systems by pipeline to agricultural areas, where—after appropriate sterilization procedures—it is incorporated into the soil. . . . Since the urban population is then no longer external to the soil cycle, it is incapable either of generating negative biological stresses upon the soil or exerting a positive ecological stress on the waters. But this state of zero environmental impact is not achieved by a return to "primitive" conditions, but by an actual technological advance, the construction of a sewage pipeline system.

It would appear possible to reduce the environmental impact of human activities by developing alternatives to ecologically-faulty activities. This can be accomplished, not by abandoning technology and the economic goods which it can yield, but by developing new technologies which incorporate not only the knowledge of the physical sciences but ecological wisdom as well.[54]

And a number of companies stand ready to deliver the technology that other companies will order whenever congressional pressure or economic feasibility dictate. Combustion Engineering, Inc., advertises that "it's going to take all our knowledge and ability to make the land, air and water perfectly clear. That means we must work with industries and businesses to come up with the technology to solve its problems. Because only technology will improve the quality of life without lowering our standard of living."[55] What greater reassurance can a consuming public ask for than that it can eat its cake and have it too?

As in the case of consumer protection, legislative measures, simply by promising relief, may assuage public fears, even though remedial action remains in doubt. Thus in 1972, after the Senate had passed the "zero discharge" bill which subsequently became the Water Pollution Control Act, a business journal analyzed the provisions and found them "more reasonable than business may think." Although the aim is to achieve water clean enough for swimming and fish propagation by 1983 and to eliminate all effluents by 1985, the language of the measure—the journal pointed out—"is careful not to eliminate affluence along with effluents." In enjoining companies to employ, at first, the "best practicable" technology and then, in the later stages, the "best available," the legislation defines these terms to take into account the age and size of plants and the cost of installing controls, thus ruling out anything "ruinously expensive." If the costs outweigh benefits, Congress is charged with making a "midcourse correction," presumably on a case-by-case basis but potentially eliminating zero discharge as a national goal altogether.[56]

A second approach to pollution control is related to the technology argument. Antipollutionists have often argued that an increase in industrial production means a concomitant increase in pollution, that goods creation involves materials conversion and disposal which necessarily have a deleterious impact on the environment. But that argument has been countered by the assertion that only through additional output can we allocate the resources to the technology that will solve our pollution problems and still have a little something left over to feed our desire for a "better" life (that is, one with more income, goods, and services). "With growth, we can handle environmental problems by allocating a bit less than one-half of the [projected] growth in GNP to this effort. Real living standards as conventionally measured would grow more slowly than they otherwise could. But the benefits in terms of a clean environment would appear to far outweigh the costs. . . . Thus the introduction of new technologically advanced equipment could foster pollution abatement. And new plants are often more profitable, compensating for some of the cost of pollution control." [57]

The Economist's Strategy:
Internalizing External Costs

Among economists, probably the preferred strategy stems from the public's realization that what was once considered a "free" good, because it was not scarce, is now an economic good, because it has become scarce. Air and water were once there for anyone to use as he chose. Somewhere along the line came the recognition that the way some people—especially industry—use air and water imposes costs on others. Our anachronistic approach to air and water as natural resources is responsible for our pollution problems. If the costs that industry now escapes, and imposes on others, were to be imposed on industry instead, then it would treat air and water efficiently. The external (social) costs to which it gives rise should be internalized (privatized), probably by some form of taxation. This would raise the cost of some goods, but only then would we have an accurate accounting of the real costs of the goods we consume.

External, or social, costs have secondary effects that compound the pollution problem. If electric power can be bought cheaply because it does not bear its full social costs, this encourages the use of household electric appliances, and the use of electric energy in the manufacture of still other products—all adding to the pollution problem. If electric power were made to bear its full social cost, not only would it become more expensive, but so would the products that were made with it and the products that used it.

A variety of plans to force products to bear their full costs have been proposed. Some would estimate the costs of pollution in terms of poorer health, reduced recreational opportunities, loss of aesthetic enjoyments, and then would allocate these costs among the polluters. This would of course involve difficult problems of measurement, but arbitrary estimates would serve the purpose. Other proposals would levy a tax proportioned to a company's emission of a particular type of pollutant, with the tax rate set at a level to achieve some overall sum. The point of all such schemes is to provide an economic inducement for a company to take corrective action. The rationale has been explained by the President's Council of Economic Advisers. After pointing out that different kinds of pollution and different sources of pollution give rise to different costs in controlling pollution, the Council has suggested: "One way that differences in control costs could be taken into account would be to set prices for the use of the air and water. If each potential polluter were faced with a price for each unit of pollutant he discharged, he would have to compare this with the costs of pollution control in his particular circumstance." [58]

If all external costs were internalized through a system of taxes or charges, the prices of some very basic commodities—food and electricity, for example—might be raised substantially. The justification for this is inherent in the proposed system—those who consume these products should have to pay their full cost, rather than force society to subsidize them by artificially low prices. It is recognized, however, that because the common components of an average household budget would be affected by rising prices, some income supplement to low-income families would be necessary simply to permit them to maintain their already low standard of living. Even so, those income recipients would, like any other consumer, be less likely to spend their supplement on the high-priced polluting items, but would economize by buying, for example, soap instead of detergents.

The taxes collected from polluting producers could be used to remedy the pollution to which they give rise, or they could go into the general treasury to be used for whatever purposes stand highest in the nation's priority list.

Already several legislative measures have been prepared or introduced embodying the effluent-tax principle. One would tax the sulfur content of fuel, beginning at one cent a pound and rising to ten cents within a few years. Another would tax the lead content in gasoline. Senator William Proxmire, an ardent advocate of the taxing device, has proposed a national tax of perhaps ten cents a pound of pollution discharged into waterways, measured by the biochemical oxygen demand (BOD) which an effluent creates. He has also proposed a tax of one cent a pound on any product that must be discarded after use.[59]

All such proposals reflect the economist's penchant for relying on price mechanisms rather than on regulations. But even economists admit that some situations are not adequately covered by the tax approach. Certain products might be banned altogether (DDT is often mentioned; Commoner would add other synthetics). Certain areas (coastlines, interior lakes) might be prohibited to industry. Courts or administrators can be empowered to suspend industrial operations or limit the use of automobiles in a particular locality if meteorological conditions threatened to trap emissions (as occurred in Birmingham, Alabama, in November 1971, when a federal judge, acting under the emergency provisions of the Clean Air Act of 1970, enjoined twenty-three companies from continuing production because of a health threat created by a protracted temperature inversion).

Environmental Deterioration within the Corporate System

The strategies of environmental protection that have been identified as compatible with maintenance of the corporate system would, of course, not be embraced by corporate managers on their own volition. We have already noted business opposition to environmental-protection programs generally. Nevertheless, given the realistic prognosis that some additional measures will be called for, actions along the above lines—technology and taxation, supplemented by regulation—would leave the system itself securely in place. This can safely be predicted for two reasons: first, there is nothing in these approaches that drives them to any "logical" conclusion threatening to the corporation; second, as we have seen, a general coalition of concerns (cost and profit consciousness on the part of management, price and employment consciousness on the part of the public) can be counted on to confine environmental legislation to relatively limited intervention with the present order, whatever strategy is employed.

The consequence is that environmental controls, as they unfold over time, are almost certain to be something that corporations can live with. There will of course be substantial costs in meeting federal and state requirements. A McGraw-Hill survey in 1973 projects annual capital spending for pollution control of approximately $6.2 billion for all industry, but this amounts to only a little less than 6 percent of total capital spending. The cost, to be sure, is spread unequally among industries, ranging from 2 percent of capital outlays in gas utilities to 42.5 percent in paper and paper products. In fact, of 26 industries surveyed, 9 expect to be spending less in 1976 than at present—on the basis of present expectations as to standards likely to be prevailing then.[60] But a substantial proportion of these expenditures will be passed along to consumers—just how much depends on varying price elasticities of demand as between one corporation's products and another's, between one industry's products and those of other industries, and between U.S. products and those of competing economies.

Although industrialists seem to anticipate, fatalistically, a continuing tightening up of pollution standards over time, thereby exacerbating their problems of "survival," one could make out a good case for just the opposite. As the price effect and consumption inhibition of controls manifest themselves, industry will be joined by the consuming public in urging a relaxation of pressures for environmental protection. For one thing, as René Dubos has emphasized, people have a marvelous—perhaps even dangerous—capacity for adapting to changed conditions. "Human beings can even become accustomed to articles of diet that appear at first unpalatable and may even be physiologically objectionable. Similarly, city dwellers commonly develop such a degree of apparent tolerance to certain air pollutants that they become unaware of the presence of these substances in the air they breathe." [61]

Moreover, the presence—and removal—of pollutants from air and water is not always physically visible. Some of the most noxious and toxic effects are virtually unobservable. Further, the long-range effects of contamination are not even known. The first administrator of the Environmental Protection Administration of New York City has observed that "there is as yet no satisfactory way of appraising the health effects of air pollutants at the concentrations experienced where reasonable abatement procedures are in effect. The results of [present] studies are highly equivocal at the levels of atmospheric pollution that will be reached when the present control program is fully implemented in 1972 to 1973." [62]

With America's urbanized population conditioned to want more consumption goods and to regard that as the principal measure of achievement over time, it seems highly unlikely that it will divert resources to remedy environmental conditions whose incidence is sometimes not discernible, which are of uncertain or unknown danger, and to which in any event they have become accustomed, even though they may grumble a bit about those conditions.

The consequence is that government, in the name of the democratic process, can be responsive *both* to the public at large and to industry as the dominant interest by undertaking only modest remedial measures and indeed some retrograde steps. Thus, at the invitation of the federal Forest Service, private developers were invited to bid to turn Mineral King Valley, in the Sierra Nevada of California, into a year-round recreation area. "The Walt Disney interests won the bidding with a plan for a huge complex of hotels, motels, restaurants, ski lifts and a nine-level parking garage. The plan anticipates a tourist traffic twice as dense as now clogs Yosemite on a busy day." [63] The prospect may sound appalling to the environmentalist, but the political process to which we are committed virtually dictates this result. Recreation and entertainment for the many takes precedence over environmental protection championed by the few. The issue has been posed with compelling simplicity by Edward Hoagland: "Understand that a bear, for example, needs a minimum of about five square miles to forage in for his food supply. . . . Yet if an acre is now to become worth $1,000 as a recreational property, is a bear worth $3.2 million?" [64]

Or take the question of the environmental impact of synthetics, which has been brought into public consciousness by Barry Commoner. The Economic Research Division of the Chase Manhattan Bank notes:

> The solution, say many ecologists, is to return to the use of natural products and economize on the use of energy. This would involve such shifts as from detergents to soap, synthetic to natural rubber, plastic to paper packaging, returnable bottles, private to public transportation.
> To make large-scale, rapid substitutions in this manner would be exceedingly costly. A considerable part of American industry would be subject to severe dislocations in jobs, materials and plant during the transition. The political consequences would be unacceptable short of clear and present danger which has not been demonstrated.[65]

In sum, the threat of environmental catastrophe *may* be real, but it is certainly not immediate, and may never materialize. Why sacrifice what is now available and good—consumer income—for the problematic? It is not simply a few self-interested corporate magnates who raise that question in their own interest. It is the public at large. The public policy consequence is clear enough: incremental adjustments, as called for by particular or developing circumstances, without disturbing the present way of life.

Behind this populist position stands a cadre of professional experts ready to give it a philosophical validation. Foremost among these are the economists. The Council of Economic Advisers speaks for what is undoubtedly the dominant view in the discipline:

> Since society places a value both on material goods and on clean air and water, arrangements must be devised that permit the value we place on each to determine our choices. . . . What we seek, therefore, is a set of rules for use of the environment which balances the advantages of each activity against its costs in other activities foregone. We want to eliminate pollution only when the physical and aesthetic discomfort it creates and its damage to people and things are more costly than the value of the good things—the abundance of in-

dustrial or farm products and efficient transportation—whose production has caused the pollution.[66]

The fact that industry itself has been largely responsible for so firmly implanting the consumption orientation, whose *social value* is placed against environmental protection, is not alluded to in such intellectual attempts at evenhanded trade-offs. Moreover, the economist can add to his stature as disinterested philosopher by pointing out that the price system can be brought into service to protect the environment, whenever we will it. Do we worry that certain resources may be exhausted by commercial exploitation? The price system will come to their rescue by increasing their price concomitantly with their scarcity. "We will not suddenly 'run out' of fossil fuels. Long before the last drop of oil is used, oil will have become much more expensive. If gasoline were $5 or $10 a gallon, we would utilize it much more sparingly, with small economical automobile engines, or perhaps the substitution of some non-petroleum-based fuel altogether." [67]

The scientific fraternity, too, has lent its authority to the incremental-ist approach. On the assumption that environmental protection, if pursued vigorously, would involve setting limits to economic growth, hence limits to the technical application of scientific developments, they have tended to support the doctrine that whatever can be done, should be done (and indeed will be done). If the Supersonic transport (SST) is scientifically and technically feasible, then sooner or later the SST should be and will be produced. The scientific and technological establishment thus also validates a more "adventurous" and "experimental" approach to the use of the environment, rather than one of retrenchment. Even René Dubos, a proponent of environmental measures, has testified to this strong drive for "unlimited" technological innovation: "Progress always implies the risk of encountering new dangers, and disease ensues whenever man fails, as he usually does, in making rapidly enough a perfect adaptive response to the new environments in which he elects to live and to function." [68]

Nevertheless, however convincingly the professional experts validate the incremental policy that major corporate interests and a consumptionist society have forced upon a responsive government, the environmental problems cannot be wished away. Moreover, it seems clear that they cannot be resolved within the framework of the existing corporate system. (They cannot be resolved within the framework of any existing socialist system either, but that is a matter to which we shall return briefly later.) The consequence can only be a deteriorating natural environment, even though deterioration takes place at a slower rate.

This conclusion emerges not out of any apocalyptic vision or out of any preference for some alternative system of economic organization. The British neo-Arcadians who in 1972 promulgated a "Blueprint for Survival," though including many eminent scientists among their number, are out of touch with reality in calling for a return to "small, self-regulating communities" of about 5,000 to which industry and agriculture both are integral, groups that would be allied with other such communities by "an efficient and sensitive communications network," that would emphasize durability and craftmanship of output, that would provide "an intensity of relationships with a few rather than urban man's variety of innumerable, superficial relationships." [69] All of this—including the educational system that would inculcate the values of this kind of stable society—bears a vague similarity to B. F. Skinner's utopian Walden II. But even in the absence of a blueprint for an alternative social order, the incompatability of the corporate system with environmental preservation seems objectively evident, and the incrementalist approach to dealing with environmental problems only a protracted refusal to face them. Let us concentrate on the most compelling reasons why this is so.

Deficiencies of the Economic Argument

However presently unpalatable to corporate leadership, the idea that seems to have won most widespread interest as a means of making pollution control compatible with the private corporate system is what we can appropriately call "the economist's approach." In its purest form, this involves internalizing within the firm all costs that its operations impose on society.[70] The result is as utopian and impracticable as anything the British scientists have dreamed up with their idyllic communities of 5,000. Or, to change the comparison, an effort to juggle market prices to incorporate all external costs (however these might be measured, a problem to which we will come shortly) would surely match the Communist effort to bypass the market and control prices for political objectives.

Given that such power over the pricing of products could not be vested in any board or agency, within anything approximating our present frame of government, the purist approach of the economist would inevitably melt into some form of politically feasible effluent charges, not necessarily (or not even likely) closely calibrated to the use or misuse of natural resources. Such charges would of course constitute some inducement for industry to curb pollution, but the degree of inducement and the amount of curbing would be problematic at best. Of one thing we could be sure: if politically acceptable, they could not *stop* environmental deterioration.

To the extent that industry was content to pay the effluent charge, because the costs of controlling the last 10 or 20 percent of pollution were greater, the revenues would probably flow into the general treasury, rather than be earmarked for the control that industry had not found profitable to undertake.[71] Even if government were to segregate these funds for environmental purposes, they would have to be supplemented from general revenues if the desired level of pollution control were to be attained, so that particular industries and the consumers of their products would be subsidized to that extent, contrary to the economists' intent. But such supplementation would be most unlikely, because we could at that point expect emergence of the coalition of interests against heavy federal funding of environmental projects, the value of which (from both the industry and consumer point of view) would not outweigh the value of the consumption foregone.

A second consideration, weighty though it is, need simply be mentioned. All economists who favor internalizing external costs of production agree that the result would be weighted against the needy. Thus Solow: "The principle of assessing environmental costs on the activities that cause them would lead to material goods (which play a relatively bigger role in the budgets of the poor) becoming dearer relative to services (which play a proportionately bigger role in the budgets of the rich). It might lead to the taxation of the necessities of life of the poor to pay for the protection of the recreational amenities of the rich."[72] The way out of this dilemma, as Walter Heller points out, is that "as we end industry's free ride on public air and water and land and thereby raise the price of goods bought by the poor, we simultaneously compensate them through more effective measures to redistribute income and opportunity."[73] How easy a solution in logic! How difficult in political reality! If little headway has been made toward redistribution of income in the last quarter century (even though rising GNP has raised the proportion of the population above the poverty level), how much would the redistributional problem be compounded by throwing in a compensatory factor to offset the income effect of the new system of prices?

A third weakness in the economist's approach is one which he generally considers his strength—the matter of measurement. It is easy to talk about "assessing environmental costs," as Solow does, but far more difficult to measure them. Heller speaks of the economist as one who "thinks in terms of marginalism, trade-offs, and a careful cost-benefit calculus," as one who strikes "a balance between nature and man, between environment and growth, and between technology and ecology," as one who would push depollution "to, but not beyond, the point where the costs—the foregone satisfactions of a greater supply of additional goods and services—just equal the benefits—the gained satisfactions of clean air, water, landscape, and sound waves." [74] But what market measures these benefits of clean air and water? How do we impute a value to health or longevity that may (can we even be sure?) be attributable to a less polluted environment? Is the value of a fresh fish dinner to be measured in what it costs now, or what it will cost ten or twenty years from now, when fresh fish has become a rarity, and if the latter, how do we know what that future price is likely to be? We are not now talking about so-called "incommensurable" items, but those things that economists are accustomed to add up, in one form or another, in computing gross national product, except that we are now talking of hypothetical rather than real values.

But this, to the economist, is the talk of philistines. "For planning purposes, an overall valuation must be defined, even though the precise form of the common measure (or *numéraire*) is undetermined. Can money perform service as a *numéraire?* Is it not obvious that it can, and that only an unwillingness to admit to the so-called ignoble side of man's nature stands in the way of this admission? Each of us must supply our own answer as to whether money can buy, for example, respect, fame, and love." [75] The authors of this bit of moral philosophy, William Ramsay and Claude Anderson, might indeed have turned to higher authority in support of their pecuniary calculus. Over 150 years earlier Jeremy Bentham had said, in similar vein: "I beg a truce here of our man of sentiment and feeling while from necessity, and it is only from necessity, I speak and prompt mankind to speak a mercenary language. . . . Money is the instrument for measuring the quantity of pain or pleasure. Those who are not satisfied with the accuracy of this instrument must find out some other that shall be more accurate, or bid adieu to Politics and Morals." [76]

But Ramsay and Anderson pursue the matter farther. "This is all very well in theory," they allow their philistine to observe. "But how can we evaluate smog in practice [to take a relevant example]?" They have their answer. "It is consistent with the price-market approach to follow a method that might be called 'deterministic pragmatism.' An example of evaluating smog by this method would be to look at the motives of people who vote on the issue with their feet, that is, people who leave the Los Angeles Basin with the avowed purpose of escaping the smog. Naturally, the human tendency to add excess drama to other decision variables must be reckoned with . . . but a study of such *émigrés* would still serve to help determine how much the negative value of smog is. The Los Angeles Basin is, in general, a region of high wages. After all extraneous factors have been averaged out, such as the days of sunshine, the relative absence of rain, the lack of distinctive seasons, and the possible presence or absence of mothers or mothers-in-law, a value set by emigrating people in terms of lost-wage opportunities might give an indication of the actual market value of smog." Nor need we stop there. ". . . the investigation of land values, comparing smog-free to smoggy environments, seems a promising approach." [77]

Any reader, with this elementary instruction (and indeed the authors describe their book as "an economic primer"), could go on to make his own calculations as to the market value of avoiding emphysema or of a day spent in recreational fishing. He might indeed be a little discouraged by the considerable range in the figures which are now quoted as the "cost" of pollution—those benefits foregone by the absence of clean air, water, landscape, and sound waves, as Heller would put it—but not nearly so discouraged as when he got around to measuring what even Ramsay and Anderson admit still present a difficult problem—matters involving aesthetics, for example. What is the relative value of bringing recreation to the masses (more Disneyland entertainment centers) as against unspoiled valleys? How compare the relative costs and benefits of the highway into a scenic mountain area as against leaving the scenic mountain area free of concrete?

For Ramsay and Anderson, the problem is not insoluble; we only have to work at it a little while longer. "In theory, all this could be handled from an economic point of view. In some way, which we cannot precisely put our finger on, the wild areas have a value to us, and this value should be, ideally, expressible in money terms, just like anything else. This value, if we knew it, would then be greater or lesser than the recreational value to the tourists who would come into the area through the proposed new highway. By comparing these two values, the highway department could make a decision for or against the road." Of course, in our efforts to quantify values which are still vague today, we recognize that aesthetic values are not the same for all. The price system has always taken such differences in taste into account, however. "The river need not have the same utility to a fisherman and a nonfisherman, in order for us to set a price on it, any more than a five dollar steak dinner has equal utility to a hungry football player and to Miss Gibbs, the vegetarian church organist." [78] There is, of course, the slight difference that the football player and Miss Gibbs are both free to express their respective tastes, but if the fisherman has his way, the recreational boater cannot have his, and vice versa. The choice is all or none, highway or unspoiled mountain valley, which is to say, that the choice is political, not economic.

On this point ecologist Barry Commoner stands on firmer ground:

Confronted by decisions on nuclear power, radiation, nitrate levels, photochemical smog, bacterial warfare, and all the other technicalities of environmental problems, one is tempted to call in the scientific expert. Scientists can, of course, evaluate the relevant benefits: how many kilowatt hours of electricity a nuclear-power plant can deliver, and at what price, or the yield of corn to be expected from the use of nitrogen fertilizer. They can also evaluate the related risks: the radiation dose to people in the vicinity of the power plant and the hazard to infants from nitrate levels exacerbated by fertilizers. Those evaluations can be derived from appropriate scientific theories, principles, and data.

However, no scientific principle can guide the choice between some number of kilowatt hours of electric power and some number of cases of thyroid cancer, or between some number of bushels of corn and some number of cases of infant methemoglobinemia. These are value judgments; they are determined not by scientific principle, but by the value that we place on economic advantage and on human life.[79]

But the problem of measurement does not end here. There is a time aspect to the things we value that cannot be passed over lightly. Economists tend to think of social assets—natural resources, for example—in the same way they conceive of corporate assets. Their present value is calculated by discounting future uses, at some appropriate rate of interest. This is based on the obvious psychological preference that people have for a bird in the hand instead of two in the bush. A future dollar is worth less than a dollar today, because a dollar held today can be invested and hence will wind up on that future date being worth a dollar plus interest, instead of just a dollar.

But to use a principle that is understandable enough when applied to the lifetime of an individual as though it applied equally across the lifetimes of innumerable generations yet to come, is to convert the principle into nonsense. It implicitly assumes that we who live today are the only ones to whom natural resources have value. We estimate the value of these resources by *discounting* their future uses down to the present, that is, down to our own immediate use. The value of those resources to innumerable future generations is of less account than their value of us today. So use up our land and mineral deposits in accordance with a corporation's method of valuation, which makes their future "realizable" value something that *we* discount, in terms of present worth. Land that could not be used until the year 2000 would have less value than that same land without such a restriction, to any corporation, and we apply the same principle to the resources that we as a society "own." Thus Ramsay and Anderson, in expressing their optimism that we will still learn how to measure aesthetic values, argue that "the wild areas have a value to *us*," even if we have difficulty in calculating it, as against the values to tourists, which we hope also to learn to calculate, and that when these two estimates have been made, the highway department can lay them side by side and choose. Choose, that is, not for future generations, even though they will inherit the effects of the decision, but choose for *us*, on the strength of our conception of the *present* value of the respective uses of that now unspoiled territory.

Carl Madden, chief economist for the U.S. Chamber of Commerce, has stated the issue succinctly: "What is of 'value' for the human species *as a whole* can be determined only if *all* future generations can make a *simultaneous* bid on resources." [80] Clearly no such dynamic general equilibrium is possible, any more than is the Walrasian static general equilibrium, even though like the latter it is logically impeccable. Nor is it any answer to say that because we can never know the future uses and values of resources presently available, the principle is unworkable and therefore we are entitled to calculate values as though we alone were the sole inheritors of the earth's resources. By insisting that the value of all things can be measured in money—"respect, fame, love," and the value of resources to future generations—economists have simply claimed more for the price system than it can deliver. Thus a defensible alternative case could be made for an arbitrary reserve of raw materials—including unspoiled natural environments—for future generations, immune from any present-generation claims based on a stream of future values that we impute and then discount.

One conclusion of enormous importance that flows from our present methods of valuation is that corporate title to natural resources *encourages* present use and discourages preservation for the future, simply on the principles of investment and asset evaluation which are taught in every business school. Indeed one could go further by saying that the corporate system, with its gospel of consumption as the focal value of life, as the *standard* of living, is likewise indirectly responsible for public policies geared to the gratification of its *present* population, resulting in the environmental effects that now concern us. The former president of Midas International, Gordon Sherman, an offbeat businessman whose iconoclast views led to his departure from that company, shared his misgivings on this score with corporate stockholders in the company's 1969 annual report. Let us admit, he urged them, "that there is no natural consonance between our desire to show *present* profit, and the desperate *long-range* needs of our people and our environment." Sherman was concerned with the toxic gases that the company's exhaust system products were "innocently" conveying into the atmosphere, and with the "happy but despoiling presence" of company-produced recreational vehicles in "our waning wilderness." Economists would, of course, have been ready to pacify this troubled corporate executive by urging on him effluent charges to compensate for the external costs his company was imposing on society. But then they would have been faced once again with the measurement problem. What is the (negative) value of the toxic gases, what is the lost value—thinking of the future as well as the present—of the waning wilderness, so that charges could be imposed sufficient to induce preventive action?

But perhaps, in a grotesquely ironic way, the discounting of future values is after all justified. As Dubos has so pointedly reminded us, man adapts, and as he adapts the value of what he has given up declines.

> Millions upon millions of human beings are so well adjusted to the urban and industrial environment that they no longer mind the stench of automobile exhausts, or the ugliness generated by the urban sprawl; they regard it as normal to be trapped in automobile traffic, to spend much of a sunny afternoon on concrete highways among the dreariness of anonymous and amorphous streams of motor cars. Life in the modern city has become a symbol of the fact that man can become adapted to starless skies, treeless avenues, shapeless buildings, tasteless bread, joyless celebrations, spiritless pleasures—to a life without reverence for the past, love for the present, or hope for the future.
>
> Man is so adaptable that he could survive and multiply in underground shelters, even though his regimented subterranean existence left him unaware of the robin's song in the spring, the whirl of dead leaves in the fall, and the moods of the wind—even though indeed all his ethical and esthetic values should wither. It is disheartening to learn that today in the United States schools are being built underground, with the justification that the rooms are easier to clean and the children's attention not distracted by the outdoors! [81]

Thus the value of the lost environment, in terms of Ramsay's and Anderson's pecuniary *numéraire*, falls over time on the open market. If, then, we try to anticipate the future, we should perhaps allow for this effect, writing down our *present* estimates of *future* environmental benefits, considered as opportunity cost relative to our present uses of that environment. To be sure, we might experience an instinctive revulsion at the prospect of such a future existence, but we could comfort ourselves by the assurance that *they* will not feel the loss as keenly as *we* imagine it, and in any event, who knows what technological advances may not compensate for natural resource displacements?

But let us waive further discussion of the measurement problem, which as we have seen is not simply a methodological issue, as economists have tended to portray it, but a substantive and conceptual matter. Let us move on, assuming that costs and benefits can indeed be measured, to consider the impact of such "trade-offs" on the environment. An economist helps us see the matter from an economist's point of view: "Costs must inevitably be paid for by consumers, and therefore consumers ought to know what environmental protection costs. As always, the question is, 'How much are you willing to pay?' . . . If people are given the impression that it will cost nothing to eliminate pollution entirely, they'll want that. But since they are going to have to pay for it, they should have a chance to decide whether they can afford, or even want, Rolls Royce standards instead of Chevrolet standards." [82] The syllogistic reasoning is evident: (1) a Rolls Royce is the equivalent of an unpolluted environment; (2) the average consumer cannot afford a Rolls Royce; (3) therefore he cannot afford an unpolluted environment.

But this is not exactly a philosopher's dream of a free and unstructured choice. There is no need to repeat here the conclusions of the preceding chapter, that while no corporation individually can control consumer choice, the corporate system in the aggregate has promoted consumption as a social value, has indeed won public acceptance for a value system with which its own interests are identified. This has not been the product of a sinister plot, but simply the ability of an interest group to persuade the public to a way of thinking. That way of thinking has become so ingrained in people's consciousnesses and so promoted through all our major social institutions that we accept it as a preferred way of life.

René Dubos supplies an interesting example of this value process at work:

In a recent issue of the *Bulletin of the Atomic Scientists* a professor of nuclear engineering at Massachusetts Institute of Technology advocates the rapid development of fast breeder reactors because, in his words, 'An abundant supply of electricity . . . is essential to civilized society. . . .' What the MIT professor really meant is that an ever increasing supply of electricity is essential for a kind of civilized society that measures civilization by power and therefore by the amount of electricity it consumes—something of a circuitous argument.[83]

Thus in considering trade-offs—how high a price in consumption we want to pay for environmental protection—the consumer is more than likely to come down on the side of what he has been *taught* to prefer. Who, then, we may ask, profits most from this democratic choice, the conditioned consumer or the producer whose dominant role in society in fact depends on the conditioned consumer?

This is not the same as the argument we earlier encountered, that pollution control would benefit the well-to-do more than the poor. Rather, it suggests that the consumptionist way of life to which the general public aspires derives in some significant measure from those who have most to gain from the public's consumer aspirations, those who control the large corporations. This is not intended to level a finger of accusation. Social values must always derive from some group that has been able to identify its values and interests with those of society at large, and history shows there can be far worse systems of values. But it does belie any notion that the "trade-off" between consumption and environment is unstructured; values built into our corporate society tip the scales in favor of consumption. In light of which, we have further basis for doubting that environmentalism, any more than consumerism, is likely to stem a deterioration in the quality of that to which it addresses itself.

Deficiencies of the Technological Strategy

In addition to internalizing external costs (or effluent charges, or cost-benefit trade-offs), the second major strategy for dealing with environmental problems within the context of the present system is through advanced technology made possible by economic growth. It is now coming to be conceded by economist and ecologist alike that reliance on technology really means a successful and encompassing recycling of resources. Economists may be more willing to accept some environmental deterioration as part of a trade-off, but to the extent that technology is viewed as a solution to the pollution-depletion problem, it is through recycling.

Economist Solow thus reminds us that "to 'eliminate' air and water pollution means to transform them into the problem of disposing of solid

75

waste, another pollution problem. The only 'solution' to the combined problem is the recycling of materials (or the greater durability of material things or the increased efficiency of conversion of fuels into energy). The rest is a choice of the socially best way to dispose of a given weight of residual material." [84] Ecologist Commoner, using the picturesque figure of "closing the circle," concludes that "We must learn how to restore to nature the wealth we borrow from it." [85]

But if recycling is the only effective technology for environmental solutions, then we face certain problems that cannot be dealt with by this method. First, some natural resources cannot be recycled, notably natural recreational areas, scenic grandeur, a variety of habitats for particular species of life. Once used, these are destroyed.

Second, some synthetic products cannot be decomposed or converted, but only buried or destroyed. Indeed, as we have seen, Commoner imputes to this class of products perhaps the principal reason for the rapid acceleration of environmental pollution since World War II.

Third, technology capable of recycling even all natural compounds is not presently available, nor is it likely to become available within the near future. Even if and when available, its use in particular situations may be so costly, especially in eliminating that last fraction of pollution, that it will be rejected in any "trade-off" with equivalent consumption benefits. We will settle, after all, for a Chevrolet rather than a Rolls Royce environment so that we can continue to have our Chevrolets.

Fourth, new technologies, whether designed to meet present pollution problems or simply to present us with new consumer gratifications, carry their own potential problems. Again Dubos offers a warning:

Developing *countertechnologies* to correct the new kinds of damage constantly being created by technological innovations is a policy of despair. If we follow this course we shall increasingly behave like hunted creatures, fleeing from one protective device to another, each more costly, more complex, and more undependable than the one before; we shall be concerned chiefly with sheltering ourselves from environmental dangers while sacrificing the values that make life worth living.[86]

Fifth, the technological advances that are relied on, however partially or dependably, to meet the problems of pollution are made possible by economic growth. There is no need here of going through the endless argument that has been generated around the concept of "no growth" or the stationary state. But it is gaining only a debater's point to rebut the "no growth" position without seriously considering whether growth per se, growth in any form that adds to levels of gross national product, should continue to serve as a prime national objective. If we concede that technology is not available to meet all our pollution problems and that public preference for consumer goods will not support full use of available technology, then continuation of the growth psychology will sooner or later bring us hard up against the pollution problems from which technology is supposed to save us. More appropriate and effective technology may slow the rate of environmental depletion and pollution, as Commoner has suggested, but with the passage of time and continued economic growth, the resources will diminish and the wastes accumulate as at present. We will have bought only a little time at best.

Nevertheless, we can be reasonably sure that the growth psychology will persist, in part because it comports with our focal objectives, but also in large part because it helps us to buy out of political problems that would be far more difficult to solve otherwise. Walter Heller has made the point forcefully: "Even with the aid of a rise of 55 percent in GNP and 34 percent in real per capita personal income from 1959 to 1969 (in 1969 dollars), we have found that our inroads on [social] problems have not kept pace with our rising aspirations and expectations. Imagine the tensions between rich and poor, between black and white, between blue-collar and white-collar and other workers, between old and young, if we had been forced to finance even the minimal demands of the disadvantaged out of a stationary national income instead of a one-third increase in income." [87]

In sum, any expectation that technology, made possible by economic growth, will provide escape from the environmental problems we confront is illusory. Appropriate technology can alleviate them, but such technology simply superimposed on the present technology-powered growth-oriented economic system is a brake that will not hold.

Corporate Social Responsibilities

In concluding that environmental deterioration (even though decelerated) is all that can be anticipated under the present corporate system, I do not wish to imply that this unwished-for consequence is escapable under socialism. The problems of depletion and pollution have been present in societies under socialist forms of economic organization, and if this has not occurred on the same scale as in the West, it is only because the scale of economic activity itself is less. Some historical burden may weigh upon Western societies for having fostered so undiluted a consumptionist, quantity-oriented, growth-focused, technologically based philosophy that has been seized on by other societies and made part of their own cultures, even if not in the same degree,[88] but in that regard the good and the bad are mixed in very uncertain proportions, and in any event the notion of historical guilt is one I find repugnant. I do believe that the drive for economic gain at almost any environmental price has been stronger under private-enterprise systems, for the very reason that we cite in extolling their greater accomplishments—the driving force of personal gain is a strong stimulus indeed, and as Tocqueville observed of America in the 1830s, it is likely to be pursued to the point where public welfare is not adequately attended to.

The burden of this assessment is not, at the end, to pull an economic rabbit out of the hat and offer an alternative form of economic organization that will "solve" our environmental problems. I know of none. It is only to suggest that present institutional arrangements are not likely to cope very effectively with environmental problems. I suspect that when these become too pressing to be evaded any longer, they will not be met by any comprehensive system of effluent charges, by any novel technologies, or by any resettlement of populations in small-scale agricultural-industrial communities, but by some more authoritarian form of government intervention.

What can we say, then, about the social responsibilities of the individual large corporation in the matter of environmental protection, given the present corporate system?

Those who argue for the Social Responsibility Thesis must face the fact that while some costs of pollution control can be assimilated as general expenses of doing business, competitors, stockholders, and employees collectively place limits on that amount. Such expenditures are viewed by management as "nonproductive," and hence something to be held down. What is not required by law becomes a marginal item, to be indulged in in years of high profit, but giving way to cost reduction and profit maintenance in the lean years.

Those who argue for the Social Engineering Thesis have a larger vision. Athelstan Spilhaus, former president of the American Association for the Advancement of Science, speaks eloquently for this view: "In the next industrial revolution, industry must close the loop back from the user to the factory. If American industrial genius can mass-assemble and mass-distribute, why cannot the same genius mass-collect, mass-disassemble, and massively reuse the materials? If American industry takes upon itself to close this loop, then the original design of the articles would facilitate their return and remaking. If, on the other hand, we continue to have the private sector make things, and the public sector dispose of them, designs for reuse will not easily come about." [89]

Unfortunately, such a vision cannot be pursued by any individual corporation. It would require a more concerted effort, with a grant to some corporations of powers comparable to state planning agencies. At the same time, other corporations would have to be denied the discretion to continue activities deemed incompatible with the recycling on which Spilhaus's "industrial revolution" depends. Obviously what would be involved here would be massive industrial reorganization, not simply something that American industry could "take upon itself."

In the last analysis, then, we are driven back upon the Limited Responsibility Thesis. Henry Ford II phrases it nicely: "In fact, there are severe limits to what business can do, entirely by itself, to solve environmental problems. The reason is that in the absence of appropriate government regulation, there is only a limited market for the main solutions to environmental problems. Few consumers, for example, will pay much for lower vehicle emissions unless their choices are limited by government regulation. Business lives and dies in the market, and no company can survive if it voluntarily assumes pollution control costs far out of line with those of its competitors." [90]

Once again we conclude that however pervasive is the influence of corporate values in American society, the power of any single corporation, however large, is limited. It is caught within the system of relationships it has helped to weave, subject to constraints that, by channeling and concentrating its activities, have given it the freedom to grow great, but that likewise limit its freedom to move in other directions.

[4]

THE CORPORATION AND ITS

INTERNAL COMMUNITY

A COMPANY produces something more than a product or a service. It produces people. By the way it structures its employee relations, by the attitudes it adopts toward its employees, customers, and suppliers; by the behavioral priorities it sets within the workplace, it helps to mold character and shape values. Companies differ from one another in this respect: like individuals, they can be said to have personalities. At the same time some characteristics are more or less common to them all. In this chapter we are concerned with the more general and common impact of the large corporation on the character formation of those who compose it. As religious orders mold their members, as military organizations make of their recruits a particular type of man, so do our dominant economic institutions help to create individuals to their own specifications. Although the phrase is less commonly used now, corporations still produce "organization men." If Americans have become concerned with "life styles," the corporations are among the chief stylists.

The large corporation still operates on a pyramidal form of organization, even though the hierarchical element may have been de-emphasized by the introduction of committees or "task forces" cutting across levels of authority. It remains true that there is a large body of the so-called rank and file (industry's equivalent of foot soldiers and lay officials) at the bottom of the pyramid, with a successively smaller number of people with incrementally greater authority at each higher level.

Influence of Labor Unions

This simple pyramidal model of any large-scale bureaucratic organization has been modified, in the case of the corporation, by the introduction of labor unions. The large body of rank and file is no longer controlled so directly by their managerial superiors. The latter's authority has to conform to the terms of an agreement, a contract, negotiated between union leaders acting as agent and representative for the workers, as one party, and top management, as the other party. The collective agreement helps to frame the "civil rights" of the rank and file and establishes certain conditions over which management relinquishes sole discretion and authority. Although there is some dispute over the precise impact of the agreement on management authority, in a rough and realistic way it can be said that management retains its traditional authority outside the areas in which it has made concessions—subject always to the realization that its relationship to the rank and file is basically one of relative bargaining powers, regardless of the terms of the contract, which represent only a temporary statement of that power relationship.

The presence of the union has thus curbed the corporation's control over its employees. There is no need to recount here the familiar contrast between preunion conditions in the major corporations, when employees had virtually no independent rights, even to join a union, and the contemporary state of affairs, when the individual worker is protected against arbitrary discipline by the equivalent of an industrial common law, when he possesses safeguards against layoffs and discriminatory favoritism in job assignments and promotions, enjoys paid holidays and vacations, and is entitled to health benefits and pensions.

In the ranks of management, however, from first-line supervisor on up, a different situation prevails. The financial emoluments and job perquisites tend to be greater, but security and independence are lacking. For individuals in the managerial ranks there is no "due process" in matters of discipline or job treatment, though there have been eloquent arguments on the need for such.[1] Managers take their chances on what they say and how they behave, both inside and outside the company. By and large, corporate authority has become too sophisticated to exercise the autocratic control over the conduct of its managers that characterized IBM in the days of Thomas Watson, Sr., when white shirts and a prim personal life were requisites for advancement. Nevertheless, there is such a thing as an appropriate "life style" in most corporations, and the individual who deviates from it is risking his chances for promotion if not his job itself.

Even in the case of the rank and file, the union contribution to worker autonomy carries two limitations. First, the union bureaucracy is patterned on the corporate bureaucracy, and the individual member must accept conformity to union standards as the price of his partial release from corporate conformity. This may not weigh so heavily on him; presumably he exercises a measure of control over the union bureaucracy in a way that he does not over the corporate bureaucracy. But in large-scale organizations (unions no less than corporations) the degree of *self*-government becomes diluted in proportion to size, and the control that the individual worker exercises over his union, particularly in matters affecting corporate-wide policy, often seems tenuous indeed. He may console himself with the rationalization that such union centralization is necessary if corporate policy is to be affected at all, but however rationalized he cannot help but be left with some sense of personal powerlessness and the feeling that policies are being made for him rather than by him. What else can one expect in the face of the scale of corporate operations? But the consequence is that the character of the individual continues to be molded by the corporate bureaucracy, except that the union has now become a functional part of that bureaucracy.

The second limit on rank-and-file self-government lies in the fact that his union does not touch, or touches only lightly, major corporate decisions such as the location or termination of a plant, the products to be manufactured and the technical processes by which they will be made, the quantity of output and hence of employment—in these areas management largely retains its old discretion.

In this chapter we shall not be much concerned with the role of the union (significant though it is, limited though it is) but with the more general way in which the attachment of the individual to a corporation affects his way of life and the extent to which he in fact is a product of the *corporate* way of life.

Alienation from Work

In Chapter 2 we contrasted the artisan who took pride in his work and possessed a capacity to carry an operation through from start to finish with the modern worker who is specialized to a particular task, whether of an assembly-line or clerical nature. Even as one goes up the hierarchical ladder, specialization remains the key to corporate organization: most individuals have a responsibility for a certain operation, whether it is the tightening of a single bolt or the marketing of a product line within a single area. Only relatively few general managers (whether at plant or corporate headquarters) escape the constrictions of specialization.

However much we exaggerate—as we surely do—the transition from an earlier day when an individual was concerned with a whole operation to the present day when he is concerned with only a small part of the whole, some such transition has in fact occurred.[2] The knowledge is commonplace. Indeed, we ascribe to such increased specialization a large part of the increased productivity of our industrial society. Such specialization does not necessarily rob a job of its interest; in particular situations, it may enhance it. Moreover, not all jobs can be minutely broken down, even within an organization large enough to permit extensive specialization of functions: the telephone installer and airline pilot are examples of occupations that still command integrated knowledge and skills, and many similar types of work could be identified even in large bureaucracies. Nevertheless, exceptions do not make the rule, and the general tendency of specialization in industrial life has been to reduce the responsibility and interest inherent in a job. As the general manager of General Motors' Lordstown, Ohio, plant said, in explaining the wildcat strike of workers at the new and highly automated facility, it is difficult to get a worker "to take a pride in our product—if a man drops a bolt and he doesn't pick it up and put it on, he's more apt to let it go the second time." While the Lordstown operation made the job simpler and easier, it also succeeded, in the opinion of some industrial engineers, in "removing the last traces of skill."[3] If a man's contribution is reduced to holding on to a bolt long enough to give it a few turns, his lack of pride in such an accomplishment is scarcely surprising.

As we noted previously, the consequence has been that workers have traded off some—and sometimes a large part—of their interest in the production process for a bigger share of consumer goods. "A sizable number of automobile workers . . . have reached a level of affluence—an accumulation of goods—unmatched in the history of the working class."[4] People may have differing views about the desirability of such a trade-off, but this has hardly been a matter of individual choice. Once the trend was set in motion, in a competitive market economy, a person's livelihood came more and more to depend on his acceptance of the system. The corporation, to survive, had to be efficient; to be efficient required technical specialization; for the worker to survive, he had to go along—however reluctantly—with the company's requirements. He solaced himself with a rising standard of living, with more goods, more consumer satisfaction. Ineluctably this substitution of consumer interests for producer interests has had its effect on the character of those who man the corporations. The worker who drops the bolt and forgets it— who can pin it on him?—and who erases the memory of a degrading day by driving to his own home in a late-model car and having a beer while watching the night game on the color television screen, perhaps in air-conditioned comfort, is simply a different person from the worker who prided himself on his technical capabilities and lived more frugally —whether a better or inferior person is anyone's judgment.

Sometimes lack of interest in a specific job can be compensated for by identification with an institution or cause. Many a common soldier, called upon to perform routine and even meaningless tasks sometimes only "for the sake of discipline," has nevertheless identified himself with his corps and looked back on his service with nostalgia. Religious and charitable workers have accepted menial tasks out of belief in the rightness of their cause. The corporation offers little such possibility for identification. What difference does it make to the clerical worker, the IBM programmer, or the assembler if his company surpasses a competitor in sales or makes its target rate of return? Can he achieve any sense of organizational pride in his company's product line (in a large corporation, often numbered in the thousands, many short-lived, each distinguished trivially from some competitor's product)? Above all, can he identify himself with an organization whose ultimate purpose is to earn a maximum profit for thousands of stockholders whom he does not know and who are themselves totally unconcerned with his work?

As one advances up the hierarchical ladder, one does indeed come upon individuals who take satisfaction out of having "made budget" or oversold their quota, but this is the kind of satisfaction experienced by a sportsman who bowled well or fished his limit or won a hand at poker: it comes not from any sense of unity with the organization, but from pride in being good at the game. Nor, except in upper executive circles, does one identify with the corporation because he helps to develop its strategy—that is defined for him by higher authority, and as in any large bureaucracy his contribution in effectuating this strategy is frequently lost in the complexities of divided responsibilities, themselves the product of specialization.

One need not be a socialist to find difficulty with the concept that the significance of one's lifework hinges on maximizing returns for a mass of rentiers. And if one tries to substitute for that prime function of the corporation some proxy function—turning out needed goods, producing high-quality products, being innovative in product development, linking the company with community development—one is sooner or later caught up short and forced to realize the insubstantiality, the secondary and dependent nature, of his proxy objective. When the profit squeeze is on, or stockholders become restive because the value of their shares is not keeping pace with that of other "comparable" companies, or chief executives begin to sense a sharper tone behind the questions of influential directors, particularly those from the financial community, or when a corporate raider casts a greedy eye on the company's unused potential, somehow the proxy objectives fade away before the ineluctable profit prerequisite. The question reemerges: Can one "identify" with a balance sheet? [5]

For most of its employees, the large corporation carries on with a seeming life of its own. What products it makes, whether it is found guilty of violating some law, who are its officers, what politics it supports—these are matters of little concern to them as long as their security is not affected. For most of them, the corporation exists not as a cause or social function, not as a purveyor of social values or as an essential institution, but simply as a provider of income for their consumer needs (and in the upper ranks, as a provider of status). Each corporation does this in ways that are more or less pleasant or crude, arbitrary or systematic, demanding or permissive. In this sense, a corporation may be a good or a poor provider.

But most employees would probably be less aware that the corporation was also shaping their character, making them more submissive and dependent rather than autonomous, more conditioned to hierarchy rather than self-governing (how indeed could it be otherwise in a large organization?), more oriented to finding the meaning of life in what they consume in their leisure time, rather than in what they do in the time that they sell.

The demands of a mass-consumption society thus lead to the alienation of many workers from the production process itself. Mass production provides few satisfactions of its own to those engaged in it; the overwhelming consideration is its efficiency in terms of economy, which means no waste motion, no special attention to a particular unit, no added touch, nothing in fact that makes the output of a worker something other than an expense to the company. The worker's role is not one of participating in a creative process—bringing something of his own, however humble, into being—but of participating in a mechanical process, according to the blueprint of the industrial engineers.

Only by devaluing work in this fashion can we achieve the levels of consumption we have achieved. The result is paradoxical enough: unbounded admiration for the *total* production process, the intricate interrelationships of men and machines, the highly specialized and auto-mated equipment, the mechanical monsters and computerized operations, but disrespect, on the other hand, for the trivial roles that the individual plays in making this production miracle come true. The automobile assembler who drops the bolt and lets it pass with a "so what?" attitude is the same person who buys with pride a car made by a similar assembly process. He takes a statistical chance that no bolt was dropped from the car he purchases and reassures himself with a car warranty if a bolt should have been dropped.

In the wildcat strike at GM's Lordstown plant in 1972, management accused workers of sabotage such as breaking windshields and rear-view mirrors, slashing upholstery, bending signal levers, dropping washers in carburetors, and breaking off ignition keys.[6] Such mass action is unusual, but it is easy enough to imagine that any average worker might, on a bad morning when things were not going right, have spitefully engaged in some comparable action. Why not, when his part in the production process means so little to him? Small wonder, then, that we have been moving towards "no-fault" consumerism and strict liability for producers when the very production process itself engenders attitudes that erode the concept of personal responsibility (let alone pride) on the part of those engaged in it. Strict liability may be protection for the consumer against the consequences of the loss of worker responsibility and pride, but what can one say of its effect on the character of the worker himself?

Corporate Remedial Efforts

Management and students of management have not been unmindful of the unrest engendered by extreme specialization, repetitiveness of operation, and paced production. A variety of solutions have been proposed and some attempted. One of the most frequently mentioned goes by the name of "job enlargement." It would reverse the historical trend toward increased specialization and recombine operations in such a way that workers would once again have responsibility for a "whole process." One official of the United Auto Workers (UAW) has, for example, suggested scrapping the traditional assembly line and replacing it with a system under which a team of workers would follow an automobile—or a major component—through from start to finish. He argues that "the average guy wants to do a decent job," that such a revamped system would give workers a chance to take pride in their work."[7]

The Corporation and Its Internal Community

A few companies have in fact experimented with job enlargement, but its applicability has thus far been limited to a small number of situations in profitable companies with relatively protected markets. I have yet to hear of the extension of such experiments to the main body of employees of any large firm.

A second approach has been to encourage greater participation by employees in decision making—for the most part, in decisions affecting their own operations, but in some instances extended to decisions affecting corporate policy. This is one of the most time-honored forms of inducing work satisfaction on the part of employees, going back at least to the studies of Elton Mayo at the Harvard Business School during the interwar years. "Social cooperation" is viewed as a healthy form of personal interaction, and to involve people in arguing over "what should be done" or "how it should be done," with some consensus ultimately emerging, is considered a means of drawing people into the corporate community and making them feel citizens rather than outsiders. This theme has taken many variant forms, acquiring increasing sophistication over the years. Nevertheless, there is no great gap between Mayo's earlier simplistic regard for the therapeutic value of worker cooperation in the achievement of goals *defined by management* and the later more elaborated versions by experts such as Douglas McGregor who argued that people are not passive by nature—they are made so by organizations—and that management's major function is to foster methods by which people can organize themselves, satisfying their own goals, *in achieving corporate objectives.*

But "participation" within the constraint of objectives imposed by higher authority is likely to carry with it a sense of being manipulated. In the face of unrest in the automobile assembly plants in 1971–1972, managements became enamored of the idea that instead of fitting the man to the assembly line, the assembly line might be fitted to the man. "Experiments" were begun, in the form of consulting workers about the organization of the work flow. Workers were shown how their part fitted into the whole, comments were solicited, and an effort was made to engender a "team spirit." A reporter investigating the development commented:

Although workers . . . may feel better about their jobs, there is some question how long it will last—especially as they go on working with the same parts in the same way on the same line as before.

It is hard to try to change work on assembly lines. Even a seemingly simple change such as letting workers follow a car along and assemble a large part of it would mean a major cost increase.

87

Chrysler management is also worried that frustrations may only be intensified if expectations are raised and workers are involved in decision making and then, for whatever reason, no important change results.

What is often implied by "participation" in structuring the work process is indicated in the following example:

> At the Detroit Gear and Axle plant, workers are being allowed to control the flow of assembly lines. William White, a 44-year old worker, sat on a stool in front of a line where gear assemblies moved past him. There was a pedal he could hit with his foot to stop the line if he wanted to get a drink of water or take a break.
>
> He is still expected to turn out 1,000 units a day, but now he has a choice of working ahead and then shutting off the line for a while. "It's better," he said. "You've got more control now." [8]

If pushing a foot pedal to stop the line, without affecting in any other way the nature of one's specialized operation or the quantity he is expected to produce over a period of time, constitutes "control" and "participation," this only underscores from how low a level of involvement this motivational "revolution" starts. Moreover, it also emphasizes the tight constraint within which such "participation" must function: whatever discretion it gives to the worker cannot be at the expense of efficiency. In the words of GM's Lordstown manager: "If we are to remain competitive, we will have to take advantage of those sections of the contract on making the work more efficient." [9] Ultimately, then, the question reduces to whether "participation," by placating workers, contributes to efficiency. There is no change in the overriding objective: from Mayo to McGregor, it is the corporate objective that controls. The issue is simply whether the worker can be motivated to contribute more effectively to that objective. If not, Theory Y is no better than Theory X.

Nor is it only the rank and file who have been subjected to the allures of participation. In the period of collegiate disillusionment with American business beginning in the late 1960s, corporations began to worry that they were not getting the ablest of the graduates. Institutional advertising began to appear. Addressed to "the college generation," its message was: You don't like the world around you? Neither do we. Come join us, and together we'll see what we can do to improve matters. *Participate* with us in making the decisions that will do something about our ailing system.

Thus Bethlehem Steel advised the young idealists it was trying to enlist in its service:

> Here are some typical problems that would face you as a participant in the steel industry today.

- Your company's earnings are low: five cents per dollar of total revenue. Your costs are high. Yet a deep sense of public responsibility urges you to spend many millions on air and water pollution abatement equipment, and on beautification projects . . . beyond those required by law. Such facilities drain investment dollars, add tremendously to operations costs, year after year, and produce no income. On the other hand the same investment in new or improved production facilities would produce income and provide jobs. How do you strike a balance?

- You want to hire members of the "hard-core" unemployed. You want to provide livelihoods for so-called unemployables. You want to provide absolutely fair and equal opportunities for minority group members to work and progress. And you're willing to make extraordinary efforts to train them and to help them develop skills. But, at the same time, you must be equally fair to other workers. How can you reconcile all of these objectives?

- You would like to make larger corporate contributions to worthy civic and social projects that desperately need support, and to colleges and universities. But vocal shareholders protest "giveaways" when payouts to them are meager because of low earnings. How benevolent can you afford to be? And how do you allocate the funds?

These are the kinds of problems that make careers in management so difficult, so trying, so challenging.

There is a beguiling innocence in such a message. We *want* the same things you want, it says, but . . . there are limits. Come join us and *discover those limits for yourselves*. These are the problems in which you, as one of us, would participate.

But this is a participation in impotence, not in decision making. The cards are already stacked by the facts recited: earnings are low, costs are high, vocal stockholders protest. The degree of participation in affecting the situations cited is on a par with the degree of participation which William White has in controlling the gear assembly line by pressing his foot pedal. If the recruit remains and seeks to make his way up the corporate hierarchy, he learns soon enough that the real decisions that affect his future are efficiency and corporate earnings.

Nevertheless, the higher a person rises within the corporate hierarchy, the more valid his participatory role. In the upper reaches of management he does indeed begin to feel part of the team. He joins with other executives in task forces to carve out the company's future, he is energized by outside consultants, stimulated by substantive training sessions with officials from other companies, subjected to sensitivity training to improve his relations with his colleagues. He acquires increasing responsibilities within his own specialized area, and makes decisions on which others act. But "the price of sophisticated production is that the fragmentation of jobs moves upward from the assembly line." [10] And all these involvements occur within a framework where his success—his "*self*-development"—is conceived in terms of his contribution to the *company's* success and development. And why should the latter be important to him? We are back full circle: not because of the corporation's preoccupation with the enrichment of a population of unknown stockholders, not because the price of its stock rises on "the big board," not because the products his company produces are essential to social welfare and endow him with personal pride, but solely because his success as a manager and a specialist is the basis for his income and status. He is the man on the assembly line in a more exposed position, where he dare not ignore the bolt if he drops it. His work is intrinsically more interesting because it demands more of him, and by concentrating on his specialized function he may derive a sense of satisfaction in bringing it off. But if he stops to ask himself what rationale determines his actions and gives them meaning, by what criteria he assesses his development, he finds himself "self-actualizing" in terms of a balance sheet.

Certainly there is no self-evident basis here for criticizing the corporate system. The fact is that the corporate stress on efficiency *has* permitted social achievements and a standard of living that few Americans would care to dispense with. The profit drive, which is the measure of efficiency, is the basic mechanism.

But we would be less than candid with ourselves if we failed to recognize that this result has been bought with a philosophical contradiction: our political ideology is founded on individualism and self-government. Even in its failures, we still revert to those principles. Our economic institutions were consistent with such philosophical beliefs as long as they rested on small-scale enterprise and a potential for every man to become his own producer. With the ascendancy of the large corporation, we have substituted an ordered hierarchy, in which the individual worker is no longer independent and self-governing. How could it be otherwise within a large bureaucracy? He does not participate as much as he takes orders. His job is structured on lines whose sole criterion is efficiency. His work is specialized often to a mind-numbing degree. He is compensated for this de-individualizing role by a mounting pile of consumer goods, which gives him a substitute sense of achievement. But the fact remains that the form of economic organization inherent in the corporate system drains from the individual any sense of personal integrity, of a wholeness or unity to his way of life. The "control" or "participation" he is offered in his economic role bears little resemblance to the control or participation provided by his political institutions, at least in principle. How can he reconcile political independence and economic insignificance, one man one vote and one man one bolt?

The camaraderie in office and shop that is characteristic of American corporate life eases the impact. There is no sense of inferiority to others or of subservience within a caste system; the sense of egalitarianism remains strong. But all are "equal" within a system in which each counts for little; the sense of inferiority is not relative to others but relative to what one might himself be. Year by year, the corporate system shapes and reinforces his character. Benign in its objective, it sees only the good it disseminates in the form of economic prosperity. What it *does* to the man it employs, it has not even considered its obligation to understand.

It is supported in this one-sided view of its impact by the national ideology of free choice. No person is compelled to do what he does not want to do; no individual is required to work at a particular company or a particular occupation. But the fact that the corporate system is so pervasive in its influence that companies and occupations may be interchanged and affect one's work situation only in degree deprives "free choice" of much of its significance. Or perhaps the proposition should be restated in reverse. The basic similarities among so many jobs, in their lack of a participative role, exaggerate the importance of such small differences as there are.

The Limited Corporate Objective

None of this suggests that the United States is less sensitive than other societies to the impact of its economic institutions on the self-conceptions of those who man them. My own judgment is that there is probably more opportunity in the United States for discovering and cultivating one's potential, for a higher proportion of its population, than in any other country in the world. But this provides little basis for complacency. The fact remains that the corporate system produces people more stunted in their development than need be, and that this will continue as long as we make rising incomes for consumption objectives a goal that justifies any structuring of productive activities in order to gain greater efficiency.

Our conception of what constitutes a "whole" person has become warped; we demean our productive and integrative capabilities in order to inflate our accumulative capacities. The consequence is discernible, in varying degree, from top to bottom of the corporation's hierarchical structure, from the assembler to the production manager. The production of "whole" people is not the function of the corporation. Its specialized task, as we have been so often told, is efficient production of goods and services. Schools, churches, and homes are the "people producing" institutions. But this formulation ignores the inescapable impact that people's working lives have on their identities, and in our unconcern for that effect we have sold ourselves for steak and plumbing.

The corporations have been aware of this impact on people only insofar as it has shown up in absenteeism, poor quality workmanship, lack of discipline—effects that undercut the efficiency they seek. Their sophisticated personnel experts have sought to meet these evidences of alienation by conscious attention to employee motivation. But as we have seen, their approach is to search for a mechanism—job enrichment, employee participation, whatever—to *motivate* the employee to better performance measured in company terms. "Job design, *with its promise of higher productivity*, is a concept embraced by behavioral scientists and managers alike." [11] It is all so self-evident. Employees are being paid to produce, not to make themselves into better people. Corporations are purchasing employee time to make a return on it, not investing in employees to enrich their lives. Employees are human capital, and when capital is hired or leased the objective is not to embellish it for its own sake but to use it for financial advantage. But somewhere in this philosophy there is an inconsistency with the notion of a society of self-governing individuals. The large corporation has become an organizer of people, a *user* of people, a molder of identities, according to criteria that it has evolved, without regard to the effect on those people except as this is registered on the balance sheet.

The primacy of this objective has been revealed in the very experiments that some companies have conducted with respect to job enlargement and participation.

Some jobs connected with highly automated processes cannot be changed if the company's profit picture is to remain favorable. . . . For example, if an automated process were redesigned to make the job more challenging for the employee who monitors it and reports on it, the cost of the change might not be offset by increased productivity for many years. One line manager addressed himself to this point: "We have at least one set of jobs that are performed in connection with a greatly automated process. The jobs require a lot of constant reporting and recording data. Our studies showed that it would cost us half a million dollars to redesign the process to make the work more interesting for the employees. We rejected the possibility because it would take us nearly ten years to recoup the expenditure, and by that time the process would be obsolete anyway." [12]

A large pharmaceutical firm pioneered in job redesign to increase employee interest and hired a behavioral scientist to supervise the changes. Plant management found the productivity results encouraging. Within two years, the company's financial picture had changed. Its principal product line was virtually discontinued. "As the profit squeeze hit, the company laid off a large percentage of its production workers and changed its operations back to a fractionalized, assembly-line way of production." [13]

The overriding pecuniary consideration was emphasized by the director of personnel research for an electronics firm. ". . . We looked at one series of jobs and decided initially to redesign them to give employees more control of their work. As we took a closer look, it became evident that the cost of revamping the whole work flow and buying new equipment could not be changed within the organization's long-range requirements."

When his company elected not to redesign that series of jobs, another consideration arose: What kind of persons should be selected to perform the jobs? The director of personnel research explains, "Since the ideal changes were too expensive to carry out, we were stuck with a group of terribly boring jobs— jobs that anybody with any intelligence couldn't stand. Our problem has been to get people whose capabilities fit the job requirements and who can be content doing 'idiot' jobs. We've tried to do this, but we haven't yet faced up to the possibility that these employees may eventually want to be promoted to higher-level jobs, which actually they cannot handle." [14]

Of course, selecting people because they fit "idiot" jobs is scarcely an appropriate means of increasing their capabilities to do higher-level work. An idiot job either takes an idiot or makes one. But the company's concern is not with the impact on the individual, but with a possible future impact on the efficiency of the company. The same consideration applies, though with significant differences, in the upper levels.

Richard Todd, surveying the type of corporate executive that America is producing, was exposed to "the rhetoric of management development," and came away disillusioned. "You listen in vain, for instance, for acknowledgment of the moral ambiguity implicit in reconciling the needs of human beings and the needs of their offices. So much is promised, nothing less than selfhood; and the extravagance of the promise trivializes the very idea of self." Todd notes the "army of men" in the large contemporary organization "existing in the middle of a seemingly infinite chain of command, managing, but being managed, and longing for a dignified rationale for work, the center of which is too often the continual sophistication of styles of obeying, and of commanding obedience." [15] That last encapsulates the corporate rationale for all the paraphernalia of sensitivity training, growth opportunity (GO) plans, "plan-do control," semiautonomous work groups, and the like.

But in making such an evaluation, are we not giving way to utopian expectations? Is there any reason to believe that work can be made interesting, creative, self-fulfilling, and identity expanding for many people? Many individuals can accommodate themselves to the demands of the organization without psychological loss—particularly as the organization's demands themselves become more permissive (the foot-pedal control on the assembly line). Even labor leaders have been known to argue that only starry-eyed idealists claim that workers want control over their own lives and a greater opportunity to participate in decisions affecting them. Most workers want only to be left alone by the boss, free of arbitrary discipline, provided with economic security—period.

There is a great deal of validity to this view, and yet it is strangely irrelevant. One may equally say that most Americans want primarily a rising standard of living—forget the job, what can it be but dull? One puts in his time not because he gains any satisfaction from what he is doing, but only for the consumer rewards he reaps at the end of it. The disinterest in his productive and integrative identity is the other side of his absorption in his consumer identity: he trades one for the other. *Both* attitudes—toward work, toward consumption—are the product of his social conditioning, of the values implanted in him by the corporate system itself. If he has been oriented toward consumer objectives, he has equally been oriented toward production *non*objectives. The lack of interest and significance in his fractional, trivialized, devalued work function is the price he has paid for a standard of living that has made him the envy of the world. He no longer even consciously thinks of it as a trade-off, as his worker predecessors of the nineteenth century did. He takes it for granted. He expects little from one side of his life, just as he expects much from the other. If one then argues, "That's the way he wants it," one could make the same case for any conditioned behavior.

Corporate Potential

What can we conclude with respect to the potential of the large corporation in providing a fuller identity and integrity to people in their work capacity? In this respect, the corporate Social Responsibility Thesis seems likely to play a minor role, giving rise to a number of disjointed and unrelated palliatives. The idea of a corporate ombudsman who will listen to any employee's problem, whether from the union ranks or not, without respect to the presence of a formal grievance procedure, trying to assure some sense of "due process" or justice, has been instituted at some corporations, as at Xerox. A few prosperous companies—Xerox, again, as pioneer—have conceived the idea of paid leaves of absence for selected employees to carry out some self-conceived welfare program, a kind of private Peace Corps. Efforts at job enlargement and job enrichment can be expected to continue in particular situations, without offsetting the more general continuing trend toward specialization. As we shall see in the next chapter, most corporations support their employees in extending their education. The overall results, however, are meager, in respect to bolstering the employee's sense of individuality.

The social engineering approach flourishes in the large corporations, as it has from the time of Frederick Taylor down through Elton Mayo and a spate of contemporary specialists in the motivational field, but the intent continues to be to secure the loyalty of the employee at no cost to the company. "A prime objective of job design in the behavioral sense —increased productivity through more efficient use of resources—is also economic in nature. However, the current emphasis is on gaining internal motivation from the employee so that he performs his tasks with more dedication and commitment, as contrasted with coercion, robot-style control, and machine-like pacing." [16] But commitment to a system, however internally motivated by the system's experts, leaves little discretion for the individual to develop along his own independently conceived paths. In a large bureaucracy, it is easier for one to take his place if he has learned to make peace with the system, and the systems engineering approach facilitates this adjustment.

In terms of the central issue, the corporation's responsibility for the development of its members' capacities, we move inescapably to the Limited Responsibility Thesis. The corporation—given the competitive network within which it must operate—has an imposed function, the production of goods and services for a profit. In the performance of this function it can engage in related and peripheral activities as long as these have no adverse effect on its profit position. But it cannot afford to recognize what in fact is the case—that the way it structures its operations and the expectations it has of its employees inescapably have their impact on the kind of people they become, and that whether that impact is desirable may be—should be—judged by other standards than, or in addition to, efficiency in the production of consumer goods.

To raise that question would be to jeopardize the position of dominance of the corporate system in American society, based as it is on a consumptionist philosophy, which can be satisfied only through mass production and distribution. But if the individual American corporation cannot afford a conscience with respect to the kinds of people its operations produce, that does not mean it is therefore heartless. In the years of its maturing, it has learned how to upgrade the workplace, just as it has downgraded work itself: it has created an environment of informality and first-name camaraderie, landscaped its grounds, installed recreational areas, brightened its cafeterias, published "family" magazines, and sponsored art and photography exhibitions of employee work. To the best of its abilities, it has sought to confer, in Milton's poignant line from *Samson Agonistes*, "bondage with ease, in a land of plenty." [17] But what is the consequence? Do we then write off any idea of self-government or self-development (autonomy for individual or group) as largely illusory in the world of work?

[5]

CORPORATIONS
AND EDUCATION

IF BUSINESS values have permeated American society, endowing it with a conception of the good life cast in a consumption mold, emphasizing an individualistic ethic that accommodated a predatory attitude toward the environment, devaluing work as only the medium of exchange for goods, one would expect these values to be transmitted and secured through society's principal institutions of learning, notably the family and the school. This has in fact been the case. But the shaping of an educational system to the needs of an increasingly business-oriented society has been a complex process.

The system of public education in the United States did not emerge as a continuous evolutionary development of the egalitarian ideal, as is often imagined. On the contrary, it constituted a patchwork of conflicting purposes. In its earliest forms, it borrowed the European pattern of the private, aristocratic, classical academy ("Latin grammar" and "dame" schools), preparatory for the handful of elite sectarian colleges. In the few places where public schools were established, they either took on the same character as the private schools, winnowing out the elect by a trial of endurance of both purpose and finance, or were viewed disparagingly as "pauper schools." Education was distinctly not for working men, and the latter—to whom classical philosophy, theology, Latin, Greek, mathematics, and rhetoric were of little utility—felt no special deprivation in not being included in the colonial educational pattern.

It was not until the stirrings of Jacksonian democracy in the 1820s that agitation began for some form of general elementary education, and not until mid-century that a network of tax-supported "common schools" became a significant part of the educational scene. These schools took strongest root in the rapidly developing Middle West, which on the whole lacked the patrician heritage of the East. Even this development, however, did not much change the aristocratic flavor of American education. Though the common schools taught the rudiments of reading, writing, and arithmetic, they did little to encourage working-class children to aspire to the higher forms of education, which retained their same classical ("foreign") flavor. Nor did this weigh oppressively on the independent citizenry. The tradition of the self-made small producer, the artisan who, having served his apprenticeship, burgeoned into a self-employed proprietor, remained strong down to Civil War days, and for the sons of such men there was little need for or interest in the pursuit of higher learning. As for the professions—law and medicine in particular—these could, like other occupations, be learned through the apprenticeship route.

For most of the nineteenth century, then, the pattern of American education was of a limited "elementary" education for the average youngster, and a classical education leading to an upper-class college for the more privileged. This pattern was, on the whole, satisfactory to all concerned. A few pre–Civil War efforts at more vocationally oriented instruction failed for lack of support.

The Rise of Vocational Education

A monumental change in the character of the American educational system, which redirected it into more utilitarian and egalitarian channels, came with the passage of the Morill Act of 1862, which provided for grants of public lands to support state colleges devoted to the agricultural and mechanical arts. Passage of this act did not follow from any great surge of support for a more utilitarian brand of education. Indeed, there seems to have been remarkably little enthusiasm for the substance of the act, but some vague political sense that the farmers, having fallen behind in the dispensation of federal favors, were entitled to some material token of esteem. But out of this uninspired background there emerged a number of colleges and universities that were to introduce sweeping changes into the nature of higher learning in the United States.

In the new institutions, education was to combine practical instruction with the traditional liberal arts, the two integrated into a single curriculum. Their student constituency was to be drawn from the public at large; education was no longer to be viewed as a privilege for the already privileged. In sponsoring extension programs and experimental stations as part of their practical orientation, the new state universities broke down the antipathy of the still largely rural population toward "fancy" learning, thus engendering popular support for popular education, especially as some of the farmers' own children began acquiring college degrees.

The new state college was hardly on a par with the older (Eastern) elite colleges and universities. For one thing, its students normally entered at an earlier age than is now the case, its faculties were less distinguished, and its curriculum less demanding. "Considering the age of the students, the course content, and the level of the instruction, the early land-grant colleges performed a function similar to that of a good comprehensive high school today." [1]

So we have the curious phenomenon of vocationalism entering the colleges of the United States before being introduced into the high schools. At the time the Morill Act colleges and universities were being established, the "high school" was in fact an institution of many forms and shapes. Some were public, some were private. Some ran for one year, some for as long as four. It was not viewed as a self-sufficing educational program, valuable in its own right, but simply as a preparation for those who were going on to college. It constituted a kind of "forced educational feeding" that made it possible for those less well grounded to make the transition to "higher" education. "In 1870, for example, eight out of ten high school graduates entered college, where six of them received degrees; there were more than twice as many college graduates in the country as there were people with high school diplomas only." [2]

If the land-grant colleges had modified the elitist character of education generally, they by no means capped a system of public education serving the population generally. The formal education of most youngsters continued to be a rudimentary knowledge gained in an elementary common school. This pattern began to change in the last quarter of the nineteenth century. Especially in the cities, more and more students began to enter the high school, remained to graduate, but did not continue on to college. The increase in high-school enrollment, while substantial, still did not encompass a large part of the relevant age group. By 1890 only 7 percent of those between fourteen and seventeen years old were in high schools. Compared with earlier periods, however, this represented an extraordinary gain.

The high schools were in fact going through a period of finding their role. Still serving largely as preparatory schools for colleges, they continued to alienate large numbers of workingclass youngsters who found no intrinsic satisfaction or pecuniary advantage in learning dead languages, memorizing chunks of the classics, or being exposed to great thoughts of the past. On the other hand, with the expansion of industry and technology in a rapidly developing economy, there was need for a lower-level version of what the land-grant colleges were attempting—an education that would combine instruction in the useful with some exposure to "cultural" subjects.

Business interests were already pushing for such a change. Beginning in 1900, the National Association of Manufacturers (NAM) threw its support behind "the establishment of free public commercial and technical schools" or at least departments offering such instruction in the established high schools.[3] Such a purely vocational approach was, however, offensive to certain educators who, while themselves pressing for curricular changes that would make high-school work more relevant to the average youngster, nevertheless continued to regard education as an instrument of intellectual advancement, social conditioning, and the making of a "whole man." One method of accomplishing this was to develop manual training programs that were not geared to particular occupational skills, but to the cultivation of the "mechanical faculties," so that a graduate would emerge trained in physical, no less than mental, dexterity.

The manual-training movement conceived in these terms won wide support in the cities in the 1880s, boosted by the impressive exhibit of the Moscow Imperial Technical School at the 1876 Philadelphia Centennial Exposition. Contrary to the types of industrial training developed in Germany, France, and England, which attempted to combine schooling with actual industrial experience, the Moscow plan created a shop within the school, where manual control could be learned free from the intrusion of practical production requirements.

The manual-training movement constituted the transitional link between the academic (college preparatory) high-school program, which had prevailed till that time, and the vocational program that was to follow, but the transition took some time. Traditional educators saw manual training as only an entering wedge for vocationalism, which was viewed as a perversion of the education process. The labor unions joined in opposing vocationalism in the public schools, seeing it as a scheme by the industrialists to circumvent union-controlled apprenticeship programs.

Objective pressures were building up that strengthened the hand of the vocationalists, however. By the turn of the century, industrial production was expanding rapidly. Population increased, but not by enough to satisfy the demands of industry, particularly because the new wave of immigrants from southern and eastern Europe came without the industrial skills possessed by many of the earlier northern European immigrants. The nature of the skills required was itself changing. The need for some institutional mechanism for socializing the new immigrants and training them to meet the requirements of an expanding industrial economy was great enough to break down the barriers of resistance to educational change. A coalition supporting vocational public schools was skillfully effected, a coalition that included the NAM, the American Federation of Labor (AFL), the National Grange, and the National Education Association (NEA). By 1910 more than twenty states had set up programs of high-school vocational training. Following a series of political compromises in the Congress, a Commission on National Aid to Vocational Education was established in 1914. Its report, recommending federal support for teachers' salaries and training costs in high schools devoting at least 50 percent of schooltime to instruction in specified types of "productive" work, led to passage of the Vocational Education (Smith-Hughes) Act of 1917. Its passage was accelerated by a growing sense of the need to "catch up with the Germans" at a time when war seemed imminent (just as passage of the National Defense Education Act, at a later date, was to be spurred by Russian success with its *sputnik*).

It was primarily with this shift in orientation of the high schools, supplementing their college preparatory role with a "terminal" diploma, that the American educational system became truly "public." In one sense, vocationalism can thus be said to have been the principal democratizing force in the American school system. From this perspective, it would seem that education was not so much co-opted in the service of business as made a more widely available instrument by means of which individuals could benefit themselves economically in a society which had made economic betterment its democratic objective.

Philosophical Validation and Leadership Accreditation

But this relationship between business and education is not all there is to the story. Business derived other benefits from the educational process. From earliest beginnings to present times, the school system has served two other functions: it has been a transmitter of the values underlying the society and a screening process for sifting out those who are to be allowed into positions of privilege and power.

Although the composition of what has constituted the business "class" has changed with the passage of years, that class has remained the dominant influence in American society since at least the early nineteenth century. Its values became identified as the national values, as Tocqueville so eloquently elaborated in his *Democracy in America* (1835). These were embraced in the philosophical traditions, passed on unquestioned by the educational system even at its most elementary levels, emphasizing individualism, vocationalism, ambition (translated into competition), private property, and the sanctity of contracts. At the same time, the products of the higher educational institutions—a restricted class—provided the dominant leadership of the influential organs of industry, finance, and commerce. The educational process thus identified and authenticated the leadership class, and at the same time validated and inculcated the underlying philosophical premises on which that leadership role—and the social order—rested.

E. Digby Baltzell has effectively identified this "gatekeeper" role of the American educational system. Between the Civil War and the Great Depression, successful Anglo-Saxon Protestants joined descendants of colonial and pre–Civil War merchants and statesmen in contributing disproportionately to business and banking leadership, the professions, and government—in short, in populating the positions of influence and power. The children of these newly rich and powerful business families were assimilated into the traditional upperclass ways via the prestigious New England boarding schools and Ivy League universities. "These exclusive institutions were run and supported by families with a nationally recognized monopoly of power and caste-like security of social position." [4]

To be sure, some provision had to be made for talent that came without family credentials. The lore of American history is filled with instances of poor boy, illiterate immigrant, and Jewish peddler who made good, rising to the top ranks of American industry or finance. Without such exceptions the system would have lost its credibility. On a continent that encouraged individualism and competitiveness, stressed equality and abundance of opportunity, there were bound to be a number of fresh successes, but not so many as to challenge the dominant position of the inner circle. Others, by following the prescribed educational path, often with the aid of sponsors, made their way into the circle of privilege without benefit of breeding: education has always been a means of advancement for those who have been able to use it.

Those who thus achieved success by their own effort had no wish to upset the system by which they had made good. If there were deep-seated social distinctions between those business leaders deriving from old settler stock and those of new immigrant background, the division was forgotten in their joint support of the system under which both prospered. Hence there was a mutual interest on the part of those who formed the dominant business class—both those born to it and those who had achieved it on their own—to use the public school system not merely to train hired hands (indeed, that function came later, as we have seen) but to assure society at large of the ethical rightness of the system under which they lived.

The common school's mission was to maintain and transmit the values considered necessary to prevent political, social, or economic upheaval. Daniel Webster said public education is a "wise and liberal system of police by which property, and life, and the peace of society are secured." Horace Mann viewed the school's chief function as a social and economic "balance wheel" balancing conflicting interests and thus protecting the social order. The common school would protect the rights of property, first, by teaching the children of the propertyless to believe that the economic system was reasonable and just, rewarding to people according to their natural abilities and real contribution to society; and second, by teaching that if one practiced those Puritan virtues, he too could be successful.[5]

William T. Harris, U.S. commissioner of education from 1889 to 1906, voiced the same conviction that "the purpose of public education was to preserve and save our civil order. The school was the 'great instrumentality to lift all classes of people into a participation in civilized life,' meaning order, self-discipline, civil loyalty, and a respect for private property."[6]

The College Screen

To speak of business leaders as the dominant class carries no connotation that the population was neatly divided into one small class of the advantaged and a large mass of the disadvantaged. There were gradations of privilege, positions of prominence to be held *near* the great, of power *close* to the top. As the local family-held business firm was absorbed into the national corporation, the latter's need for executives increased, bureaucratically. If the old aristocracy chose to retire on the proceeds from sale of the family firm, new professional managers must take their place. As the economy leaped forward, openings for executives grew apace.

This need for middle managers, plant managers, professional managers was increasingly met out of the expanding college population. The tradition of the self-made man, making his way up through the ranks by dint of persistence and ability, retained its validity, but the incidence of such successes declined as the number of college graduates increased. If most top corporate officials came out of an Ivy League background, their supporting cast might come from the University of Wisconsin or Purdue. The educational screening process continued to function. The Morill Act of 1862 made a major contribution in this respect, as we have seen, but in 1881 the University of Pennsylvania took a further step by establishing the first collegiate school of business—the Wharton School of Finance and Commerce, made possible by a gift of $100,000 from Joseph Wharton, a Philadelphia merchant. Several other universities soon followed suit, and by the turn of the century half a dozen colleges had established departments of business. This new development—at first regarded with suspicion by many educators, just as high-school vocationalism was being regarded at about the same time—won its respectability with the founding of the Harvard Graduate School of Business Administration in 1908.

How the trend from family business to public corporation, on the one hand, and the increase in the collegiate population, on the other, affected admission to the ranks of management, is suggested in two surveys of American business leaders. The first was undertaken in 1928, the second in 1952. Both sampled a quite comparable group of top managers. Over the twenty-four-year period, the proportion of managers who had been to college rose from 45 to 76 percent, and there was a strong statistical inference of a decline in the number of managers who had inherited their positions.[7]

In a sense, the increasing reliance on the college degree for accreditation to managerial position, coupled with the growth in collegiate schools of business (which by the 1950s accounted for one out of every seven baccalaureate degrees) simply extended the screening functions of the educational system. Both values and skills were inculcated in those being groomed for leadership positions in industry.[8] Many of these persons would remain in subordinate positions all their lives, scattered throughout the length of the management hierarchy, but nevertheless reaping differential rewards over the noncollege population, who were more and

more excluded from managerial position above the rank of first-line supervisor. Presumably these college-educated managers would also retain
a strong conviction, implanted in their educational experience and held
to as a matter of self-respect, that the large corporation constituted
America's greatest source of strength. This confidence was reinforced by
the emergence of a concept of the social responsibilities of business, par-
alleling and reflecting the rise of the large corporation as the major national institution. This was a necessary reinterpretation of the traditional
values transmitted through the educational establishment, since a large
social institution must reflect large social interests.

In short, at least through World War II the educational system, both
public and private, served business by providing (and reinterpreting as
need be) a philosophical validation of the role of business in a free society and by accrediting its graduates at various levels (high school, college, graduate professional schools) for appropriate types and levels of
business employment. It thus contributed a stability to the social order,
which in effect meant a widespread satisfaction with the distribution of
the rewards passed out under the system. By maintaining relatively
open access to the educational system and by making the educational
system a vital factor in the distribution of social advantages, it preserved the credibility of equality of opportunity, even as it continued to
concentrate in the hands of an educational and social elite a disproportionate degree of influence in the management of the corporate system.

Recent Changes

The years following World War II brought a marked alteration in the
relationship between business and the educational establishment, the result of certain changes in the objective conditions underlying American
society. Perhaps the most significant of these was in the composition of
the cities, which became gathering points of the black population. The
story is told in summary form by the National Advisory Commission on
Civil Disorders, which rendered its massive, thoughtful, and pessimistic
report in 1968, the year following the outbreak of racial riots in most of
the major cities.

"Almost all Negro population growth is occurring within metropolitan
areas, primarily within central cities," the commission noted. "From
1950 to 1966, the United States Negro population rose 6.5 million. Over

98 percent of that increase took place in metropolitan areas—86 percent within central cities, 12 percent in the urban fringe." By contrast, "the vast majority of white population growth is occurring in suburban portions of metropolitan areas. From 1950 to 1966, 77.8 percent of the white population increase of 35.6 million took place in the suburbs. Central cities received only 2.5 percent of this total white increase. Since 1960, white central-city population has actually declined by 1.3 million."

The effect on the population composition of America's urban areas is written in those figures. "Central cities are steadily becoming more heavily Negro, while the urban fringes around them remain almost entirely white. The proportion of Negroes in all central cities rose steadily from 12 percent in 1950, to 17 percent in 1960, to 20 percent in 1966. Meanwhile, metropolitan areas outside of central cities remained 95 percent white from 1950 to 1960, and became 96 percent white by 1966." [9]

The larger the city, the greater the concentration of blacks. Moreover, this locational differential of the races did not end in 1966, the latest date for the commission's figures. Two demographers, projecting trends to 1985, have concluded that between 1960 and that date the white population residing within central cities will experience a decline of 2.4 million, or 5 percent, while more than doubling in the suburbs. By contrast, nonwhite population in the central cities will almost double, expanding to more than 20 million. [10]

In the major cities the blacks have been joined by a major in-migration of Latin and Caribbean populations, primarily Puerto Ricans and Mexicans. Though minorities in the nation at large, these outcast groups, disadvantaged economically and socially, are rapidly becoming majorities in the principal central cities. This result has come about not simply because of the influx of these groups, but because of a resulting efflux of native whites to the suburbs, as the statistics reveal.

We are not now concerned with this population shift except for its impact on the educational establishment, which has been monumental. Overall figures describing the breakdown of populations by color do not reflect the differential age composition. Nonwhite birthrates exceed white birthrates, with the consequence that the color contrast in the younger age-groups is even more marked than in the population at large. Demographers Hodge and Hauser project that between 1960 and 1985, whites under fifteen years of age will increase by 26 percent, while nonwhites in the same age group will increase by 60 percent. This differential increase in the younger age-groups is obviously reflected in school enrollments, particularly in the cities. Integration and assimilation have thus become receding goals.

Corporations and Education

Racial isolation in the public schools is intense throughout the United States. In the Nation's metropolitan areas, where two-thirds of both the Negro and white population now live, it is most severe. Seventy-five percent of the Negro elementary students in the Nation's cities are in schools with enrollments that are nearly all-Negro (90 percent or more Negro), while 83 percent of the white students are in nearly all-white schools. Nearly nine of every 10 Negro elementary students in the cities attend majority-Negro schools.[11]

This racial polarization has resulted in a marked deterioration in the quality of public education in the cities. Black experience, from an early age, with discrimination and inequality of opportunity has belied the traditional philosophical validation of the existing social system and has undercut respect for, and the authority of, the educational establishment. To put the matter more bluntly, in the face of higher unemployment rates and limited job opportunities, there is less interest by black youngsters in education for its own sake and less belief in its economic value. For the lower-income ethnic groups who are left behind in the city, some of the former respect for the educational process and belief in its relevance to achievement remain, but it is harder to maintain those attitudes in the changed environment.

Corporate recruitment patterns reflect these alterations in the effectiveness of city school systems. Higher-level jobs, requiring more social skills, literacy, and motivation, tend to be filled by suburban-schooled white youngsters who join their parents in commuting to the city. Thus a notable postwar feature of the large city is the "busy-ness" and whiteness of its central business district by day, and its emptiness at night as the daytime occupants return to their suburban residences.[12] The lower-level jobs are left to be filled by inner-city residents. A 1968 survey of the management of the largest firms in fifteen metropolitan areas disclosed that although 86 percent of those interviewed accepted a "social responsibility to make strong efforts to provide employment to Negroes and other minority groups," almost the same percentage believed that very few Negroes are now qualified for white-collar or professional-level jobs, 69 percent felt that few were qualified for skilled-level jobs, and 23 percent were even skeptical of the Negro's qualification for bottom-level work. "In brief, employers as a group tend to see Negroes as simply not qualified—by preparatory institutions or by past employment experience—for good jobs." While actual employment practice is somewhat less discriminatory than these perceptions, these attitudes indicate the nature of the work opportunities, if any, which a black is likely to be exposed to.[13]

For companies anchored in the big cities, whether because of corporate charter (like the utilities), state regulations (as in the case of some banks), or heavy capital investment (some industry), the high-school diploma is still relied on as a screening device to sort out the more acceptable from the less acceptable or unacceptable in filling the myriad of routine entry jobs. But the content of the high-school education has itself been devalued in the personnel manager's eyes; the diploma is symbol rather than substance—symbol of some degree of perseverance, some degree of discipline, some degree of acceptance of the social order. What better screen for the mass of lower-class youngsters could be substituted?

Business no longer relies on vocational training in the high schools to provide it with recruits possessing wanted skills, as it did in pre–World War II days. It may still talk of the need for upgrading vocational-technical education, as for example in the report of the U.S. Chamber of Commerce Task Force on Economic Growth and Opportunity, which criticizes the present quality of such instruction: high schools are too college-oriented, vocational training is not directed toward the types of jobs found in today's labor market, educators and businessmen should work together to make such functional training more relevant.[14] These expressions of concern are in reality, however, a carry-over from an earlier day. In contrast to the enthusiastic business backing for the Smith-Hughes Act in 1917, "not one business spokesman testified at the hearings on the 1963 Vocational Education Act." "Business in general has long since lost its enthusiasm for vocational training in the schools."[15] The increased fractionalization of the work process, clerical and industrial both, has made skill training less necessary. The company can move, train, and retrain its lower-level employees with a minimum of lost time.[16]

Obviously some jobs require special skills that some companies are unwilling to teach—shorthand and typing, for example—and to this extent high-school or proprietary-school education cannot be dispensed with. Even in these instances, however, the quality of performance demanded has, of necessity, been downgraded, and substitutes for skills in short supply have been found: the duplication of materials has eliminated a vast amount of typing, computers have substituted for armies of low-level clerical and accounting functions, electronic controls and equipment displace manual skills and judgment.

Corporate Reaction

Largely as a consequence of the race riots of 1967, a number of major corporations developed an interest both in improving the quality of high-school education in the major cities, and in embarking on special programs to train the so-called "hard-core" unemployed, who were generally high-school dropouts, often with a police record or drug problem. At least thirty companies "adopted" high schools in at least twenty cities. The relationship sometimes involved supplying part-time instructors (for example, Kodak, Xerox, and DuPont), equipping vocational programs with more modern equipment (General Electric in Cincinnati, for example), conducting earn-learn programs leading to post-graduation employment (Chrysler and Michigan Bell in Detroit), and assisting in overhauling the management of the public school system for greater efficiency and economy (Olin in New Haven, for example).

For training the hard-core unemployed, numbers of corporations joined in a National Alliance for Businessmen to establish the JOBS program (Job Opportunities in the Business Sector). "Businessmen were suddenly asked to start hiring persons they wouldn't have let past the plant gate a few years ago." [17] This program, while widely publicized and favorably commented on, proved to be less than a major success. An impartial inquiry commissioned by the Urban Coalition was generally skeptical in its findings. Of 224 companies with a total workforce of 8.7 million, "less than 10,000 recruits can be identified as receiving special training. While publicized figures indicate that industry has hired over 100,000 'hard-core' nationally, it is beyond doubt that this figure includes a large percentage of persons who would have been hired whether the term 'hard-core' existed or not." Many sympathetic corporate officials were critical of what they described as a "phony numbers game," with a pressure to report numbers of recruits, leading to dubious counting and higher turnover.[18]

Nevertheless, some corporations—particularly those anchored in the cities—did undertake new and expanded training programs, recruiting high-school dropouts and putting them through remedial courses in mathematics and English, coupled with preliminary job training, and leading eventually to employment. Such recruits were paid during their weeks of instruction (with the expense often subsidized by the federal government). Experience with such programs has shown that the greater the emphasis on specific job preparation, in contrast to more academic subjects, the greater the motivation and the lower the dropout rate. As a consequence, many such programs have tended to move toward job training with the educational component minimized.[19]

To make a rather broad judgment on corporate involvement with training programs specifically directed toward blacks and Latins in the cities, I would conclude that where companies are committed to their existing urban locations they will continue to operate, and perhaps even to expand, their own training programs as a supplement to public education, on which they will rely less, except as a broad screening device. Separate, socially oriented programs for the *really* hard-core unemployed (the alienated) will wither away; high-school dropouts who cannot make it through the regular corporate training course will simply fall back into the pool of the unwanted. I would judge corporate involvement with the public schools themselves ("adopting" or cooperating with them) to be a passing phase. The white-managed corporations will not be wanted to patronize the black-populated schools.

The major corporation that requires a high proportion of well-educated recruits for specialized, even though still routine, jobs, and that seeks to maintain a corporate atmosphere emphasizing the social amenities, stability, and employee congeniality, is likely to commit more and more of its operations to suburban locations. Because public schools in these communities tend to be more college oriented and to maintain higher standards for that reason, the high-school diploma is a respectable terminal degree for those who do not continue their education. The generally more conservative attitude of residents is more favorable to educational emphasis on what are regarded as "America's values," which are reflective of business values. Business representatives often sit on boards of education, and some corporations make financial contributions to school systems educating large numbers of their employees.

Management Education and Development

The closest educational link of the large national corporation is with the colleges and universities. For one thing, as a national institution, the corporation finds it easier to deal with other national institutions, such as the major private universities. Top management speaks to top management, as it were, while local managers deal more directly with local school systems and regional or community colleges. But of dominant importance is the fact that corporations rely on colleges and universities to breed their managers and professional employees.

Corporate officials sit on university boards of trustees and influence the university's educational programs—not in devious ways, for selfish advantage, but obviously in ways that reflect their own value perceptions. Corporate financial contributions, both direct and indirect (via wealthy industrial benefactors), are vital to the private universities, whose endowments, in turn, are partly invested in the securities of the major corporations. Through the initiative of three corporate board chairmen (Irving S. Olds of U.S. Steel; Frank W. Abrams of Standard Oil of New Jersey; and Alfred P. Sloan of General Motors) a Council on Financial Aid to Education was established in 1953 to serve as a conduit for the flow of funds from private business to primarily private universities.

The youthful unrest on the campus of the past decade strained somewhat the closeness of this relationship between higher business and higher education, but the relationship has nonetheless held. How could it be otherwise, when each needs the other?

Thus there has been a growing emphasis on the need for "higher" education for those who are to play the principal professional, administrative, and executive roles in the major corporations. If there has been a downgrading of the importance of education with respect to the routine, rank-and-file jobs, there has been an upgrading of its importance for the responsible innovative and policy-making positions. Thus on the technical side: "As engineering continues to become more complex and specialization is delayed, graduate education will become a must for the engineer, and, by the same token, it is probable that within the present decade the bachelor's degree will become a must for many technical occupations. Similarly, the skilled crafts are now making their appearance on the junior college level." [20] And with respect to the administrative need: "Perhaps the most important educational task in business today—and one, certainly, essential to its continued growth and survival—is the development of its managerial resources." [21] If class distinctions are hardening in the United States, it would seem to be along educational lines, with the gulf widening between those with a high-school education or less and those with a college education or more. Such a gulf always existed, to be sure, but it was much less consequential when the number of the college educated was small.

Thus education at the higher levels appears to have become the *passe-partout* to management positions. If the strength of American society lies in its great corporations, then leadership of those corporations constitutes a social responsibility of the highest importance, to be entrusted only to those who have prepared themselves for it. But the matter is not quite as simple as that. Strict "meritocracy" does not apply, and all college degrees are not equal. In the method of selection of top managers, by incumbent management and with ratification by board members who have been chosen by incumbent management, there still runs a strong current on behalf of the "old stock"—white, Anglo-Saxon, Protestant—by no means so strong as in an earlier day, but still strong enough to make itself felt.

Baltzell has put the matter in perspective, using Philadelphia as his laboratory. The old upper class is relatively unconcerned with local operations, especially because the changing composition of the cities has meant a considerable loss of political influence and involvement there. Their interests are on the national scene. "It is socially acceptable to become a junior executive at General Motors but hardly proper to run the local Buick agency." [22] Local managerial positions are more likely to fall to the college graduates among the ethnic groups.

Even in the corporate headquarters, the managerial and professional positions to be filled are too numerous to reserve exclusively for a privileged class, and the college-educated ethnics are also being admitted to positions of national corporate power. The modern large corporation, simply by virtue of its position of influence in society, can in fact *confer* status on an individual by the act of elevating him to a top-management post. At the same time, the progressive large corporation has "elaborate devices for acculturating its new executives into the kind of social life proper to their achieved positions in the corporate hierarchy." [23] Just as in the previous century the "self-made" first- or second-generation immigrant who made good was more interested in preserving than upsetting the system, notwithstanding its social exclusiveness, which excluded him, the college-educated ethnic who becomes knighted in the corporate boardroom today is just as anxious to uphold the system by which he benefits, with its greater social inclusiveness, which now includes him.

Nevertheless, as the number of college-trained young people has increased, the degree as the key to upward mobility has lost some of its credibility. Particularly because of pressure from minority and ethnic groups concentrated in the cities to open the colleges to them, with a consequent swelling of the number of such graduates, the large corporations have found that college alone is not enough to certify the professional or the manager. The U.S. Equal Employment Opportunity Commission reported in 1968 that in the greater New York metropolitan area alone, 32,000 nonwhites had completed four or more years of college.[24] Nor is this democratization of the colleges confined to the blacks and Puerto Ricans. When New York City established its policy of "open enrollment," among the beneficiaries were large numbers of Italian and Irish first- and second-generation youngsters. The same experience is being repeated in kind, if not in degree, in most of the major cities across the nation, where state universities have been pressed into establishing branch campuses where they are easily accessible to ghetto and lower-income residents.

The numbers of students crowding into these colleges, many of them poorly prepared, have had a deteriorating effect on the quality of instruction offered and the education received. Like the high-school diploma, the college degree issued from some institutions has become a symbol for the substance, a cachet for persistance. Standards of performance sometimes cannot be maintained without risking political upheaval.

With the college degree losing some of its luster and scarcity value, the corporation finds screening both more difficult and more important in determining who shall be hired for its managerial and professional positions, who shall be advanced to various levels, and especially who shall rise to the top. In the absence of an almost religious dedication to the principle of equal opportunity to all, preferential treatment for some groups or classes is unavoidable. What is more natural than that the forms of screening tend to give expression—perhaps even unconscious expression—to the preferences of those in control? If there is stiff competition for the better jobs, that competition still tends to be limited to those who have been sifted out by a process that produces a desired social type.

As part of that process, there is one peculiarly effective device that American corporations have developed—the executive development program. Sometimes offered internally, sometimes in conjunction with a university, sometimes shared with other corporations, the content ranges from cultural enrichment to technical instruction, from sensitivity training to business games. Programs may last for a day or a year, and an individual may go through none or many. Both the programs themselves and the employees chosen to participate in them are carefully evaluated, and when it comes to promotion this information can be interpreted in a way that advances or retards a candidacy.

The Effect of Business Influence

The most significant impact of business on education in the United States has been to give it a strong utilitarian and vocational flavor. This has by no means been wholly pernicious. If it has tended to de-emphasize the cultural content of education, it has also democratized it. For all its deficiencies, the American school system has reached and benefited more students than has been the case in countries following a more nonfunctional, but elitist, pattern of education.

But as the characteristics of work itself have changed in recent years, building on fractionalization and specialization, the consequences of this utilitarian approach have been less appealing. Work requiring no special aptitudes except the ability to repeat simple, segmented, and easily taught tasks has downgraded the *functional* value of high-school training and has undermined the economic motivation to learn, which had been learning's greatest appeal in a pecuniarily motivated society.

At the other end of the work spectrum, professional and managerial specializations have placed a premium on functionally oriented college and graduate instruction. This democratization of higher education, as it were, again carries certain social benefits but also, by putting a pecuniary imprimatur on higher education, tends to undermine the cultural motivation for advanced study. In terms of a people's intellectual, aesthetic, moral, and emotional development, this impact at the higher levels of learning is more serious than at lower levels, because it narrows the leadership base for American civilization, reinforcing the utilitarian, consumptionist standard we explored in Chapter 2.

This materialist preoccupation with education as functional training shows up in the economist's contemporary infatuation with education as investment in "human capital." It is revealed in the growing corporate resort to "manpower planning and development" programs, particularly at management levels, where the individual, viewed as "manpower," is "developed" for his value to the company, as a corporate instrument. Thus the corporation's effect on education has been to drain it of its moral quality and to fill it with functional utility. This is the basis for a strong economy but not a great society.

If this general evaluation is accepted, what can we say about the prospects for a corporation's exercising social responsibility in this field?

We can only conclude, once more, that insofar as it operates within a competitive framework, the individual corporation can do very little to change the existing situation. It prospers by encouraging a materialistic philosophy and survives by adopting the most efficient production routines, whatever their impact on the individual—in both ways supporting the functional stress in education. Its effective social contribution is thus largely confined to doing what it can to improve, incrementally, the educational system as it exists. This means cooperation with the public schools where possible, improvement and extension of its own training ("educational") activities, and financial support for colleges and universities within modest limits.

On the social engineering approach, there are those who believe that the most progressive and sophisticated corporations can apply their proved efficiency to upgrade the educational process, conceived as a production system. This heady view was more prevalent in the late 1960s than it is today, though it still has its proponents.[25] In any event, it would only strengthen a functional approach to education.

In short, the individual corporation, for all its seeming influence and financial strength, can do very little to aid the present educational system. This is not for lack of goodwill. There is ample evidence that many individual business leaders are anxious to cope as best they can with what they regard as an undesirable present state of affairs. But in trying to cope, they are limited to doing so in a way that perpetuates the character of the society whose values they have helped to mold, making incremental adjustments, but being incapable of making fundamental changes.

The consequence is likely to be a growing number of educational and social misfits—those who are unmotivated to learn and disinterested in trivializing work—particularly in the cities, where black alienation from white society is becoming a fact of American life. This would mean acceptance of more public employment and public welfare for those whom the educational system cannot or does not prepare for the labor market, or whom the labor market is unwilling to accept, or who are unwilling to accept the labor market.

[6]

CORPORATIONS
AND THE CIVIC COMMUNITY

HISTORICAL perspective is useful in examining the relationship between the large corporation and the civic community of which it is a part. Because the subject is vast, that perspective can be gained only at the price of oversimplification, but in this terrain any position involves oversimplification. Our objective is to explore the influences of the large corporation on the communities in which it operates and the extent to which it may be made an effective instrument for urban improvement.

The Natural Community

The fact that the United States had its beginnings on a bare continent only three centuries ago gives us greater confidence in describing the growth of its communities: it is almost like looking over one's shoulder. Thus when Percival Goodman generalizes that, as historically understood, a "natural community" is

a group living in face-to-face proximity, having common interests, a way of life conditioned by their special material resources, technology and tradition. The group, individually and as a body, acts to protect and enhance the commonly held values. To belong means loyalty to the commonly held belief, continuity of personal relations, and permanence in geographical location. The organization of the community is a result of slow growth, not intentional plan,[1]

his generalization sounds remarkably like the picture that the historian Sam Bass Warner, Jr., draws of Philadelphia on the eve of the American Revolution, when it was a town of not quite 24,000 people:

116

Corporations and the Civic Community

The real secret of the peace and order of the eighteenth-century town lay not in its government but in the informal structure of the community. Unlike later and larger Philadelphias, the eighteenth-century town was a community. Graded by wealth and divided by distinctions of class though it was, it functioned as a single community. The community had been created out of a remarkably inclusive network of business and economic relationships and it was maintained by the daily interactions of trade and sociability. Because it was small and because every rank and occupation lived jumbled together in a narrow compass the town suffered none of the communications problems of later Philadelphias.[2]

Philadelphia was of course a northern town, where slavery had relatively little presence. The enumeration of the Middle Ward of the city for 1774 showed seventy-eight Negro slaves and sixty-five bound servants in residence out of a total population of 1,401. Still, even in southern towns of the time there existed the same sense of an ordered "natural" community, despite the much larger slave population. Tocqueville, to whom slavery was America's greatest blemish, nevertheless commented that it was capable of acquiring a "kind of moral power which it derived from time and habit."[3] It was an accepted pattern of everyday life, held together by rules that did not have to be written to be understood, that created a community out of a population.

In such towns (again drawing on Philadelphia for example):

> The wealthy presided over a municipal regime of little government. Both in form and function the town's government advertised the lack of concern for public management of the community. The municipal corporation of Philadelphia, copied from the forms of an old English borough, counted for little. Its only important functions in the late eighteenth century were the management of the markets and the holding of the Recorder's Court. A closed corporation, choosing its members by co-option, it had become a club of wealthy merchants, without much purse, power, or popularity.
>
> By modern standards the town was hardly governed at all.[4]

The system of social values that underlay this network of relationships was subscribed to by lower and upper classes alike, in part because such class distinctions were not fixed. Growing out of the common philosophical heritage that found expression in such broadly based statements as the Declaration of Independence, Paine's *Common Sense* and *Rights of Man*, and the Constitution itself, it was built around the constitutional value of individual autonomy and self-development, with a minimum of government controls. After all, the upperclass merchants and businessmen who served as the community's leaders, prizing as they did their own freedom of action, could hardly deny it as equally valid for all others. They believed with Locke that security of property was the mainspring of economic motivation, and to the numerous aspirants for economic advancement around them that was equally self-evident. In terms of the distribution of material advantage, the businessmen— merchants, shopkeepers, master artisans—had no qualms in asserting equality of opportunity for all, with no inheritance of privileged posi- tion. Though divided on the issue of whether the vote could be en- trusted safely to every male adult, even those who favored property qualifications agreed to the desirability of affording everyone a chance to acquire property. Here the Puritan ideal of salvation through work (the full use of one's talents, whatever these may be) and the "covenant with God" that linked spiritual and material advancement compatibly were focal. The ideal was a society of equals, even if nature itself frus- trated the fulfillment of that ideal by endowing some with less talent and ambition than others, slaves being the most notable exception to this social ethic.

The National Market

Yet these simple social values of a relatively simple community, with their stress on private initiative and private reward, inevitably gave rise to disparate fortunes and disproportionate political influence. By the time of Tocqueville's visits, he could readily foresee the rise, out of con- ditions of equal opportunity, of a class of business magnates who would organize the activities of a multitude of workers—not Marx's proletariat, but a prosperous middle-class citizenry, preoccupied with making money and getting ahead and not much else.

This development could only come about through the spread of the limits of the "natural" community. Warner sets 1830–1860 as the period during which "the communitarian limits of a city of private money mak- ers were reached and passed." [5] For our purposes, we can speak of this nationalization of the sphere of business activity as extending over the century from the mid-1800s to the mid-1900s. The causes of this expan- sion were several and interrelated. One was the growth in population of the cities themselves, and of the country as a whole. The Philadelphia community about which Warner writes was earlier described in much the same terms by John R. Commons, one of the pioneer students of in- dustrial relations. He was interested in explaining the rise of national labor unions and took as his example the shoemakers, whose organiza- tion into a local union had come under the disapprobation of the Re- corder's Court in Philadelphia as early as 1807. Why had they had cause to join themselves in an association antagonistic to their employers?

The reason, according to Commons, was that down to the end of the eighteenth century, the production of shoes, like other commodities, had gone on in small establishments operated by a master, who invested his limited stock of capital in materials that he fashioned into boots or shoes only after receiving a customer's order. These small-scale operations were almost an adjunct to the master's own household. In this close relationship, the interests of a master and his journeymen and apprentices were very similar. They all wanted to obtain a good price for their product, but were aware that driving a hard bargain would turn trade away and injure their reputation. Social pressures, as much as the possible competition of other shoemakers in the community, prevented them from exploiting their customers. There was thus a community of interests and personal relations—masters trying to build up their little stock of assets, journeymen seeking to earn a good living and desiring eventually to set themselves up as masters, apprentices aspiring to journeymen status, and customers who were neighbors and likely enough to be making something themselves for sale to the shoemakers. It was a system of mutual forbearances and mutual interests—a community.

But as the seaboard towns began to expand, the personal nature of relationships broke down in the face of numbers. By 1800 Philadelphia was a city of 70,000. Retail establishments now competed with one another for trade. In periods of rising prices, a master shoemaker-retailer would hesitate before raising his prices, for fear that his competitors might not follow suit. The consequence might be a squeeze on his journeymen workers. But other population influences were at work as well. The larger retail establishments began seeking out business in the hinterlands, investing their growing capital in prefabricated goods, like shoes, to sell to customers in the interior settlements. Indeed, the retailers became wholesalers in the process, and wholesalers from Philadelphia found themselves competing against wholesalers from New York for the trade of retailers in Pittsburgh and Cincinnati. Such intercity competition drove the merchant to try to lower his prices; to do this he had to shave his costs. The method to which the growing business establishments turned was specialization—the journeyman ceased to produce a whole shoe and specialized on the uppers, while less exacting work could be farmed out to younger workers and women. The skill was literally disintegrated as the businessman strove for efficiency.

It was, according to Commons, these competitive pressures on the journeymen which drove them into the self-protective organization of unions. But he does not rest his analysis there. As population increased and markets became extended, competition changed the position of the small businessman himself. Lacking the capital to operate on a large scale, he sold his entire output to a master merchant, who disposed of it through a network of wholesalers and retailers. Thus the little workshop of the small community had metamorphosed into a complex economic network of manufacturers, merchandisers, wholesalers, and retailers. But behind this network stood also the bankers, whose financing was necessary to the whole operation, and who—to preserve their investments—sometimes intervened to reorganize the production process itself, sometimes effecting mergers, dictating economies, and insisting on more efficient methods. The final stage in this process, in Commons's analysis, comes toward the end of the nineteenth century, when the segmented parts of this stretched-out process become integrated into the large corporation, which finances, produces, and markets its own products, all in one organization operating on a national scale.[6] If Commons had lived to carry his analysis further, his extended market would have carried into the international sphere—not just in terms of the marketing operations of a national firm, but the total operations of a multinational firm, and might have encompassed the conglomerate corporation as well, extending its activities across industry and product lines into "free-form" sectors of the whole economy.

The technological changes that accompanied this consolidation of local markets into a national market, encouraging production on a large scale in anticipation of, rather than in response to, customer orders, were at first of the kind that Commons documented—the breaking down of a whole operation into specialized tasks, repetitively performed. Mechanization played an increasingly important role, but the assembly of pools of capital equipment tended by workers was a phenomenon that by and large followed, rather than preceded, the widening of the market. In effect, a mass market created the demand for mass production, eliciting from inventors the mechanical devices and inventions to accelerate output.

Improvements in transportation and communication were of vital significance throughout this period. In the earliest stages they took the form of toll roads and canals, but as the nineteenth century wore along railroads became of overriding importance. Indeed, the rapid development of the steel industry in the United States was attributable largely to the insatiable demand for steel rails, in the production of which the United States soon became so proficient that it surpassed in productivity the mills in England, which had pioneered the basic processes by which they were made.[7]

Corporations and the Civic Community

In the process of creating a national market, cities themselves became specialized into particular economic functions in the overall network. Warner provides a nice description of how the changes we have been discussing—population spreading through the country, population growth in the cities, specialization of workers' jobs, introduction of mechanical aids, improvements in transportation links, and concentration of particular economic contributions by cities—had their effects on the makeup of the city's industry.

"By the 1850's Philadelphia's artisans had been organized in a curious network of large and small enterprises in which large-scale production emerged from a mixture of old and new ways." Most of the city's 7,000 shoe workers had been affected by mechanization and interregional specialization. Their specialty had become ladies' shoes and expensive men's shoes and boots, which they produced in quantity for jobbers and retailers. The production process itself was still fragmented—skilled cutters prepared the materials at central manufactories and the finishing operations were carried on by men and women in their own homes or in little shops scattered around the city. Cheap shoes were made elsewhere, notably in Lynn, Massachusetts, though some Philadelphia shoe manufacturers imported parts from Lynn for local assembly.

In clothing the same dispersed operations prevailed, though in the field of men's and boy's garments larger factories were coming into existence, employing highly specialized and "rationalized" processes. Carpet weaving followed the same pattern. Hosiery production, which had been a Philadelphia specialty since before the Revolution, at mid-century displayed every stage of historical development "from the cottage use of wooden hand-powered knitting frames to factory-organized power-driven circuit knitters which 'will do a day's work before breakfast.'"

"The whole city was a mix of old and new. At the Baldwin and Norris locomotive works hitherto unprecedented industrial armies of 600 workers using the latest machinery turned out these novel machines. Philadelphia's foundries and chemical companies, though not all large, had a national reputation for quality and modernity." [8]

Effect on Community Leadership

Favored by particular circumstances of location, leadership, population characteristics, and capital availability, some communities grew faster than others, becoming, like Philadelphia, centers of national or regional economic activity. Others were more tied to their rural past or to a particular resource, such as lumber or iron or copper, and remained centers of supply of materials and sources of demands for manufactured goods.

In the smaller towns and cities, there was a tendency for local business, especially if family owned, to play a leading role in community organization and activities. Around the turn of the century a number of one-industry or one-company towns answered this description, in whole or part—the Pullman Company in Pullman, Illinois; the Ball Company in Muncie, Indiana; the Hershey Chocolate Company in Hershey, Pennsylvania; Cannon Mills in Kannapolis, North Carolina; the Armco Steel Corporation in Middletown, Ohio. A number of such instances remain today, and new ones have been added as some large corporation relocates in a suburb. In other cases, towns once so dominated have grown large and diversified enough to shake off any single pervasive influence. The influence in all these cases may have been beneficent or constricting, paternalistic or destructive—each situation was more or less peculiar to itself.

Over this same period, "second-tier" cities, such as Cleveland, Pittsburgh, Cincinnati, St. Louis, Philadelphia, came under the control of a clique or oligarchy of business families. These families were known to one another, shared the same set of social values and beliefs in civic virtues, and gave the city some cohesiveness or unity through support and direction of its institutions, but they were less personally involved in the more public aspects of community life. As these cities expanded and became more economically diversified, and as the family-owned companies were increasingly bought out and merged with national corporations, the relationship between business leadership and community involvement underwent a marked change. Those whose economic functions oriented them toward national markets tended to become disengaged from local affairs, while those whose economic functions tied them to the city either as a market (as in the case of department stores and public utilities) or as a fixed supplier of materials or services (as in the case of transportation and extractive operations) continued to exercise such influence over civic matters as they could, but found their position weakened by the defection of their former business associates and by the rise of other local interest groups, ranging from labor unions to ethnic societies.

Because of the diversity of size, geographical location, and economic specifications of towns and cities across the nation, let us concentrate on those that have become significantly integrated into the national economy. This would certainly include most towns with populations of 50,000 or more. For this class of cities, the rapid nationalization of the U.S. market since the mid-nineteenth century, accompanied by the gradual disengagement from civic affairs of the expanding large national corporations, has had a catastrophic effect.

Once again we turn to Warner's reconstruction of Philadelphia's history for an example of what was occurring throughout the United States over the century since the Civil War. He describes the changes in terms of the focus of interests of the business leaders of the city. "The great strength of the old merchant system of government lay in the variety of talent, experience, and opinion which it could harness to public commissions, private boards, and elective office." Henry Gilpin, attorney general under President Van Buren, sat on numerous civic boards dealing with activities as wide ranging as transportation and education. Stephen Girard, a merchant, left his fortune to Philadelphia for various public works that had occupied his lifetime interest. Matthias Baldwin, the locomotive builder, served on numerous public and private boards and was among those instrumental in effecting the County Consolidation Act in 1854. "This style of leadership died out in Philadelphia about the time of the Civil War."

Characteristic of the successor breed was Jay Cooke, a self-made man, who rose from clerk to founder of an investment banking firm. Tocqueville's warning as to the possible neglect of public interest arising from excessive preoccupation with private advancement was exemplified in Cooke. "Though he was lively, curious, and open-minded, the sheer discipline of work precluded his making any meaningful contribution to his society outside the specialty of his career of private banker and investment broker." This was in line with the prevailing social ethic, which held that one's personal advancement was coincident with his contribution to society. What was different was that no longer was there the constraint of local public opinion, a fear of disapprobation, which had previously held private interests within appropriate bounds. For Cooke, in whose lifetime banking became a nationalized activity, "the city of Philadelphia did not serve . . . as it had served for previous merchant generations, as an important frame through which he saw the world. . . . No deep knowledge of, or concern for, the general welfare of his city informed Cooke's business, politics, or philanthropy." His political concerns were with Washington. His financial concerns were largely with New York.

Nor was Cooke singular in this regard. "The new habits of business taught the mid-nineteenth-century Philadelphia businessman that the city was not important to their daily lives, and in response these business leaders became ignorant of their city and abandoned its politics." [9] In turn, the city lost the active involvement of an important segment of its business leadership. The resident managers of branches of national corporations were incapable and unwilling to assume the civic positions vacated by the old-family business elite. Their time was their company's, not their own, and their career advancement lay with the national corporation, not in the politics and policies of a city in which they were at best transient residents. Their participation was limited to noncontroversial forms, like lending their name to Red Cross and United Fund drives, the Police Athletic League, and more recently to some aspects of the Urban Coalition.[10]

Nor was such noninvolvement purely a personal choice on the resident manager's part. How much discretion can a national corporation afford to give to a plant manager in certain sensitive areas of community relations, such as those that concern labor and black activist groups? Vigorous participation in a controversial area might set a precedent that would embarrass the company in other locations. Whatever the manager of U.S. Steel's Birmingham, Alabama, mill may have felt about the racial controversy that erupted in 1963 over employment practices in that city, Roger Blough, as board chairman, enunciated corporate policy binding on all its operations. In an unusual exposure of the effects of corporate nationalization, Blough declared in effect that *any* policy that the company adopted in such a field would be an imposition on the communities in which it operated. Because a company can hardly act without policy, if only *de facto*, the neutrality implied by Blough's statement was more apparent than real. The implication that was more real than apparent was that the national corporation would make its own policy, abstaining from active or open community involvement, despite the importance of its position in the community.

Corporate Power in the Community

The Blough incident points up the power over community life that resides in the national corporation, despite its apparent disengagement from the community. That power lies in the "negative decision," the capability of effectively vetoing local actions unpalatable to it. The threat of moving its plant from town in the event of community actions considered unfavorable to its interests is always present, and even if such drastic retribution may be unrealistically disproportionate to a particular action complained of, it cannot therefore be wholly disregarded: corporations cumulate records of community dispositions toward them, favorable or otherwise, and displeasure may be expressed, not on the occasion of a particular event (perhaps a change in tax policy, or regulatory treatment, or refusal to grant a zoning exception), but at the time when a decision must be made whether to remodel or expand facilities or reduce activities in favor of other locations.

The national corporation thus continues to influence community affairs without actively participating in them, or being sensitive or responsive to community needs or welfare in the way that a permanent local leadership would be. Moreover, its managerial personnel—transient though they may be—become members of local organizations, their occupational status merits them respect, and their views on particular issues carry weight. Considering that such individuals have cast their careers with the corporation and are unlikely to endanger their chance for advancement by views prejudicial to their employer, they can act only as conduits for corporate positions—negative or otherwise—concerning local actions affecting corporate interests. The uninvolved corporation thus takes precedence over their own involvement as citizens of the community.

The fact that the national corporation has limited its community interests means that business no longer exerts the controlling influence in community life that it once did. Local business organizations continue to play an active role, for their own protection, as permanent residents with personal interests at stake. But the weakening of the business hegemony in local matters has opened up opportunities for other groups to exert their own special interests: in some towns labor plays an influential role; in other cities certain ethnic groups are cohesive and must be listened to. The political scientists have pointed to this rise of multiple-interest groups, seeking to effect some consensus, as the essence of democracy. Under the term "pluralism," it connotes the absence of any single dominant power and the presence of numerous fragmented interests that must be reconciled to one another, through compromises, if community life is to be viable.

But this construction neglects the effect of the historic and still prevailing social ethic under which community life in the United States operates. That ethic stresses the importance of private initiative as against government action and emphasizes individual (and corporate) autonomy as against social order. For all the expansion of governmental activity since New Deal days, we still operate on a premise of limited government. Nowhere is this philosophy more practiced than in the local sphere. If, then, the disengagement of the large national corporation from community life has tended to strengthen a pluralism of interests, it is a pluralism that is relatively powerless. The issue is less how much power business can exert, affirmatively, over others than whether there is any opportunity, within the private enterprise ethos, of developing public institutions that can act effectively on behalf of the public, particularly with regard to the problems that plague the cities.

The antipathy to governmental power inherent in the social values of a business culture, coupled with the withdrawal of our major business leaders from direct personal community responsibility, has turned America's towns and cities into shells empty of power, facing major social issues that are beyond their capacity to solve. The rise of the national corporation, autonomous in its actions under a philosophy of private initiative intended originally for persons, but extended to it by interpretation, has made communities—like the physical environment—something to be exploited for pecuniary advantage. The national corporation, with its subsidiaries and satellite plants, is free to move in and out of communities at will, with limited concern for its impact on the community as a place to live. Its effect is twofold—on the physical environment, which is shaped according to the corporation's economics rather than a community's needs, and on the social environment, which becomes for the corporation's personnel a short-term place of assignment, as temporary officials in the colonies on behalf of the metropolitan corporation.

Influence on Community Environment

Because we have previously explored at length the pollution effects of industrial activity, let us concentrate here on the aesthetic impact. The very *shape* of American cities in which hundreds of millions of people must spend their lives derives from the decisions of large corporate organizations whose interest is not in the environmental effect on the inhabitants but in the effect on the balance sheet. If a Charles Luckman, himself an architect, as president of Lever Brothers designs a corporate office for Park Avenue in New York that sets a high standard for beauty, enhancing the physical environment, that action constitutes a gratuity bestowed on the public, which it has no reason to expect. What it could expect was that the imaginative use of glass in that unique structure would be reproduced, unimaginatively but economically, in boxlike

structures providing more square feet of office space for a given investment, the formula repeated over and over again, with modest variations,
so that for years to come the residents of New York will be forced to live
with a graceless architecture, as boring and repetitive as most of the
jobs which go on within their walls.

In an article carrying the apocalyptic title, "A City Destroying Itself,"
Richard J. Whalen commented:

> New York has become a failure in human arrangements. This failure has
> many sources. It can be traced to the apathy and venality of the city's politi-
> cians; to the cold unconcern of the city's builders, among whom a kind of
> Gresham's Law of architecture prevails: to the remoteness and indifference of
> the city's business and financial leaders; to the selfishness of competing groups
> and interests whose actions and demands take little account of the general
> welfare. . . .
>
> Through their collective decisions, the speculative builders and, even more
> important, the mortgage lenders in the banks and insurance companies have
> reshaped the contours of New York, determining how the city functions and
> how its inhabitants live. Provided with incentives by every level of govern-
> ment, these private decision makers of great public power have feverishly torn
> down, rebuilt, and expanded, profitably manipulating the land beneath build-
> ings and even the air above. In the process they have established the rule that
> in New York the land and the buildings define the place of people. People are
> not people but economic units. Even in the aggregate, their wishes are out-
> weighed by columns of figures.[11]

Others have echoed this lament. *The New York Times*, bidding adieu
to the Fifth Avenue that had once been the city's pride, commented:
"Like the other avenues, Fifth Avenue is to be turned into bland blocks
of banks sleekly embalmed in a corporate pall. The problem is that land
prices have been bid up so high in the real estate game that retail rent-
als will no longer support them. Stores cannot compete with the return
to be squeezed out of corporate tenants. . . . It is absurd that the form
and future of the city, for whom and how it functions, are determined
by the insane spiral of escalating land prices. The city be damned, if the
return is good." [12] And economist Wilfred Owen of Brookings Institution
has remarked: "Instead of seeing land as a public trust, we believe
everyone has a constitutional right to exploit it. When anyone demands
public controls on the pursuit of the dollar, we cry that our freedom is
in danger. But we use our freedom only to despoil and destroy." [13]

Most economists have been brought up to believe that pecuniary valuation can be equated with social good; if corporations bid up land
prices and erect their own bland buildings on the parcels they buy,
however centrally located, however conspicuous in the life of the city,

this only means that land is going to those uses that yield the highest returns, within a system of prices that reflects society's own preferences. The major difficulties with this argument are two. It fails to consider the so-called "externalities," which are in fact incommensurable. (As Whalen says, "What, after all, is a vista worth?") And it does not take into account that the authority over money is distributed in a way that carries with it an undemocratic aesthetic control over a people's physical environment.

The autonomy of the national corporation, its freedom to move its plants and people, and its understandable withdrawal from active participation in communities of which neither its headquarters staff nor its plant managers are an integral part, however long it may operate there, creates a problem in town and city governance. The institutions on which government is most dependent are beyond its reach, and those whose leadership capabilities could be most beneficial to it cannot be counted on. With growth in population, particularly through immigration, and with the massive movement from farm to city, particularly of the blacks, the old unity under a recognized leadership characteristic of the natural community becomes only a memory. There is neither leadership nor unity.

Party Leadership and the Consequences of Reform

The social values of a business culture have discouraged the development of public institutions and public authority. For a time, the vacuum created by the withdrawal of the most active and effective business talent from civic life was filled by a new breed, the professional politicians. These men hammered out a political party organization that itself carried no public authority but, when in office, managed to serve as an integrative mechanism for the maintenance of order, an instrument for effecting compromises, striking bargains within a more diffused power structure where the dominant weight was still swung actively by the local business interests and passively by the national corporations operating there.

In effecting compromises—partly to maintain public order, partly to maintain themselves in power—the new party professionals resorted to tactics that were often offensive to members of the older patrician families. Corruption was overt; vote buying was commonplace; the "machine" ran on patronage, not principle. The first decades of the twen-

128

tieth century saw a good deal of journalistic muckraking, perhaps the best known being Lincoln Steffens's brilliant, but ineffectual, polemics "The Shame of the Cities." Steffens regarded the corruption of party politics as a process by which the new "natural" leaders of a diffuse urban society, the party bosses and ward heelers, acquired power only to "sell out" to a business plutocracy for personal gain—a species of democratic disloyalty, if not treason.

It was in this period, lasting into the depression years of the 1930s, that cities spawned "reform" movements, often led by sons of the old business elite, some of them still active in local mercantile affairs, others (like the younger sons of British nobility) having elected to enter the professions, particularly law. New city charters were drafted and sometimes put into effect. But perhaps the favorite objective of the reformers was a civil service based on merit, which would presumably deprive the politicians of the patronage on which their power rested. As a college student in Cleveland in the late 1930s I was myself caught up in the final stages of that reform movement, serving as executive director of a campaign to amend the city charter and bring all nonpolicy city employees under the merit system. The campaign (which benefited from a one-night stand by Mayor LaGuardia of New York) was successful by a margin of a few hundred votes. I had no realization at the time that in fact I was helping to undermine the only authority—the party machine—that exercised an integrating influence on an increasingly diffuse society.

The decline of business leadership in the smaller natural communities of the nineteenth century was thus followed by the decline of party leadership in the larger, more heterogeneous, disorganized urban conglomerations of the twentieth century. The reformers believed that the leadership role could be filled by technically trained, efficiency-minded, public-oriented city managers. "Honest, well-intentioned amateurs band together to drive out the forces of organized plunder, corruption, incompetence, and partisan politics and replace their rule with the benign effects of civil service-recruited experts." [14]

The consequence was something different from what had been expected. The basic functions of the city—police and fire protection, education, health, sanitation, housing, and welfare—were in effect turned over to bureaucracies performing each of these services. Protected by civil-service commissions, increasingly independent of executive control, more recently acquiring in many jurisdictions a *de jure* or *de facto* freedom to strike, these groups have each sought the advancement of its own bureaucratic interests, without regard to any impact on the city as a whole. The city's government has been parceled out among organization officials who are not themselves elected by the citizenry, and who are not responsive to public officials who are elected by the citizenry. Reviewing the major fields of city government, a former deputy mayor of New York City has concluded: "the political party has no voice in any of these important areas of city government. In all of them the bureaucracy is vested with the overwhelming preponderance of political power—so overwhelming a preponderance that no combination of forces outside the bureaucracy is capable of controlling it." [15] Norton Long draws the only reasonable inference: "In practice this has meant that no matter who won at the polls the likelihood was that things would remain much the same." [16]

Disintegration of the Cities

In the earlier years of American cities, before the rise of large industrial establishments, the population distributed itself by income and ethnicity to only a slight degree. As the cities expanded and the size of the mills grew with technological advances and mass-production techniques, drawing workers from all sections of the city, a change in the residential pattern began to take place. The more skilled and well-to-do began to move toward the outskirts of the city, away from the older, more crowded, more heterogeneous central district. Ethnic neighborhoods became more sharply distinguished. In Philadelphia, for example, the Italians, Russians, and Poles were more segregated in 1930 than had been the Irish in 1860 (at that time the major disfavored ethnic group).[17]

This centripetal movement accelerated. By the 1920s the exodus of the middle class to suburban neighborhoods, graded by income levels, was well advanced. The post–World War II influx of blacks from rural areas gave it fresh momentum. As we have previously noted, this movement was accompanied by some transfer of business to the white suburbs and the open areas around them. Within the space of half a century the form and functioning of many large towns and most major cities had undergone radical transformation. Particularly in the cities, the keepers of the establishment had become the downtown business institutions and the professions relating to them, the city bureaucracies, the building trades and related unions (still dominantly white), and the older elite who presided over the cultural institutions—all with disparate and frequently opposing interests. These keepers had their wards—an increased population of the aged, the poor, alienated blacks and Latins, the deviants and rejects. No mechanism existed for coordinating these contentious and often embittered elements, no public authority was capable of creating out of this maelstrom of separatist and self-interested groups some viable civic order.

As we have seen, the schools no longer were accepted as transmitters of traditions and values but had retreated into an intrenched and beleaguered bureaucracy seeking to preserve a culture that those whom it tended largely rejected. Among dissident elements, particularly among the blacks and Latins, demands were raised for decentralization of the city's functions to permit neighborhood control—a challenge to the existing bureaucracies and hence a further basis for confrontation and contention. But decentralization of a major city, in the absence of any effective coordinating authority, could lead only to greater disintegration and conflict. What is totally lacking is any means of eliciting from, or imposing on, the city's constituent elements a sense of responsibility for the city as a corporate entity. The sense of community has gone out of the American city. Lacking leadership, it lacks cohesion. Lacking effective common values, it is only a locus for opposing interests, which are held together by a set of fragile accommodations and mutual weaknesses.

The future consequences of this social fragmentation have been pictured dramatically by the National Commission on the Causes and Prevention of Crime:

In a few more years, lacking effective public action, this is how these cities will likely look:

• Central business districts in the heart of the city, surrounded by mixed areas of accelerating deterioration, will be partially protected by large numbers of people shopping or working in commercial buildings during daytime hours, plus a substantial police presence, and will be largely deserted except for police patrols during nighttime hours.

• High rise apartment buildings and residential compounds protected by private guards and security devices will be fortified cells for upper-middle and high-income populations living at prime locations in the city.

• Suburban neighborhoods, geographically far removed from the central city, will be protected mainly by economic homogeneity and by distance from population groups with the highest propensities to commit crimes.

• Lacking a sharp change in Federal and state policies, ownership of guns will be almost universal in the suburbs; homes will be fortified by an array of devices, from window grills to electronic surveillance equipment; armed citizens in cars will supplement inadequate police patrols in neighborhoods closer to the central city, and extreme left-wing and right-wing groups will have tremendous armories of weapons which could be brought into play with or without any provocation.

• High speed, patrolled expressways will be sanitized corridors connecting safe areas, and private automobiles, taxicabs, and commercial vehicles will be routinely equipped with unbreakable glass, light armor and other security features. Inside garages or valet parking will be available at safe buildings in or near the central city. Armed guards will "ride shotgun" on all forms of public transportation.

• Streets and residential neighborhoods in the central city will be unsafe in differing degrees and the ghetto slum neighborhoods will be places of terror with widespread crime, perhaps entirely out of police control during nighttime hours. Armed guards will protect all public facilities such as schools, libraries and playgrounds in these areas.

• Between the unsafe, deteriorating central city on the one hand and the network of safe, prosperous areas and sanitized corridors on the other, there will be, not unnaturally, intensifying hatred and deepening division. Violence will increase further, and the defensive response of the affluent will become still more elaborate.[18]

Corporate Efforts at Reinvolvement

The major corporations have not been blind to the increasing fragmentation of city life, with accompanying special-interest confrontations. Nor have they been altogether unaware of their role in the process. Beginning in the 1950s a number of major companies looked beyond their long-standing participation in safe local causes, chiefly of a fund-raising nature, to concern themselves with restoring their diminishing influence in local affairs. Stung by accusations that their plant management people were uninvolved with civic issues because of the transiency of their attachment to the community in contrast to the permanency of their attachment to the corporation, some companies—Texaco and Johnson & Johnson, for example—sought to encourage greater local involvement of their managers by assuring them that their community activities would be taken into account in considering them for promotion. But perhaps more important than uneasy conscience in stimulating community "reinvolvement" was a fear that groups antagonistic to business could create a climate "inimical to the health and vitality of industry." [19]

General Electric led the way in spreading this philosophy. In addition to an initial appraisal of such considerations as "labor psychology, local government efficiency, relationship of taxes to services provided, educational and cultural facilities," the corporation urged its managers "to take a periodic inventory of their climate, to set out specific goals for its improvement, and to become in part the architects rather than merely the victims of their environment." [20] To achieve these ends, partisan political activity, no less than neutral civic activity, was necessary. Other corporations—Ford Motor Company and Monsanto Chemical Company, for example—followed suit.

The civil rights movement of the 1960s caused a marked shift in the nature of these corporate efforts at reinvolving themselves in the life of the cities. Confrontation with black activists inescapably drew a number of corporations into local policy matters, particularly in the area of employment, which many would have preferred to avoid. Eastman Kodak is perhaps the outstanding example here.[21] Other companies undertook initiatives of their own in such matters as minority housing: Quaker Oats, for example, applied pressure on the officials of Danville, Illinois, to pass an open-housing ordinance before committing itself to locate a plant there.[22] Chrysler and Michigan Bell undertook to contribute to upgrading the educational offerings of two Detroit high schools, Olin and Southern New England Telephone Company assisted in the reorganization of the New Haven school system. In some cities—notably Atlanta, Georgia, and Hartford, Connecticut—local business institutions joined national corporations with local plants in taking leadership roles in large-scale rehabilitation programs. On a wider front, businessmen across the nation participated in the much-publicized Urban Coalition and the National Alliance of Businessmen. In a survey of executives of 250 major corporations, nine out of ten averred that this renewed involvement in urban affairs was not just a passing phase but marked a permanent change in corporate policy.[23]

Despite the good intentions of such programs, they represent only modest incremental efforts to palliate an urban condition so grave as scarcely to be touched by them. Although the disengagement of nationally oriented corporations from the life of the community was critical to the subsequent disintegration of the cities, corporate reinvolvement cannot now resuscitate the cities.

Proposed Solutions

The enfeeblement of civic life in the United States has been plain for all to see, but what can be done about it is less apparent. Some analysts have suggested the need for new local public authorities to supplement existing city governments. "Every metropolitan area in this country desperately needs a social planning commission . . . looking for ways to better coordinate the great varieties of local effort, whatever the source of funds, directed toward the widest possible range of social and educational problems, . . . to constantly study our ever-changing picture . . . and seek to guide our efforts accordingly." [24] Legal "neighborhood corporations" have been suggested to bring "the people of the community together into an effective body to determine, plan, and implement the kinds of programs of self-development and local authority which the community requires and which it can manage." [25] "Community corporations" have been proposed, "somewhere between a kibbutzim and a company town," that would share in the profits of businesses which adversely affect the community and undertake remedial action.[26] Perhaps the most idealistic proposal has emanated from the realistic Norton Long, who believes the city can restore its viability only if it reevaluates its assets, poor though they may be, and reestablishes itself "as it once was as a cooperative device for its inhabitants to pool their resources and meet their needs." [27]

All such proposals are wistful and wishful efforts to recover the past of the natural community, to reestablish an effective local leadership, to restore a sense of community and purpose. They make no sense within the contemporary environment. In the face of the national corporation, no community corporation or reorganized city government is capable of exercising genuine autonomy or decision-making power. It remains dependent on the goodwill of the corporate hierarchies, whose basic interests still lie in corporate rather than community development.

The state of affairs was pathetically demonstrated when the Western Electric Company decided to move part of its headquarters out of New York City, relocating in Bedminster, New Jersey, a largely rural community of 2,700 people, zoned only for residential use and single-family homes set on five acres of land. The company appealed to the town to grant it an exception that would permit construction of "campus-like office buildings" on 300 acres of land. The administrator of New York City's Economic Development Administration took the highly unusual step of appearing before the Bedminster planning board to urge it to reject Western Electric's petition on the ground that many of the company's employees would then be unable to live in the community where they worked. The company, he argued, would become "an employment site surrounded by a moat of five-acre zoning, in a county which makes no provision for moderate-income housing. This gulf between where people may live and where they might work can be crossed by some but clearly not by a significant proportion of our society."

"If businesses and communities continue in the present mindlessly selfish way," the New York administrator argued, "we will Los Angelize our land, Balkanize our region's finances and South Africanize our economy." [28]

What potential lay here for either the major metropolis of New York or the rural town of Bedminster to cope with Western Electric? If Bedminster rejected the company's request, the company need only turn to another community, one that would welcome its contribution to local finances. New York had no authority to require the company—or another community—to make provisions for its citizens whose jobs went with the company. The problem lies not in the size and scope of the corporation's operations, but in the lack of any matching public authority to deal effectively with it, on behalf of the communities involved.

We may expect that as a society expands in population, it must reproportion itself. The institutions suitable for a small, agricultural nation are inadequate to a populous, industrialized one. As the United States grew, its business institutions went through that reproportioning process, developing into nationally oriented organizations, decentralizing their operations into numerous, but centrally coordinated, subsidiaries and plants, located in equally numerous communities.

This nationalization of the market, and the reproportioning of the economic institutions that served it, was a logical accompaniment of the country's own growth. But the communities themselves, for which a comparable development would have been equally logical and desirable, were inhibited from moving to reorganize their governmental arrangements by the political philosophy of local self-government. As small businesses became subunits of the large corporations, so communities could have become subsystems of the larger political system, no longer fully self-governing, but exercising, within a system of decentralization comparable to corporate decentralization, a degree of discretion backed by federal political power. No longer would it have been within the corporation's sole discretion to move, autonomously, in and out of powerless communities as suited its own convenience. Its private discretion would have been constrained by public authority, in the public interest. The towns and cities would have lost their illusion of self-government, but they would have acquired a competence to deal more effectively with their physical and social environment.

And indeed, as the cities have become weaker and less capable of dealing with their mounting problems, they have tended to throw themselves on the mercy of the federal government, pleading for financial assistance, grants in aid, and the assumption of welfare or education costs. At the 1971 Conference of Mayors, Mayor Lindsay of New York went so far as to propose that the federal government designate major cities as "national cities," for which Congress would assume responsibility. The illusion of self-government is now being rudely shattered; how much better it would have been if a restructuring of federal-local sharing of political power had taken place concomitantly with the restructuring of national-local economic relations.

The federal government is the only political authority capable of dealing effectively with national corporations, but the principle of the decentralization of power and discretion can apply within the political as within the economic sphere. The numerous experts who have asserted the importance of local leadership are right. Nothing can be done without it. But leaders must have some strength from which to lead, and that cannot be supplied only locally, or even primarily locally, but chiefly from federal exercise of authority on behalf of the public welfare, power that would be delegated as feasible to the local leaders.

Given the numerous social action areas confronting a major nation, the federal government would have its hands full in designing appropriate policies or guidelines for national economic and social objectives. How those many-faceted programs are coordinated at the local level, and how the discretion allowed to communities is exercised, would provide ample challenge to the best of the city's leaders, and presumably would provide suitable power as well.

The Social Responsibility Issue

Thus, when we confront the question of the likely role of the corporation in bringing about some amelioration of the condition of our civic communities, we really confront the question of the extent to which they are willing to acquiesce in an accretion of federal authority over their activities, an authority that can be shared with the communities. If the social responsibility approach calls for corporate support of such a policy, the answer is clear that no such response will be forthcoming.

The social engineering approach offers another possibility, one that is more appealing to some business leaders. It involves a closer working—contractual—relationship between the federal government and national corporations on behalf of the cities. One executive sees business as performing the coordinating role that we normally associate with local government:

Corporations and the Civic Community

What we need most today is to revive the executive "Minute Men" expediters of World War II. They would come into town with a briefcase full of authority from all relevant government agencies. They would go over a local proposal to meet an emergency need in two days. They would draw up a contract, sign it the third day. Within 24 hours a new factory to produce an urgent war need was under construction and was in operation six months later. If we would apply this same sense of urgency to urban affairs projects, the private corporations of this country individually and in consortia would perform some peacetime miracles just as they performed some wartime miracles.[29]

Similarly, from the president of Urban America, Inc.:

The private sector needs the support and direction of government; government needs the highly developed tools and management approaches. A most promising means of coordinating efforts to achieve urban goals is through application of the private sector's successful problem solving and management tool, systems analysis. On a nationwide basis, such system management would look into all the components of our urban life—schools, water, utilities, transportation, government structure and operation, industrial development and business location, social patterns and services, relation of one metropolitan area to another, and so forth.[30]

Despite the appeal to some business leaders of such a "systems" approach, one might readily surmise that many other business executives would be less than enthusiastic about being drawn more tightly into a network of federal authority. Daniel P. Moynihan has commented on "the willingness [of American business] to be regulated, for any purpose whatever, so long as profits and oligopoly situations are maintained." [31] But an expanding federal control over the economic and political life of the cities could strike at the roots of business's basic value commitment to organizational autonomy for private advantage.

The social engineering approach to meeting America's social problems has a more plausible prospect than the social responsibility approach, but less, I would judge, than the concept of limited responsibility.

With limited responsibility, the major corporations would continue to mount piecemeal programs attacking facets of urban problems, as lured by government contract, spurred by public pressures, necessitated to protect sunk investments or to salve individual and corporate consciences. Those whose operations do not require their presence in the cities will experience less risk, both to physical assets and to the social structure of their organizations, by locating outside the central cities. They will continue the process of disengagement, but now in terms of physical plant as well as personal participation. On the other hand, the same concern for preserving the value of their assets is likely to encourage those companies rooted in the cities to continue programs to recruit and train more blacks and Latins, advancing them into managerial positions as necessary. Because these efforts arise more from necessity than from conscience, their extent and intensity are likely to reflect the companies' reading of the pressures on them. Despite the rising proportions of blacks and Latins surrounding them, it is difficult to conceive of their reflecting this change in any ways that basically affect the structure and control of the company, whose ownership will still rest largely in white hands.

Cities now present too complex and high-risk an environment to be viewed as attractive potentials for exploitation in the near future. At a later stage, when urban deterioration demands the assertion of greater federal authority, the cities may once again "open up" for profitable investment. In the meantime, an ad hoc, incrementalist approach seems most likely, concentrating on the rejuvenation of those downtown areas that can be most nearly self-contained and most effectively joined to the outer suburbs, new towns, and open spaces by "sanitized corridors."

[7]

THE CORPORATION

AND NATIONAL

OBJECTIVES

HISTORICALLY, the corporation was a governmentally sanctioned body organized to function for a particular specified purpose, whether religious, educational, eleemosynary, or economic. As such it was viewed as an arm of the state, a public agency whose only reason for existence lay in its conduct of public business. Thus the industrial and commercial corporations that came into existence in the latter part of the eighteenth century, in conjunction with what we now refer to as the industrial revolution, were formed for the development and exploitation of a particular invention or resource, and constituted an "opening" for private venture in an otherwise governmentally restricted field. Even though giving rise to exceptional advantages for those who organized them, they were still conceived as extensions of the state and were justified only because they were deemed to serve the national interest.

Individualism and the Private Corporation

The "modern" *private* corporation (which we can identify with the rise of liberal economics) inherited this ascription of serving *public* purpose only by virtue of a profound change in social and political philosophy. That change was the culmination of a number of circumstances all heading up to the philosophical principle of individualism, whose early

139

spokesmen were, among others, John Locke, Adam Smith, and Jeremy Bentham, a principle that took deepest root in England and its American colonies. It had as its cardinal tenet that the individual's unfettered pursuit of his own advantage conduced, in the final analysis, to the public welfare. To achieve this end, the powers of government were to be severely limited to those functions that protected private liberties and property, powers that were not inherent in government, but rather were grants from the citizenry.

Thus came about in the nineteenth century a truly amazing reversal in the role of the corporation. Where it had once been public agent, it now enjoyed the private discretion of a citizen, justified by the principle that its private advantage cumulated to the public advantage. And the political powers that the older corporations (of all forms) had been specifically authorized to exercise in such designated fields as religion, education, charitable activities, foreign representation, were now withdrawn from them and reserved to government on the premise that, as unrepresentative bodies, corporations could not be allowed to exercise political powers that could be granted only by the citizenry at large to a representative government. "So great is the change from the old to the new that a superficial view of the subject almost justifies a doubt whether a study of old corporations is profitable as a preparation for the study of modern corporations"—so wrote John P. Davis in the last chapter of his two-volume classic history of corporations. The historical continuity is preserved *only* by regarding private enterprise as public purpose.[1]

The change in attitude toward the corporation was rapid, but not precipitate. In the early years of the nineteenth century, Davis points out, "it was not considered justifiable to create corporations for any purpose not clearly public in nature; each application was considered by itself, and if favorably was followed by a legislative act of incorporation. Not only was it always difficult to distinguish between public and private, but the view that individuals should have the freest possible opportunities to create wealth encouraged the presumption that every business was of public importance in the respect that it might increase the aggregate wealth of society. . . . The climax was reached in some states when general acts were passed permitting the incorporation of associates 'for any lawful purpose.' Thus the innumerable 'private corporations' came into existence."[2]

General incorporation laws—present in most states by 1880—permitted the incorporators, rather than the legislature, to define their own purposes, in the pursuit of which they were accorded privileges respecting their financial and fiduciary status. "The new style of corporation statutes in effect judged that corporate status had no social relevance save as a device legitimized by its utility to promote business. The obverse of this judgment was that regulation of business activity was no longer to be deemed a proper function of the law of corporate organization. The function of corporation law was to enable businessmen to act, not to police their action." [3] By judicial construction, the expanding corporation retained the same freedom from government intervention that the doctrine of individualism had preserved for the natural individual.

Moreover, under the prevailing philosophy of individualism and limited government, the "scattering" of sovereignty, to use Davis's phrase, and the restraints placed on any extension of governmental activity gave a virtually clear field to private business. Numerous studies have shown that state and federal governments, even in the nineteenth century, did in fact engage in a variety of projects that seem to transcend the concept of limited government. The inconsistency is more apparent than real. What was generally opposed was the idea of an accretion of government's political authority over the operations of private persons and organizations, or in competition with them. Specific projects did not threaten private autonomy; a more authoritative government did. Specific projects were often beneficial to the encouragement and extension of trade. Hence the fierceness of the debate in the 1930s over the meaning implicit in the Constitution's grant of authority to the federal government to promote the general welfare. A too liberal interpretation threatened to go beyond specific affirmative actions and to deprive private interests of their autonomy, to make them subordinate rather than independent.

The growing importance of corporate activity in the life of the nation —the primacy of business on which Calvin Coolidge publicly remarked when president—simply reflected the readier acceptance of private as against public authority, an attitude that, as we saw in the preceding chapter, was so largely responsible for the withering away of the political viability of American cities. Until the Great Depression in the 1930s, public activity stagnated while private initiative surged ahead. It was the Depression, which elicited the political innovations of the New Deal administration, followed by World War II, which mobilized the economy as never before, that marked an end to this phase in American economic history, an era during which the national purpose of an expanding economy was correlated with a government of limited domestic power and purpose.

The Government-Oriented Corporations

Within the changed international environment following World War II, the role of the federal government in the economy likewise changed. Whereas up to that time the largest governmental expenditure had been to its own employees, now disbursements to private industry for an expanded range of goods and services—but chiefly military—dwarfed all other categories. In 1929 federal outlays had totaled $2.6 billion; by 1969 they had passed $190 billion. Approximately half of this total went for purchases from private business, with defense and space expenditures absorbing the largest share.

No longer was the federal government a lazy bureaucracy of limited powers purchasing standard pencils, typewriters, and filing cabinets under sealed bids from numerous competitors. The bulk of its purchases took and still take the form of "specialized commodities, typically highly engineered systems designed and produced to the government's own specifications and for which there are no established private markets—missiles, space vehicles, nuclear-powered carriers, desalinization systems, and atomic energy items. . . . The dominance of military and related high-technology procurement is striking. Contract awards by the Department of Defense are three times as large as the grand total for all civilian agencies. Moreover, the purchases of the civilian agencies with the largest totals—nuclear reactors and products for the AEC and aerospace systems for the NASA—bear a closer resemblance to the military than to the civilian agencies."[4]

Such items are nonstandard, and hence can only be negotiated directly with a small group of potential contractors who are capable of supplying the highly specialized needs. "By the selection of contractors, the government can control entry and exit, can greatly affect the growth of the firms involved, and can impose its way of doing business on the companies participating."[5] It can also allocate its economic favors among geographical regions as suits its political needs.[6] All this sounds far away from a government of limited powers that simply tends to the needs of private business. Indeed, Murray Weidenbaum, who has made a study of this phenomenon, concludes: "In some ways the newer relationship can be viewed as a partnership whereby both the private and public sectors work together in achieving important national purposes unattainable via separate efforts in either sector of the economy."[7]

Despite Weidenbaum's perception of the potentials of this "newer relationship," he tends to discount it as portending a major shift in the structure of the American economy. Instead, its effect is restricted to a segment of the economy that has simply seized on a new market. He points out that the bulk of the government's contracting has been with a comparatively small number of firms. By and large, these are not the giant corporations like General Motors or RCA or Eastman Kodak. They tend to be medium-sized companies, still large but a good size category lower in the scale. Moreover, the giant corporations are not dependent on government contracts, whereas the medium-sized companies receiving the bulk of government contracts tend to be heavily dependent on those contracts. Hence we wind up with a category that Weidenbaum dubs the "government-oriented corporations," firms like AVCO, Boeing, General Dynamics, Lockheed, Martin-Marietta, Newport News Shipbuilding, Raytheon, and North American Rockwell.

According to Weidenbaum, it is this specialized group of corporations, not the corporate economy generally, that has become a new type of agent of the state. With respect to this group, the Department of Defense or the National Aeronautics and Space Administration (NASA) in effect determines the products they produce, provides their capital equipment, dictates their internal operations, renegotiates price and profit under rules of its own devising. The result has been that this coterie of corporations is more dependent on the government, less capable of functioning in private competitive markets. In effect, they constitute a specialized sector of the economy.

The New Industrial State

Weidenbaum opposes his conception of the limited functions of a government-oriented sector to the more sweeping view of John Kenneth Galbraith. Galbraith has argued that government-corporate collaboration on a far more extensive scale has in fact created a radically changed economy, a "new industrial state," in which the large corporations *as a class* have become an administrative arm of the state, employed by it to effectuate national policy. In taking issue with it, Weidenbaum has, I believe, misunderstood the thrust of Galbraith's argument. Because he is himself primarily concerned with the contractual system developed by the federal government for the achievement of specific public objectives, he has failed to appreciate that Galbraith's concern goes far beyond such a dependent, contractual relationship.

While Galbraith maintains that the large modern corporation has become an administrative arm of the state, he likewise asserts that the state has become the partner of the large corporation. The two collaborate, each dependent on the other.

For Galbraith, the state cannot do without the corporate network in achieving its economic, political, and social objectives. Its world leadership depends on maintaining a sufficiently high rate of industrial and economic growth and innovation. Its domestic tranquility depends on a growth of jobs and income. But neither can the large corporation go it alone. It requires from the federal government monetary and fiscal policies that will sustain its markets. It depends on wage and price policies that will curb inflation without restraining growth. It needs federal support for scientific research and for the educational institutions that supply it with professional experts.

Because of its long-term capital commitments, the large corporation needs assurances of political and economic equilibrium. These can be given only by the federal government. But the federal government equally relies on a buoyant and progressive economy to supply jobs and income for all its citizens. This can be the consequence only of the initiatives of the hundreds of large corporations who invest for the future. Galbraith's new industrial state is in effect the U.S. equivalent of the widely publicized "Japan, Inc." The primary difference is that in Japan the relation between state and large corporation is an outgrowth of national traditions, whereas in the United States it involves a reinterpretation of national traditions.

Weidenbaum is bemused by national objectives conceived as so many specific projects—missile platforms, transportation systems, weapons systems. Galbraith, in his larger view, sees national objectives as composed not only of such specific projects, but also of a whole range of general social and economic policies, including rates of economic growth, stabilization of wages and prices, programs for tying minority groups into the mainstream, and foreign economic and political relationships. In short, he sees government-corporate collaboration as operating over the whole sphere of activities encompassed by the traditional powers of a sovereign state—hence his term the "*industrial* state." If one may be pardoned for imparting his own interpretation to another's analysis, I understand Galbraith's conception as applying, not to a fully realized state of affairs existing at the time of his writing (which would leave it open to criticism "on the evidence"), but to a state of relationships in the process of being realized—but so far along the road to realization that one can reasonably anticipate the end result and write of it as *though* realized, for dramatic effect.

As I have noted in contrasting the Weidenbaum and Galbraith approaches, the complex of government-business relations divides into two major categories. One is concerned with specific objectives, deriving sometimes from the specialized federal bureaucracies or the residual discretion of an ebullient chief executive (military systems, the Kennedy moon shot, for example), sometimes from the pressures of "publics" of varying size and political strength (small-business support, minimum-wage legislation, highway construction). The other category is more general and pervasive, dealing with broad aggregates or targets or policies (the size of the GNP, nondiscriminatory employment practices, inflation control).

In some instances the government can achieve these objectives by writing clauses into the contracts it makes with business firms—not only in the high-technology contracts with which Weidenbaum is concerned, but in contracts for more ordinary products and services, such as the construction of buildings, the purchase of automobiles, the provisioning of desks or computers or light bulbs. There is scarcely a large corporation in the United States that is not touched by contracts of such a nature, even if they represent only a small amount of its business. They may not be government oriented, but they are certainly government influenced.

In other instances, the government can achieve its objectives by simple act of regulatory legislation, as in the areas of employment and environmental control, applying to all business operating in interstate commerce, which certainly covers the large corporations, but extends downward to many that would be considered small by any standard.

These are the kinds of regulations that, as Moynihan pointed out, business can take in stride as long as its basic position of market power remains unaffected. It can comply with a new set of minor constraints —grumbling in the process, particularly at the paper work involved— but the very nature of business opportunism and risk taking have tuned businessmen to learn to cope with such measures without allowing them to affect their basic initiative and discretion. Indeed, business's powers of seeing to it that government does not go too far in limiting its discretion are very great: business retrenchment or noncooperation in the economic sphere could undermine the position of governmental administrators.

The government can secure implementation of its objectives also by positive inducements in the form of subsidies, tax abatements, insurance and lending advantages, and various indirect benefits (road construction, harbor dredging, tariffs, preferential purchasing). A study prepared for the Joint Economic Committee of Congress concluded: ". . . in the course of our history, the Federal Government has engaged in a great variety of subsidy and subsidylike programs. Originally they were limited substantially to assistance to transportation interests, to encourage foreign trade and domestic expansion and development; more recently subsidies have expanded to the point where few segments of our economy are completely unaffected by them." [8]

The degree of compliance with regulatory objectives embodying "national policy" depends on the effectiveness of the responsible agency, the cooperation of business, the persistence of public interest, the presence of organized pressure groups, the effect of subsequent amendments and interpretations. We have in previous chapters discovered the ways in which reforms passed with high hopes have been rendered ineffective and all but forgotten, just as others have become so absorbed into standard methods of doing business that they no longer irritate those regulated.

The change in attitude by business, particularly large corporations, toward cooperation with government in achieving broad national objectives is most marked in the area of aggregate economic activity. It would be pointless to record again the intense opposition that business once registered to any governmental fiscal or monetary policy that had as objective anything other than balancing the government's own budget. The Keynesian concept of using government policy and budget as an instrument for affecting overall economic activity was so bitterly opposed that as recently as the Kennedy Administration the council of business advisers, summoned annually by the Department of Commerce, forced the president's Council of Economic Advisers to abandon its efforts at computing potential GNP. The objection was that if an activist government concluded that something was potential, it would seek to make it actual, which would be likely to involve some form of public economic planning constrictive of corporate autonomy. Yet less than ten years later, with Republicans in power, the chairman of President Nixon's Council of Economic Advisers could testify before the Joint Economic Committee of Congress: "We incorporate in our view of 1971, as earlier private forecasters have not always done, the facts that $1,065-billion GNP is the target of government policy for 1971, that the government has the means to achieve the target, and that the government will use them." [9]

Mutuality of Government and Business Interest

The adjustment by business to this sweeping recasting of public economic policy reflects the increased appreciation by business that only through working cooperatively with government can it achieve its own objectives. The federal government must of course act as coordinator—who else could perform that function?—but business influence can help to shape its policies. If those policies are cast at as *general* a level as possible, then operating autonomy is preserved within the general framework. Government intervention is needed only when the general (aggregate) performance is inferior to what has been agreed upon (a level of GNP that creates excessive unemployment or excessive inflation). The assurance that some government action will be taken when needed to support overall performance provides a firmer and more comfortable base from which the major corporations can plan their own programs. Thus private business actions cumulate in public economic goals (of income and employment), and public actions underwrite private corporate objectives.

This same mutuality of interest is evidenced in the related matter of productivity. This elusive concept has at least two meanings. At the level of the firm, it is the familiar measure of input-output efficiency, an efficiency that is largely engineered by private management and is an important determinant of the firm's rate of return on investment. At the level of the economy, productivity is a measure of how effectively use is made of the economy's resources—whether manpower and industrial capacity are fully employed or partially idle—in achieving as high a level of real GNP as is realistically feasible.

But each of these levels of productivity is partially determined by the other. The efficiency with which a firm produces depends in part on its capacity utilization, which is in large part a matter of the economy's effectiveness, a governmental responsibility. And the economy's effectiveness, in the sense of the GNP that it is capable of producing, depends not only on the degree of utilization of its assets, but also on the efficiency with which they are used, which is a corporate managerial responsibility. The managers of the corporations and of the economy interact to increase one another's productivity, the better to realize both the public and private objectives for which each is, respectively, responsible.

The jointness of this interest, recognized only after World War II, is gradually casting the large corporations in a new position vis-à-vis government. Where until recently the corporation's public-service role was encompassed within its private autonomous activity (the two identified as one), now its legitimacy as a social institution depends on a greater sensitivity to the public impact of its specific activities. But the corporation whose actions are once again legitimized because they *directly* serve the national interest has not reverted to the same dependent status as the corporation of the early eighteenth century. Having grown giant in the intervening years, fattening on the political philosophy that viewed its autonomy as being in the public interest, it emerges now, not as a dependent, but as a collaborator. If the result is not quite so system-sophisticated in the economy at large as in the corporation itself, even in its more ragged shape it performs the same function. If some businessmen do not choose to call the result economic planning (which implies a loss of that autonomy to which the corporation still nostalgically clings), perhaps a substitute can be found in the French term *économie concertée*. As Pierre Massé once pointed out when he was commissioner of the French indicative planning program, a firm can reasonably take exception to any discipline imposed on it, any constraint over its actions, *provided* it is willing to give up some portion of its economic well-being that depends on an overall pattern of discipline. What is not rational, he pursued, is to expect both the freedom of individual action and the benefits that come from some degree of conformance to a larger pattern.

In this evolving relationship, the government does indeed view—as Galbraith contends—the corporation as an administrative arm in achieving national economic objectives. It is equally true that the major business corporations view the government as an instrument that can be used effectively, for the corporation's own purposes, in exploiting the opportunities inherent in the economy. The more positively they use governmental authority, through a national plan or otherwise, the more capable they are of achieving their own objectives.

Certain businessmen in the United States have recognized this possibility. Henry Ford II has remarked that business should cease thinking of rising social demands as imposing new costs on business. "Instead, we should start thinking about changes in public values as opportunities to profit by serving new demands. We have to ask ourselves, what do people want that they didn't want before, and how can we get a competitive edge by offering them more of what they really want?. . . What this approach implies for government policy, is that the most effective way to encourage business to serve new public needs is to rely, when possible, on market incentives. When the marketplace does not automatically translate a public need into a market demand, then government action may be required to change market conditions." [10]

Eli Goldston, president of Eastern Gas and Fuel Associates, has urged the same approach: "Strong forces are pushing business to face the major problems of our society, and ways exist to encourage and control business participation. Today's highly professional manager, eyes focused on profit performance, operating with excellent controls and within strict rules in the glare of a public scoreboard, needing growth opportunities, and not limited by conventional business boundaries, may be the most promising recruit for solution of the crises in our public service." [11]

The French system has been more explicitly organized to achieve this result. As one observer describes it:

The *économie concertée* defines a partnership between the managers of big business and the managers of the state. It provides big business with the active participation and support of the state while keeping broad participation politics away. From the perspective of big business, the *économie concertée* is the most satisfactory reconciliation of its potentially conflicting wants: big business needs the active participation of the state in the management of the economy, but it fears opening economic administration to popular participation.[12]

In Pierre Massé's trade-off, such a collaborative arrangement obliges the corporation to surrender some of its autonomy as part of the political bargain. What purpose would a plan have if it did not exert some compulsion over those subject to (or composing) it? On the other hand, the large enterprise has its influence on the plan, which it employs to its own advantage. Why else should it participate in the arrangement? As Earl Cheit has summarized the situation: "In broadest terms, the Plan's objective is to bring economic power under political control, a point clearly understood by American executives operating in France. 'At home we think about autonomy,' one told me. 'Over here we look for influence.'" [13]

Corporate Influence in a Pluralist Society

Decades ago John P. Davis saw this new pattern emerging. "The present tendency is for them [corporations] to become less organizations for the self-government of industries than organizations for the imposition of the conditions under which industries shall be prosecuted—essentially governmental bodies. . . . The corporate or semi-corporate organizations of society are so numerous and so pervasive of all kinds of social activity that the individual citizen, trying to attain the ideal of personal independence venerated in the theory of the political institutions of his country, finds every avenue under the control of some kind of an association in which he must acquire membership or to whose regulations he must submit. . . . He discovers, in fine, that citizenship in his country has been largely metamorphosed into membership in corporations and patriotism into fidelity to them." [14]

Davis was obviously referring here not simply to business corporations, but to all associational forms. But without detracting from the point he was making, we can avoid the error that other pluralists have so often subscribed to—that because numerous associations exercise authority over individuals and over the state, none is dominant. Among organizations as among individuals, all are not equal. Among American organizations, clearly the large business corporation has emerged as the dominant type. In a pluralist society, its influence counts for more than one. Like Galahad, but not necessarily for the same reason, its strength is as the strength of ten.

In the words of one business leader: "This is a business and industry society. We are the 'power group,' the 'lead group,' the group which has a chance to set the example." [15]

The validity of that proposition has been demonstrated in France's system of indicative planning. Theoretically, the labor unions are involved in the planning process, but practically they have had little influence except as an external political pressure that must be taken into account. Theoretically, too, the French legislature approves the social objectives and the plan as a whole, but practically the unwieldy Assembly can do little more than provide the broadest sort of directives for the guidance of the experts. Its influence is roughly equivalent to that of the board of directors in a large corporation, in that it is neither significant nor insignificant. The technical and economic considerations that business and government experts build into the plan, which becomes a kind of script for those firms that recognize that a role in the drama is rewarding, are simply tempered by political and organizational considerations as necessary to secure the assent of the stagehands.

It would be absurd to assume that business, even though dominant, can control governmental authorities and contain opposition pressure groups. In the nature of the modern democratic state, with universal franchise, concessions must often be made. Professional politicians, while sensitive to corporate interests, must accommodate numerous groups of voters if they are to win office. They serve, in effect, as power brokers, weighing the political costs of concession and nonconcession to this group and that. In playing that role they must sometimes take positions to palliate populist causes even against the interests of those who are their chief support.[16] Informal bargaining often goes on between business and government officials, sometimes with threats and counterthreats, sometimes with misleading information or efforts at confusion. We have noted this process in previous chapters, particularly in connection with consumerism and environmentalism.

Even if concessions are made to other interest groups, these concessions often prove more symbolic than real, more palliating than altering, more temporary than lasting, interpreted in ways that rob them of their initial apparent promise. Even if such concessions exact from business a new system of accommodations (as in the case of its relations with organized labor after 1935), the new arrangements usually end up leaving the essential business authority largely intact, requiring it to take into account other views and reactions, but constituting more of a nuisance than a serious constraint.

Politicizing the Market

In this continuing rebargaining of the social contract among a society's major population segments and interest groups, with the professional politicians serving as mediators and brokers of the power balance, the major serious threat to the large corporations appears to me to stem from the deteriorating position of America's cities. As we observed in the preceding chapter, the cities seem on their way to becoming concentration points of those whom society has failed to integrate—the minority blacks and Latins who have been discriminated against, the poor, the aged, the misfits and deviants. Some of these constitute little threat to the system: the elderly, for example, can be accommodated on social security as long as the city can be made livable for them.

But how do you tie a population of working age, particularly the young, into the national income stream, if jobs can no longer be depended on to do that? If the trend is for the major mobile corporations to move from the central cities, which present too high a risk for the investment or reinvestment of corporate assets; if corporations anchored to the city find it unrewarding to do more than give modest supplementary training to the increasing numbers who are unmotivated to gain much from the city's school systems, fitting them for relatively unrewarding and undemanding jobs; if, at the same time, the rising affluence of the dominantly white population outside the central suburbs cannot be flaunted without taunting those inside the central compounds, then some form of urban public employment and public assistance program must take the place of mainstream jobs. The city would become even more than today the locus of vast bureaucracies to which its residents would attach themselves (if only to the welfare bureaucracy as clients), making little productive contribution to the life of the nation, but rendering relatively ineffectual services to one another, jointly composing an increasingly dependent local population that would be financed out of the federal treasury. Under the ominous, but perhaps prophetic, title "Living with a Higher Jobless Rate," *Business Week* cited the case of a thirty-nine-year-old unskilled, unemployed black janitor, a vocational school dropout. After a succession of jobs—given and lost for a variety of reasons—he quit as janitor in a newspaper office after an argument over tardiness. "Since then, Calhoun has supplemented his $45-a-week unemployment check with pay from part-time cooking. The union offered him a $3.20-an-hour job cleaning a theater, but he did not want to work weekends. And he calculates that taxes and other deductions would reduce his pay to not much more than his unemployment insurance. Calhoun says his present income covers food and rent for his furnished room, all he needs since his wife and children left five months ago."

Admitting that one cannot extrapolate from a single case, the editors comment that "many economists insist that a society that reduces unskilled job opportunities, pays low wages for the unpleasant unskilled jobs that remain, and provides welfare benefits for workers who reject those jobs will automatically produce large numbers of labor market dropouts." [17]

In effect, the presence of these urban pockets of millions of people who are no longer *effectively* tied into an economic allocation of the GNP has converted that allocation into a political issue. The question is now being raised in terms of minimum living allowances—how much an individual or a family may be entitled to, on his or their own terms, simply by reason of existence, not for any contribution to society and in the absence of any responsibility to society. Some vague notion along this line appears to be becoming more and more acceptable to corporate philosophy, just as broader national planning is becoming more acceptable. This may be one of the concessions that business will be called upon to make as the price of its survival under changed objective circumstances. Whether such a concession would contain the underlying explosive social situation is another matter.

One concludes that national objectives are likely to be more or less in line with corporate objectives, except as professional politicians, performing their brokerage role, find it necessary to make concessions to other groups to keep the system functioning. Such concessions are not likely to undermine corporate influence, however; too many individuals and institutions are tied to corporate values and corporate interests for that to occur. Corporations dominate American society, not because people are impotent or supine, but because so many have prospered under the corporate system, in ways they have been educated to accept as desirable.

If corporations undertake to discharge a larger national responsibility, they will have to do so through more active participation in, perhaps control over, a planning program, of a social engineering nature. This last prospect would, however, involve a considerable shift in managerial thinking, perhaps a new breed of younger managers. And it would leave them still confronting the seemingly intractable problem of how to incorporate within such a system the populations of the major central cities, whose separation from the mainstream of American life is creating around them new and invisible walls, ironically contrasting with Norton Long's conception of the unwalled city.

[8]

THE CORPORATION

AND INTERNATIONAL

RELATIONS

THE corporation that outreached local markets to expand on a national scale did not cease its expansion there. The dominance of Western powers throughout the world guaranteed the extension of their institutions into other countries. Among these were the doctrines of freedom of contract, the rights of private property, the corporate form of economic organization, and a system of international exchanges based on liberal economic philosophy. One consequence was that (in the words of former Undersecretary of State George Ball) "over the years, the corporate form of business has become common everywhere and enabled business to roam the world with substantial freedom from political interference." [1]

This remarkable social phenomenon, almost Darwinian in its evolution, could not help but carry remarkable consequences. The presence of strong foreign enterprises—almost economic principalities in some instances—in politically independent nations is only the most recent chapter in the long history of international commercial relations, a history whose overriding theme is less amity among peoples than exploitation, less mutual benefit than bargains (imposed or otherwise) that carry disproportionate advantages to those with the greater bargaining power. In recent years, however, the idea has surfaced that the worldwide corporation contains the potential for exorcising the evil spirit of nationalism, replacing it for the first time with genuine internationalism. The exploitative corporation of the past, concerned with its own special interests, may have been only the forerunner—it is said—of a more politically sophisticated (as well as economically developed) institution serving all peoples everywhere with neutral beneficence. We can best explore this exuberant possibility through the background of historical and contemporary events.

The Growth of Multinational Operations

As long as a century ago United States enterprises had already undertaken a substantial amount of direct foreign investment, in both raw materials and manufacturing industries. In manufacturing alone, by 1900 there were some 75 to 100 American overseas subsidiaries.[2]

There was a more or less common pattern. A company pioneered in developing a product. Expanding beyond the national market, it would undertake to build markets abroad. For a time its head start would protect it, but then local imitators would appear. Taking advantage of lower labor and transportation costs, the local companies would make inroads into the American company's sales. The obvious counter would be to set up manufacturing facilities in the overseas market, benefiting from the same cheap labor, eliminating the transportation expense, and continuing to capitalize on an already established reputation. Raymond Vernon, examining the reasons why a number of manufacturers located plants abroad in the period prior to 1900, finds such a pattern present in seven out of ten major cases, including Colt, Singer, General Electric, Westinghouse, Eastman Kodak.

General Motors provides an excellent example of this phenomenon a few years later. Prior to 1920, foreign producers of automobiles built a low volume at high unit costs. U.S. producers, already achieving economies through mass production, could ship fully assembled cars abroad and undersell the home-based competitor. In this period GM concentrated on building a marketing network. As the European market expanded and domestic producers could increase their output, tailored to the somewhat different needs of European drivers, GM found itself under increasing competitive pressure. Duties on parts were lower than duties on assembled cars: nine disassembled Chevrolets could be shipped to Europe at the same cost as two assembled. So between 1923 and 1928 GM opened nineteen assembly facilities in fifteen countries outside the United States, and 70 percent of its overseas sales were assembled abroad. In the late 1920s it took the next step by purchasing two European-based automobile manufacturing corporations, one in England, one in Germany. By 1935 these plants were accounting for one-half of GM's foreign sales. It was only after World War II, however, that a major expansion in the establishment of manufacturing operations took place worldwide; by 1965 these operations accounted for more than $1 billion of GM's assets and 1.2 million units of its sales.[3]

Two factors are important in this explanation for corporate expansion into international markets. One, peculiar to the United States, especially after the turn of the century, was the rise of industry that was oriented toward mass production and mass marketing—that standardization of products sold at low cost under a widely advertised brand name that was noted in Chapter 2. The other factor, important from the beginning but increasingly important after World War II, was the emphasis on products incorporating a high technological component. In a detailed survey of product lines of the foreign subsidiaries of 187 major U.S. corporations, Vernon concludes that the expansion of overseas manufacturing facilities "took place hand in hand with a rapid spread in the production of 'skill-oriented' products—products, that is, in which the emphasis on development and innovation in the United States was relatively strong." [4]

Prior to World War II, some high-technology companies sought to exploit their advantage without becoming involved in overseas investment, by cartelization or combination with foreign competitors. Perhaps the most famous of such arrangements was that which brought E. I. Du-Pont, Imperial Chemical Industries, I. G. Farben, and the Belgian Solvay Company into a cartel that divided the relevant world markets among themselves and effectively excluded competitors.[5] Thus they stood to recoup with greater assurance their mounting research outlays, while avoiding costly overlapping expenditures in developing competitive products. With the outlawing of such combinations, the surest alternative way of recovering the costs of technological development was through direct investment in operating subsidiaries overseas.

So important did this technological component of overseas investment become that Antonie T. Knoppers, president of Merck & Co., has identified it as the primary reason for the "invasion" of European markets by subsidiaries of U.S. corporations in the years since World War II. Emphasizing that it is not only the development of technological advances as such which is important, but also their industrial application through superior management techniques, he argues that until very recently the United States had the edge over other countries on both counts. Because of its larger technologically educated population, it was able to spawn more ideas. Because of the heavy investment in research by both government and industry, these people were given research opportunities and provided with the necessary laboratory facilities. Because of the managerial competitive drive, innovation was relied on for growth of markets.[6]

Because this technological-managerial combination involved the exploitation not just of a single product but of a whole stream of products, it paid a corporation to establish its own subsidiaries abroad. As Knoppers points out, the trend of big, research-oriented, U.S. companies to try to operate as multinational companies with wholly owned subsidiaries meant that technology was not as readily available to European firms as theretofore. There developed a tendency for the American firm to exploit its advances first in its own organization and to consider licensing or transfer of knowledge only at a later date.

In recent years, this U.S. lead in technological application and managerial capability has been gradually eroded. New products and processes increasingly emerge from Europe and Japan, and their large corporations have demonstrated an aggressive managerial capability that in many industries has put American corporations on the defensive, even in their home markets. This development simply underscores that the multinational corporation is not an American invention or an American property. Three out of every ten workers employed by Swedish-owned firms now work outside Sweden, for example, and Japanese and German firms now have the highest growth rates in the world for foreign direct investment.

Nevertheless, the United States still outdistances other nations in the scale of its overseas operations. Their total book value, which amounted to just under $12 billion in 1950, had grown to almost $45 billion by 1960, and in 1970 reached almost $70 billion. In that year the United Kingdom had the second highest level of direct foreign investment, but this was only one-fourth the U.S. total. "The number of foreign subsidiaries of leading U.S. firms has been going up without interruption for as long as the record runs: from about 1,000 in 1930 to 2,300 in 1950, and to more than 8,000 in 1970. . . . Neither wars nor revolutions nor depressions have quite arrested the expansive trend."[7] Moreover, the importance of foreign operations in the overall activities of the major American corporate giants has been rising steadily. "As a result, for an estimated 80 of the top 200 U.S. corporations, foreign operations now account for at least one-fourth of sales, earnings, assets, or employees."[8]

The foreign operations of these global firms divide into two quite different categories. In one class, the subsidiary produces a whole product intended primarily for sale within the country in which it is located or in some instances for export to other markets usually designated by the parent company. In the second category, the subsidiary either produces a component of a product, without necessarily producing the final product itself, or it assembles the final product without itself making all the components, some of which come from other subsidiaries or from the parent company. This second group includes the more complex and technologically advanced operations.

Subsidiaries in the first category generally operate with more discretion within a decentralized organizational framework. They are represented by firms in the food, drug, chemical, paper, and rubber industries. The second category involves more complex, and therefore more centralized, coordination. A GM spokesman describes the problem as it applies to its South African plant:

> The Opel components, which in disassembled form are shipped from General Motors plants in West Germany, may reach our Port Elizabeth plant in South Africa for assembly some three and a half weeks later. This is only one shipment from one source. If the South African assembly operation and its recently added manufacturing facilities are to function smoothly and efficiently, they must today receive a carefully controlled and coordinated flow of vehicle parts and components from West Germany, England, Canada, the United States and even Australia. These must reach General Motors South Africa in the right volume and at the right time to allow an orderly scheduling of assembly without accumulation of excessive inventories.[9]

At the same time these same GM plants that are supplying South Africa are also supplying other subsidiaries. The flow of components becomes intricate, and can be effectively handled only by centralized coordination, by *system* planning. Moving from such short-term operating decisions to longer-range strategic matters, the parent company—conceiving of its far-flung operations as a single system rather than a loose association of semiautonomous production units—restricts or controls the subsidiaries' discretion in investment decisions, financing, pricing, product-line determinations, research and development, dividend policies, and purchasing.[10]

Relations between Multinational Corporation and Home Government

Just as political repercussions were created when corporations graduated from local to national operations, so do they follow the movement from national to multinational status.

The acceleration of U.S. corporate activity overseas has not occurred because of any prompting or prodding from the federal government, but has come about through business's own initiative. As the Manufacturers Hanover Trust Company of New York expressed it concisely: "The explanation for the rapid expansion of U.S. industry abroad is simply that there are markets to be served and profits to be made." [11]

The global firm cannot, however, seek its own advantage without regard to its effect on the countries in which it operates. At the same time, it cannot possibly serve the interests of them all. "On the whole, the multinational company will try to decide what is good for the company and then fit its explanation of what it is doing to the expressed objectives of each government." [12] This business *realpolitik* applies to the firm's relations with the home government as well as to relations with other governments. After all, business is business, as the American aphorism has it, or in the more diplomatic language of *Le Monde:* "For the American businessman, there are not two categories of Africans— one having a favorable attitude to the United States and the other an unfavorable attitude; but rather, Africans with whom it is possible to do business and others with whom it is impossible." Nevertheless, when there is a conflict of objectives between the policies of the home government and those of other countries in which the company operates, the former typically rules. "In almost all instances where the squeeze is tight, it is the parent government that wins." Although their interests are not identical, both the parent corporation and the home country from which it operates are, in effect, partners in enterprise. It could hardly be otherwise considering the fact that the large corporations constitute the dominant influence in American society.

Understandably, a government is somewhat loath to stress the ties that bind to it a company operating in a number of other countries. Occasionally, however, an official speaks out. When serving as Secretary of the Treasury, John B. Connally made no secret of his belief that the U.S. government should give greater support to its overseas corporations. Thus he stressed that the United States should stand behind companies threatened with expropriation by nationalistic governments. "In such situations, Mr. Connally said, Washington should put itself in the position of saying to other governments, 'You don't negotiate just with American business enterprise. You negotiate with the United States Government.'" [13] He was quoted as saying that the United States sends its business executives "out like Don Quixote, to do battle—but we don't give them much of a lance to do battle with." [14] He suggested increased tax benefits, direct subsidies, and the modification of antitrust legislation in support of U.S. firms operating abroad.

Federal support of its international corporations would not constitute a novelty. "Gunboat diplomacy" on behalf of American companies operating abroad was once carried on so blatantly as to arouse opposition even at home. Sanctions are still threatened or invoked—sometimes openly, sometimes discreetly—against countries that treat American business interests too harshly, such as freezing accounts of their nationals in U.S. banks, cutting off promised foreign aid or technical assistance, or instituting embargoes.

Formal actions or implicit threats even of this limited sort are, however, much less common than in an earlier day. Business now relies more on a federal investment guarantee program covering almost sixty developing economies. The importance of such financial assurance is suggested by one tally of major international "incidents" occurring around the world between 1959 and 1969. Excluding "minor skirmishes, unsuccessful revolts and incidental riots," there were 129 such incidents: 22 riots, demonstrations, terrorist activities; 17 assassinations of country leaders; 42 "nondemocratic" changes in national leadership; 10 major economic agreements involving aid, trade, or treaties; 42 economic-political actions that carried potential threat to a foreign corporation; 22 military conflicts, massacres, or revolutions; and the creation of 44 new states.[15] In a world of such unrest, support by one's own government of overseas business operations, in one way or another, is vital. If one adds to these more traumatic episodes the continuing negotiations over tariffs, quotas, favored treatment, unfair competition from foreign firms ("dumping"), it is readily evident that the corporation that goes questing for profits on the international scene welcomes the attitude expressed by Secretary Connally that Washington must become more of a cooperative partner with business against foreign competition. "No American business enterprise can operate on a par with foreign governments around the world." [16]

If the national government undertakes to support its multinational corporations, it does not do so simply at their bidding, even though national interests have come to be closely identified with business interests. Moreover, national interests, even when broadly supportive of business interests, need not be in harmony with the interests of any particular corporation. Public policy, whether in the international or domestic field, is not always to the liking of corporate managements, not only because concessions must be made to other groups by the professional politicians acting as power brokers, but also because the government must necessarily take a "system" point of view that puts in a broader perspective the relationship even of powerful component groups to the whole economy.

From this point of view, the multinational corporation, like any constituent interest, becomes an agent of the home government. The restraints thereby imposed on its discretion may be relatively minor, but they cannot be disregarded. "For the enterprise not to be under control of the U.S. government would mean that the government had abdicated a series of important economic decisions to the boardrooms of these companies." [17] The chairman of Dow Chemical Company, a leading multinational firm, has put the matter succinctly: "By United States law an American corporation operating in another nation is obliged to conform to the dictates of the Federal Government, executive, legislative and judicial. It is thus, through no choice of its own, to some extent an instrument of American policy." [18]

Most obviously, operations of the multinational corporations have a significant impact on a country's balance of payments. Outflows of capital for direct investment are offset by repatriation of earnings. In the United States the latter now outweigh the former by a significant margin. Nevertheless, when the negative U.S. balance of payments became serious enough to prompt corrective action, among other measures the government restrained capital outflows. (The result was not to halt the growth of investment, however, but to induce a sharp expansion in borrowing abroad by U.S.-based companies.) More recently the Department of Commerce has been exploring means by which industry can be further assisted in exploiting government-owned patents, in order to build up its trade balance. While this would initially apply to export activities more than to direct overseas investment, the latter would surely benefit in time. Thus the multinational corporation becomes an instrument by means of which the government can operate on its payments relations with other countries.

But the multinational corporation can also be a more direct implement of foreign policy. When the United States had established an embargo on shipments to Communist China and Cuba, it could impose that policy on the foreign subsidiaries of its corporations no less than on their domestic operations. The consequence was sometimes a loss in foreign-exchange earnings for the country in which the subsidiary operated, and an embarrassing display of a limitation of control over its foreign policy by that country. Thus when the French subsidiary of an American firm sold—on its own initiative—some 500 trucks to Communist China, the American parent intervened to cancel the order, as it was compelled to do under American law, even though it thereby subjected its French subsidiary to legal action for aborting the contract. After Sperry-Rand acquired working control of a Belgian firm manufacturing farm equipment, the U.S. government refused to permit the Belgian firm to export rice-harvesting equipment valued at $1.2 million to Cuba. The Belgian minister for economic affairs was asked in Parliament why a company located in an economically depressed part of the country should be forced to lose the equivalent of forty days' work for 2,400 workers because of American foreign commercial policy.[19]

Such overt use of foreign subsidiaries to advance the policies of the home country is relatively rare. Aside from the direct economic impact on balance of payments, perhaps the most important influence lies in the fact that the top managers of the multinational corporation are almost all nationals of the home country. Even in the case of the operating subsidiaries, where an effort has often been made to incorporate resident nationals into the local executive structure, the majority of management positions, or if not the majority then the key management positions, generally fall to parent-company nationals.[20] Whatever may be the local restrictions or regulations under which the subsidiary has to operate, they can never be so all-encompassing as to control all exercise of corporate discretion. In instances when corporate policy may be influenced, however unconsciously, by ingrained attitudes that favor home over local interests, the influence is likely to manifest itself. In innumerable minor decisions, the expatriate manager operating abroad is likely to reflect his own nation's interest, almost as though he were a member of its foreign staff. Almost, but not quite. The interests of the parent corporation will take precedence. It is there that his career lies. The "global" orientation of his company permits him the luxury of contemplating that no "narrow" national interest should supersede the advancement of "international" interests as represented by his firm. But such conflicts are not likely to be important. However global the scale on which the firm operates, its basic security lies in its relationship to its home government.

Relations between Multinational Corporation and Host Countries

Perhaps the most serious political effect of the spread of the multinational corporations is that they have aroused a fear that they are the carriers of a new economic imperialism. Countries playing host to subsidiaries of foreign firms see the control over parts of their economy passing to outsiders. This attitude is especially marked in the case of the American multinationals, simply by virtue of their number. To the host country, it is not particularly consequential whether that outside control is the parent corporation or the corporation's home government; in either event, it threatens a subordination of domestic economic interests to foreign economic interests, in effect an invasion of sovereignty.

There is no conceivable way in which the philosophy, interests, and objectives of an international corporation can be identical with those of the governments of all countries in which its subsidiaries do business. Indeed, its subsidiaries may be operating in countries that are at odds with each other (India and Pakistan, for example), so that the objectives of the multinational corporation could not possibly coincide with those of all countries in which it has plants. As Rex Winsbury has commented, from a British point of view: "If it is arguable whether what is good for General Motors is good for America, it is even more arguable whether what is good for General Motors is simultaneously good for France, Germany, the United Kingdom *and* America." [21]

Organizationally, the objectives of the parent corporation must take precedence over the objectives of its subsidiaries. Top management poses certain goals for the corporation as a whole—both generalized objectives, such as a target rate of return on its investments and growth of its sales and its asset base, and specific objectives, relating to its present strategy for securing its future. If the achievement of those aims can best be furthered by actions that run counter to the interests of some subsidiary, the logic of system management comes down on the side of taking the measures indicated. The system takes precedence over the subsystem. But it is the subsidiary's welfare, not that of the corporation as a whole, that accords with the interests of the host country.

In maximizing the advantage of a network of operations, the multinational corporation must centralize key decisions, as we have already noted. The executive vice president of International Harvester comments: "When you have a joint venture in Turkey, with engines from Germany, chassis from the U.S., together with a local sourcing of components, you just have to be centralized. You'd probably have to call us pretty well centralized as far as design, product development, purchasing, and financing are concerned." [22] But when the subsidiary is regarded as simply one unit of a larger system, in which centralized decisions are made for the good of the parent corporation, and one part of the system may substitute for, or be preferred over, another part, the subsidiary—and the country in which it is located—become tools for an outsider's advantage. This need not be done flagrantly: all that may be involved is a succession of normal "neutral" business decisions, based on relative pecuniary advantage, no one monumentally important. And yet the dependency effect may render the situation politically distasteful and economically sensitive to the host countries. The flexibility of the multinational company in administering its corporate empire, by virtue of the number of bases from which it operates, enables it in effect to pit the advantages of one host country against another in a form of economic gamesmanship, favoring whichever country benefits it more.

By virtue of its flexibility, the corporation may be able to bargain for certain concessions from a country. Labor unions have charged that multinationals have wrung from developing countries a promise to "control" unionization, and in collective bargaining negotiations have threatened either government or union with transfer of production to other countries unless their offer was accepted.[23] In other instances companies have won tariff or tax advantages, exclusive position, or import quotas as the price of their undertaking or continuing business in a country.[24]

Its very neutrality as among countries—on any ground except pecuniary advantage—has enabled the multinational firm to treat its subsidiaries as mercenaries in an international contest, without respect to whether the actions it requires of them are directed against their own country. Thus the parent corporation is free to provide its subsidiary with substantial sums, even if government policy is to curb aggregate spending. It is sometimes free to repatriate not only profits, but also earnings credited to depreciation, even if the government is seeking to stem deflationary tendencies. Governments attempting national economic planning may find their efforts frustrated by the authority of multinational firms over subsidiaries within their borders. As George Ball has put it: "How can a national government make an economic plan with any confidence if a board of directors meeting 5,000 miles away can by altering its patterns of purchasing and production affect in a major way the country's economic life?"[25]

In transferring funds, multinationals can sometimes—by anticipating weaknesses in a currency—exacerbate monetary situations to the disadvantage of a host country. It was reported that some U.S. subsidiaries sold sterling in the 1964–1966 crisis as "a cheap hedge against the effects of devaluation on their UK assets and thus on their balance sheets," an action that could only worsen the crisis in Britain.[26] When the pound was devalued in 1967, USM Corporation (formerly United Shoe Machinery) not only hedged against devaluation through the forward exchange market, but "encouraged Continental subsidiaries in countries

164

with reasonably solid currencies to defer payments for goods sent them by the British subsidiary for as long as six or seven months. Massey-Ferguson did much the same thing, and it got an added benefit from devaluation because of its worldwide production flexibility. Because so many of its subsidiaries produce a large line of interchangeable parts, it could switch subsidiary purchasing immediately from France to the U.K., thus taking advantage of the fall in British export prices." [27]

The significance of such actions depends, of course, on the scale of foreign operations within any given country. In Canada, political and economic sensitivity is great, in view of the fact that nonresident (mostly American) ownership runs as high as 69 percent of holdings in petroleum and natural gas, 59 percent in mining and smelting, and 59 percent in manufacturing. The situation in Europe is much less aggravated. U.S. corporations are estimated to control 7 percent of the assets of British industry and to account for about 10 to 14 percent of all manufacturing sales. The percentage of sales for Western Europe and the United Kingdom together is approximately 6 percent or a little higher. Nevertheless, in the aggregate these are not insignificant proportions of domestic economic activity, and the fact that they tend to be concentrated in certain industries, particularly those with advanced technology, often makes them strategic.

But the disadvantages of the multinational presence are not all there is to the story. If that were the case, no country would make concessions to secure the location of a foreign corporation within its boundaries, and political actions by sovereign states to prevent their establishment would have been far more effective than they have been. The multinational corporation also brings with it a number of highly desirable advantages.

As part of its effort to achieve greater economic viability, developing countries seek to reduce their dependence on industrialized nations for manufactured products. The concessions that they sometimes have made to induce a major corporation to locate a subsidiary within their territory are expected to have their compensation in producing at home, with native labor, what would otherwise have to be imported. Employment rises [28] and foreign exchange is conserved.

Such "import substitution" sometimes graduates into export expansion. Vernon points out that American manufacturing subsidiaries in Latin America in 1966 accounted for less than 10 percent of value added in manufacturing industries, but for 41 percent of manufactured exports. This export effect is possible in large measure because other subsidiaries of the parent corporation constitute outlets through which new markets

165

can be found. It is also because the multinationals, as we have seen, commonly bring with them technology that is advanced for the country or region in which they are locating.

In addition to these direct effects, there are spillover or spread effects of foreign investment. The establishment of a new and advanced facility almost always provides opportunities for ancillary business activity geared to the plant's needs—as suppliers of materials or components or services, as dealers, and as construction and maintenance contractors for plant and supporting infrastructure. General Motors has estimated that on the average about 60 percent of the retail price of its products made overseas is paid locally to supplying companies, wholesale distributors, and retail dealers. In addition, other businesses are called into existence to service car owners.[29]

The foreign subsidiary can also serve as an agent for the host country, just as the parent corporation does for the home country. Thus in the race among members of the European Common Market to build up intramarket positions for themselves, some countries found it advantageous to welcome an American subsidiary before a sister nation acquired it. And in the development of economically retarded areas, such as France's Ardeche region and Italy's Calabria, the host country has sometimes found the multinational firm more responsive than its own companies—perhaps in an effort to build favor.[30]

As we have noted, the basic charge brought against the multinational is that it undermines the sovereignty of the host country within its own territory. But this is something of an exaggeration. Despite the considerable bargaining powers that the corporation can muster, the government under which a subsidiary operates does in fact possess recognized power to regulate and control the subsidiary in a variety of ways. In some instances the intent is to extract maximum advantage from the foreign firm. Thus governments (Canada and Australia, for example) have prescribed the extent to which the manufacture of automobiles must incorporate domestic-made parts. Ancillary home industry is thus built up. Other governments (Japan, Mexico, and India, for example) have specified the amount of local capital that must be mingled with imported capital, at least in specified industries, thus encouraging the development of local capital markets by giving investors financial opportunities at home that would otherwise be obtainable only abroad and in the process assuring greater domestic participation in operations than would otherwise be the case. In some instances (England, France) restriction on the choice of location has channeled foreign capital into regions more in need of an economic injection. At times, under pressure from domestic labor unions, host governments (as in some of the Latin American states) have insisted on guarantees with respect to employment and income security. They can, if the economic or political urgency seems great, impose "regulations countering the orders of the parent government on repatriation of earnings, inflow of funds, export sales and even competitive relationships. They can also raise the political cost of interference by claiming that it goes beyond some 'rule of reason,' and by demonstrating to other countries the dangers of permitting political intervention through multinational operations." [31]

The host country may also counter with "flexible" discriminations of its own. Although the subsidiary is technically a domestic corporation, it is sometimes deprived of equal treatment with other domestically owned corporations. Government purchases may discriminate against the foreign-owned subsidiary; the latter may find access to local capital markets more difficult; tax advantages and subsidies, which are presumably open to all firms under specified conditions, may be denied it. Such treatment may be relaxed or tightened depending on the firm's readiness to cooperate with the government.

Finally, governments may intervene to renegotiate terms—for example, license fees or royalty rates, on which foreign firms were initially admitted; they may simply revoke prior concessions. The oil-rich countries of North Africa have thus demonstrated an increasing sophistication in bargaining (an historically venerated Middle Eastern trait) with Western oil companies. Expropriation without compensation is less commonly resorted to now, but the Andean group of countries has adopted a pioneering measure that would require new foreign investors to provide for a scheduled divestiture of foreign ownership as a condition of entry.

These undisputed powers of sovereign governments to counter the economic advantage of the multinational corporations may indeed appear to be overwhelming. The difficulty lies in the difference between possessing a power and being able to use it. The very reasons why countries welcome foreign subsidiaries—the advantages they bring with them—impose a self-restraint in the exercise of constraints on those operations. The heavier the load of limitations imposed by the host country, the greater the danger that these limitations may drive the firm to some friendlier country. If a country wishes the benefits that flow from direct overseas investment, it cannot avoid a bargaining relation, implying concessions. The more that it is in need of foreign capital or improved technology, the weaker is its bargaining position. ". . . there is a limit to the amount of leaning that even the French government can do.

A company as large as IBM, for example, always has the counter-threat that it just might shut down in France altogether and go elsewhere." [32] The situation is akin to that of U.S. cities which compete against one another to induce a national company to locate a plant in their jurisdiction, or when they reluctantly agree to concessions (tax, zoning, improvement of roads or schools) in order to persuade a firm to remain with them rather than respond to the allurements of another locality. Joint ventures do provide a measure of local control over the subsidiary, but the subsidiary cannot control all the decisions of the parent corporation which affect it.

"What host governments badly want is not only a sense of control over foreign-owned subsidiaries but also access to the resources they think some of these subsidiaries can provide. As long as governments feel that they need those resources, they are likely to be vulnerable. And being vulnerable, they will continue experiencing the discomfiture that foreign-owned enterprises have so commonly produced." [33]

Going National as Compared with Going International

There are both similarities and differences between the impact of the national corporation in transcending the local community in which it originated, and the effect of the multinational corporation in transcending the country of its origin. First, the differences. As the American corporation extended its operations to exploit a national market, its economic jurisdiction was paralleled by the political jurisdiction of the federal government. Even though the social philosophy of the times may have rendered the federal government effectively neutral with respect to the corporation's activities, the government's regulatory authority nevertheless existed and occasionally was used to curb business excesses. Moreover, the interests of the expanding national corporation were seen as reinforcing the interests of the expanding national economy, and because local citizens were also members of the larger political unit, they could identify themselves with the growing nation—especially given freedom of mobility and relative openness of opportunity within the larger boundaries.

In the case of the multinational corporation, there is no governmental authority of equal scope capable of regulating it and curbing its discretion when abused. Nor is there any sense of identity between a national of one country and some hypothetical "world society," which would accord him some share in worldwide economic growth, nor freedom of mobility among countries, nor anything approximating equal access to opportunity.

A second contrast lies in the fact that the nineteenth-century national corporation did not need the support of the city of its origin as it moved into a larger and more fiercely competitive (national) environment, while the multinational corporation does draw strength from its home country. In this respect it is much more akin to the trading companies that ventured forth from medieval cities; these groups were protected locally against foreign competition and were given assistance in establishing their foreign commerce.

But the similarities between the effects of expanding into national and multinational markets are as striking as the contrasts. As the American corporation came to identify itself with the national market, there occurred a simultaneous disengagement from the town or city in which it had begun. In Chapter 6 we noted how the national corporation fostered its own welfare without respect to the impact on any particular community. This was in the nature of a profit-oriented, private-enterprise economy. Its multiple local plants became components of a larger national system and were used to further the interests of the parent, not the interests of the localities in which the plants were located. We have noted that such a philosophy also characterizes the multinational corporation. The plants located in the home country are no different from those located in foreign countries in this respect: they too are simply units of the larger system. If, as Tilford Gaines comments, the international companies approach "the world as a single economic unit rather than a fragmented collection of nations," then many of the criticisms directed against them by host countries of subsidiaries are equally applicable in the case of the home country. "The fact that the parent company had its origin and often its headquarters in the U.S. has become increasingly less relevant. . . . Today, the international company exists as an entity essentially independent of its national origin. . . ." [34]

There is obvious exaggeration in this position. For one thing, the home country is in a position to regulate the parent corporation. For another, there is—as we have noted—some psychological orientation on the part of corporation top management, still largely composed of nationals of the home country, toward the interests of the society of which they are citizens. But to the extent that systems logic takes hold—as the multinational managers themselves testify is occurring—and to the extent that the home country leaves them to their discretion, the management of a global firm will treat its home operations as opportunistically as those in any other country.

In effect, the multinational corporation enters into a bargaining relationship with its own country as well as with others. The very importance of the multinationals to the U.S. government, in terms of its world economic position, gives them greater leverage in helping to frame U.S. international commercial policy and makes the home government depend on them just as they depend on the government. Multinationality, by increasing management's options in its global operations, gives it a degree of independence of its home country. This fact also increases its bargaining power vis-à-vis other interest groups, as these relative powers are mediated by the professional politicians who compose the government.

So far, the labor unions have felt most injured by the multinationals' independence. "In seeking to maximise profits, the global corporations follow a policy of 'world-wide sourcing,' which means buying human labour and raw materials in the cheapest markets and selling the products" wherever they can at the highest prices.[35] "If a multinational does not like a U.S. federal minimum wage of $1.60 an hour, it simply closes its plant here and moves the manufacture to Mexico and pays wages of 16 cents an hour. If it does not like our National Labor Relations Act, even with its Taft-Hartley and Landrum-Griffin amendments, the multinational removes its facilities to some land where unions are either nonexistent or legally disapproved. If the multinational does not like America's Fair Employment Practices Law, it can set up shop in South Africa."[36] *Business Week* contributes its testimony: "The auto unionists have seen car production move between countries, most recently into underdeveloped areas, in search of lower labor costs. If U.S. auto unionists fear Europe and Japan in this regard, unionists in those areas fear shifts to Africa and South America."[37]

Some economists have disputed the unionists' contentions. The jobs "exported" to lower-wage countries would have been lost in any event, they say, because U.S. industry could not effectively compete against such low-cost production. Moreover, by establishing subsidiaries abroad, the multinational keeps open a market for the export of U.S. raw materials and components to those subsidiaries, thus actually preserving some jobs.[38] Other economists have argued more conventionally that what is at work is simply that tendency toward equalization of wages that typically goes with open competition: by producing in areas where labor is cheaper, the multinational in fact contributes to raising wages in those areas. In due time, the competitive advantage of cheap labor will be lost.

There are good grounds for skepticism as to the validity of these counter-arguments. Profit-maximizing corporations may move operations to lower-cost areas, not because they would otherwise have to close down the home operation, but simply to improve profits. This is indeed the action that one would expect from private enterprise, whether operating nationally or internationally. The result is a loss of employment in the home country, which runs against worker interests. Moreover, the expected leveling of wages that will remove the foreign advantage will take place, if at all, over so long a time as to be of no consolation to the present generation of displaced workers—especially in view of the continually increasing populations in the less developed areas. In poverty-stricken countries, there is no seeming end to the supply of workers willing to work for a fraction of the American wage.

There is one further source of concern to the labor unions. On the conventional economic argument of comparative advantage, it has commonly been argued that a country can expect to lose those exports—and jobs—in which its advantage is relatively lower than in other types of production. Thus the United States can expect to lose those more elementary industrial operations that can be performed by any country, even one at a low stage of industrial development, but it will build on its own strength in the high-technology areas. But what the multinational corporation has been doing has been to export its high technology, too. As we have seen, one chief basis for the establishment of U.S. subsidiaries in Europe has been its advanced technology. But the establishment of those subsidiaries also means the transfer abroad of operations in which the United States has a comparative advantage on the world markets, which presumably should supply the jobs for its own workers.[39]

The impact of multinational operations on American exports, and hence on the balance of payments, is also subject to question. The indeterminacy here has been indicated by a business source, the economics department of the Manufacturers Hanover Trust Company. The output of U.S. overseas operations far exceeds total U.S. exports—by $200 billion to $33 billion in 1968. This gross difference "raises the question as to whether U.S. industry has not seriously harmed our export markets by producing abroad. To some limited extent, foreign production by U.S. companies no doubt has been substituted for exports, but *it is doubtful* that such substitution has been significantly large. In almost all cases, U.S. companies operate abroad only because of realizable cost efficiencies that enable them to compete with foreign producers in the world market. *It should be assumed* that if U.S. industry operating abroad had not produced these goods, foreign producers would have filled the gap. Precise measurement is not possible, but *it seems likely* that additions to U.S. balance of payments from the income on U.S. investment abroad substantially offset whatever exports have been lost by U.S. companies producing abroad." [40]

The uncertainty in this statement is almost explicit. A good case could be made for the reverse position, especially in view of the assumption that most of what was produced abroad could not otherwise have been sold by the U.S. firm, and that its motive was not simply to increase profit but to save sales. It is no disparagement of the profit objective to recognize that production undertaken abroad may in fact substitute for production at home, simply returning a higher profit. But it does raise a legitimate question as to whether any individual multinational may not in fact pursue its own interests at the expense of its country's economic welfare, whatever may be the present net contribution of multinational corporations as a group. And whether, if this is indeed the case, any coincidence of interests between multinational operations and home country interests may be purely temporary and even accidental. And whether, given the opportunity, the multinational may not disengage itself from the interests of its home country—pursuing a "global" point of view that in reality only masks its own interests—just as in an earlier period it disengaged itself from the interests of its home community by "going national."

In earlier chapters we observed the efforts, however limited, to undertake certain regulation of business activity in the interests of consumers, in the avoidance of pollution, in environmental exploitation. It is conceivable that the options available to the multinational corporation may limit the effectiveness of such national regulations. By threatening to remove, or actually removing, its operations to countries less concerned with such regulation, it may inhibit domestic controls over its domestic production.

Private Corporation and Public Authority

There has in the recent past been some rather heady talk by top managers as to the prospective internationalism or nonnationalism of corporate activity that lends credibility to what otherwise might be viewed as insubstantial speculation. Frederic Donner of GM has entertained such a vision of the corporation that has disengaged itself from its nationalistic ties:

It is the emergence of the modern industrial corporation as an institution that is transcending national boundaries. These great concerns of the Free World, both here and abroad, are no longer adequately described as Dutch, German, French, Italian, British or United States corporations. We may be approaching a stage where we will not think of them primarily in terms of a single country nor will we think of their benefits as flowing especially to any one country. In interests and ambitions, in investments, in employees, in customers, they are an international resource. Their benefits should be regarded as flowing to workers and customers—and to owners as well—without regard to any individual nationality.[41]

Perhaps the strongest statement in this regard has come from the chairman of Dow Chemical Company:

We appear to be moving strongly in the direction of what will not be really multinational or international companies as we know them today, but what we might call 'anational' companies—companies without any nationality, belonging to all nationalities.

We generally conceive of the multinational company as one having a fixed nationality (that of the parent company) but operating in many nations.

With the blossoming of a true world economy, these multinational bees, whether they are American or British, German or French, Russian or Japanese, will be establishing more hives in the farther fields. We will see more foreign companies with large American holdings and vice versa. They will tend for many reasons, political and economic, to become nationless companies. . . .

I have long dreamed of buying an island owned by no nation, and of establishing the world headquarters of the Dow company on the truly neutral ground of such an island, beholden to no nation or society.[42]

This dream of a stateless corporation, operating on its own, beholden to no society but somehow equally beholden to all, underscores that along with disengagement from the home country goes noninvolvement with any country. Just as in the case of the national corporation, which ceased to be concerned as a permanent resident citizen with the welfare of any single community, but exploited its multiple opportunities "equitably," so the multinational corporation—whether ultimately "anational" or not—is not involved in the affairs of the countries in which its subsidiaries operate except as these countries offer opportunities for exploitation. Systems managers cannot become immersed in, or dedicated to, the advancement of any constituent, regardless of its contribution to the system. The subsidiary—and the country it represents—are downgraded to the status of means to a corporate end.

In one of his last published statements, the late Frank Tannenbaum, a

gentle and sensitive scholar, commented on the multinational corporation: "Its total commitment is extranational. It has no concern with
boundaries, national interest, local cultural pride, regional idiosyncra-
cies except only as they favor or hinder the performance of the function
for which the corporate body has come into existence." [43] In its context,
which was laudatory of the multinational corporation as an agency for
international peace, I can only interpret this as the despairing conclusion of one who throughout his lifetime had been dedicated to a humanist
tradition, and who had ultimately concluded that raw nationalism stood
in the way of international harmony, that world government was an illusory hope, and that only the driving force of trade and commerce—
expanded to a global scale—would preserve some semblance of peaceful
order. But the depth of his despair is marked by his writing off "local
cultural pride" as something that would have to give way to international trade, as though these were incompatible.

As Erik Erikson has written so persuasively, nationalism lends itself to
"pseudo-speciation"—the pathetic fallacy that a people or a country is
different from, and better than, other peoples and countries. This self-
conception as "master race" or "chosen people" has been the breeder of
conflict and war throughout history. But this is not the same as to say
that group affinities, traditions, customs, and culture are for that reason
to be discarded, as though of no value. Some forms of kinship—
nationalism is simply one of the most recent—have given rise to much
of the human cultural heritage that we prize, no less than to some of
mankind's greatest depravities. To sweep all political kinships aside for
the latter reason is to conclude that the worst in them will prevail, and
that the good in them must therefore be sacrificed. To replace national
cultures with some form of international corporation culture is a mark
of the dominance of the large corporation over our social values, along
with recognition that the nation is an inadequate political unit from
which to cope with world economic development.

Just as in the nation the city has had to find some way of tying itself
into the national economy in order to make itself viable, so today does
the nation have to find the means of relating itself to the world economy. The seeming irresistibility of industrialization and its by-products
of economic growth and consumption orientation mean that the nation
that cannot tie itself into the mainstream of international economics will
become a stagnant backwater. The idea has been repeated in numerous
ways. ". . . to eschew the fruits of technology today would be, sooner or
later, to die politically." [44] "French nationalism would mean economic
dependence or an unacceptable retardation of growth and standard of

living." [45] "Today, whole nations are threatened with obsolescence as industry expands without reference to national boundaries." [46]

But to recognize the need for international economic linkages does not carry the corollary that national cultures must subordinate themselves to the private international carriers of trade, the multinational corporations. Yet that is an argument frequently encountered: national loyalties are archaic; supranational authorities are either infeasible on a world scale or, on a regional scale, are simply the equivalent of larger nations, and hence still archaic. Only the multinational corporation rises above such parochial attachments to join people of all nations in a functional unity. Ironically, again it is the humanistic Frank Tannenbaum who has expressed this view most starkly:

An industrialized world is held together by the large number of corporate bodies, and by their widening role. The corporation groups the nationals into a new loyalty—a functional identity across all borders. The day may well come when the majority of people in all nations will have their functional loyalties to one or more supra-national corporate bodies. They may well become conscious of basic commitments, values and interests unrelated to the state or the nation.[47]

I am not myself so pessimistic as to the potential of creating a supranational political unit capable of representing people in all their manifold interests and strong enough to subordinate the multinationals to those larger interests, regulating them instead of being regulated by them. Even though the potential may be long in realization, and may come piecemeal, I concede it at least as much likelihood as that the world should be ruled by several hundred major corporations, in the "balanced best interests of all," as their autonomous executives perceive those interests, without interference by anarchic nations or inept and impotent supranational governments. Just as the cities of the United States can recover a purpose only if the federal government first asserts national objectives and then decentralizes authority to metropolitan areas in the achievement of those objectives, so does it appear that nations can recover their political authority vis-à-vis the multinational corporation only as an international government (or a regional government) coextensive with the jurisdiction of the corporation is able to assert its authority on behalf of larger political objectives, decentralizing that authority to constituent nations.

That the multinational corporation may be an integrating force in international relationships has been urged by businessmen and scholars alike. Roger Blough of U.S. Steel believes it can "provide the adhesive which can do more to bind nations together than any other development yet found by man in his pursuit of peace." [48] Arnold Toynbee has predicted: "The businessman of the future, I believe, will be one of the key figures in a world civil service. . . . Whatever their official labels may be, most of them in the next generation will be employed in building up and maintaining the new world order that seems to be our only alternative to genocide." [49] But to argue that the expanding corporation may aid in developing an international order does not require that the nation, as a significant political unit, will wither away.

There is no reason to assume that the post–World War II resurgence of nationalism was a passing phenomenon, nor that it necessarily stands in the way of a more authentic international federalism. As an organizational unit expands and centralizes certain decisions, it necessarily decentralizes other decisions to lesser units—whether by intention or by default. This is a characteristic of organizational growth, a reconstitution of functions so that what needs, or benefits from, coordination gets coordinated and what needs, or benefits from, local expression gets expressed locally. Even in the case of the multinational corporation itself, its centralization of key decisions in the parent company goes hand in hand with decentralization of other decisions to its subsidiaries. In the same way, whatever form international authority may assume, it is likely to rely on national units for the effectuation of certain objectives.

Roy A. Matthews, director of research of the Canadian Economic Policy Committee, has, I think, stated the essence of the matter: "The multinational corporation, reflecting the imperatives of an increasingly global industrial economy, can contribute significantly to the political and cultural dynamic that will bring about such a transformation to a new international system. But it cannot get too far out in front of the total process." [50] To assume that private world-straddling corporations can supplant nations, obviate the need for any political authority capable of imposing responsibilities on them, and themselves create a world order is to confuse their specific, partial, special-interest contribution to internationalism with the more comprehensive process.

Indeed, the need for political constraints over the economic self-interest of the multinationals may itself contribute to experimentation with more effective forms of collaboration among nations. Several possibilities have been suggested—consortia of government and corporation representatives from home and host countries; "cooperation between free world governments directed toward establishing ground rules to guide the future development and growth of the supranational organization"; [51] "the establishment by treaty of an international companies law, administered by a supranational body"; [52] "an international instrument outlining obligations of multinational companies toward governments and trade unions." [53]

Some have advocated the direct chartering of multinational corporations by a competent international authority, presumably the United Nations. The latter would then be in a position to establish the terms within which the former would operate. Although the present functioning of the United Nations suggests that this would simply provide a more central forum for debate of contentious national issues, rather than a means of effective international regulation, a movement in this direction may be necessary for an ultimate "solution." [54]

Social Responsibility and the Multinational Corporation

Once again we raise the question of where this leaves the present state of relations between the corporation (this time in its international operations) and society (this time many societies, both home and host). We can readily agree that the multinational should do its best to play the part of "good citizen"—but we remain puzzled as to what this means, effectively, when there is a conflict between the interests of two or more of the societies of which it is a citizen. All the admonitions for it to become more sensitive to the cultural, economic, political, and social characteristics of its many spheres of operation cannot define for it the actions that are appropriate under such circumstances. Nor can sensitivity relieve it of the competitive pressures to make centralized decisions that are bound to be damaging to the welfare of certain of its decentralized theaters of operation. Nor does playing the good citizen resolve for it the gnawing problem of whether it should prefer the interests of its home government above those of any host, when this lies within its discretion.

In this area of activity, the possibility of a corporation's acting "responsibly" by any set of standards appears to be weakest. There are, of course, limited responsibilities that all agree it should assume— appropriate regard for its impact on employees and community wherever it operates, according to local interpretation; avoiding expatriate arrogance and "branch-plant" attitudes; upgrading of nationals and greater reliance on them in policy-making positions; respect for, and cooperation with, host country policies even if this involves some (acceptable) loss of profit. Moreover, as we have noted, some of its decisions

177

may be more socially responsible than those of domestic industry (in the matter of plant location, reinvestment of profits, training and promotion of lower-status employees, for example). But with the best will in the world, there *must* recur situations where the logic of global operations requires its being unresponsive to some society's interests.

For all the benefits that the multinational corporation brings, for all its contribution to international development, it remains an organization striving first for its own advantage, bound by the logic of its situation to sacrifice both the specific, identifiable welfare of particular societies and the far more amorphous "international welfare" when these conflict with it. Operating opportunistically (the essence of private entrepreneurship), the multinational corporation is presently unconstrained by any coequal public authority.

[9]

THE GOVERNMENT OF
THE CORPORATION

JUST as a labor union has been considered to be simply the aggregate of its members, no more and no less, so the corporation has been held in law to *be* the stockholders. This theory has not gone unchallenged, but it has enjoyed such important judicial support that a strong probability exists that cases will still be decided by courts of law on the presumption that corporations such as U.S. Steel or General Motors are merely associations of several hundred thousand people whose common interest is in profiting from their investment in the common operation.

The collection of individuals who combine to do business receive their corporate character from the state that grants it a charter. In the absence of any provision to the contrary, either in law or in the charter, the legal powers of the corporation reside in the body of stockholders. Almost invariably, however, either law or charter provides for the direction of the company by a stockholder-elected board of directors charged with acting on behalf of the body of corporators. The powers of this board are defined not only in law and in the charter, but also in the bylaws adopted by the stockholders, who commonly grant additional discretionary power to the directors, sometimes even to the extent of empowering the latter to amend the bylaws themselves.

So sweeping is the legal authority of the board of directors that it has sometimes been said that though the stockholders possess the power to elect the directors, they are virtually powerless to take further action with respect to the conduct of the business that they own. In the words of one justice: "The corporation is the owner of the property, but the directors in the performance of their duty possess it, and act in every way as if they owned it." [1] There is nevertheless an all-important constraint on the directors' authority. All decisions and actions taken by it must be in the interests of the stockholders.

The Concept of Corporate Democracy

The rights of stockholders in opposing directors who fail to fulfill this obligation of trust can be enforced by appeal to the courts, and directors failing in their obligation are subject to penalty imposed by the courts. But if this were the only remedy available to stockholders, the government of their corporation would take on all the characteristics of paternalism or a guardianship: they would stand as wards under the protective scrutiny of the law. But the stockholders are not quite so powerless. As the electorate of this incorporated body, they hold the power of naming and replacing those who shall serve as their directors. The stockholders' vote thus determines the composition of the board, to which they then alienate operating authority over their property as long as that authority is used on their behalf.

If this sounds like a minimal stockholder role, it does not differ radically from a citizen's rights in a constitutional democracy. The voters (stockholders) elect the legislature (board of directors), but the legislature, once elected, exercises sweeping powers of discretion within the constitutional framework (charter and bylaws). The voters may replace one legislator with another, if they believe he does not serve their interests well, but, once elected, he and his fellow legislators are beyond any intervention from the citizenry until the next election. Hence the nineteenth-century analogy between the government of the corporation and the government of the state, hence the conception of "stockholder democracy."

Abram Chayes has nicely summarized this legal construction of "the corporation as the Republic in miniature":

> The analogy between state and corporation has been congenial to American lawmakers, legislative and judicial. The shareholders were the electorate, the directors the legislature, enacting general policies and committing them to the officers for execution. A judiciary was unnecessary, since the state had kindly permitted the use of its own. Shareholders and directors each had functions which could not be exercised by the other. The directors managed. Shareholders could not directly affect most business decisions. The prescribed mode of review of directorial decisions was by the ballot. Only when proposed changes reached constitutional dimensions—charter amendment, merger, dissolution—was the shareholder given a direct voice in the decision. Only where a direc-

tor's conduct was ground for impeachment could the body of shareholders recall its representatives before the appointed term.[2]

The selection of chief executive became one of the principal functions of the board. The review and evaluation of his performance was its continuing responsibility. On major questions of operating policy, he would wait upon its approval. The chief executive was thus a creature of the board and was responsible to it, and the board had to accept responsibility for the actions of the chief executive, who held his position only as long as the board supported him. The analogy here was closer to the British parliamentary system than to the American Republic.

The Reality of Management Control

This was the theory of corporate government, and as Chayes has commented, it applied "with tolerable accuracy" as long as the body of stockholders, while substantial, was "reckonable," each with a sizable stake and a general knowledge of the more or less localized activities of the corporation[3]—that is, in the period before the corporation expanded beyond its local boundaries and extended its activities to the nation at large, increasing its scope and scale. The number of shareholders likewise increased, but their stake was often only a few shares, and their dispersion throughout the nation made any direct contact with their elected directors infeasible for most. Thus began that reversal of the flow of authority that was the subject of the Berle and Means treatise of 1932, which publicly documented what previously had only been speculative or special knowledge.[4]

The shareholder—now one of thousands if not hundreds of thousands —was no longer capable of having even the most general knowledge of the activities of his corporation and ceased to care as long as the financial results were satisfying. He maintained contact with "his" corporation only by signing the proxy form submitted to him by management, thus ceding any independence of vote, or by *not* signing the proxy form, an indication of protest or indifference, but not an instrument of alternative action. The principal importance of the proxy is to ratify a slate of directors—no longer nominated by the stockholders as their representatives to supervise the conduct of the corporation, but nominated by the incumbent directors themselves on the recommendation of the chief executive.[5]

The consequence is as one business executive put it succinctly: "Management, as long as it's successful and things are going well, is more than likely to have reversed the flow of authority from the boards to management so that it runs from management to boards. Because in a very practical sense the management has to pick new members of the board and present them for consideration to the board first and then to the stockholders." [6]

Berle and Means put this shift in the functioning of corporate government in historical perspective:

The corporate system has done to capital what the factory system did to labor. As the factory system separated control from labor, so the corporate system has separated control from ownership. The one brought the labor of a multitude of owners under a single control, the other is bringing the wealth of countless owners under the same unified control. [7]

Berle and Means had said that "Control rests with a group which can dictate the choice of all or a majority of the board of directors and which therefore exercises ultimate [legal] authority over the enterprise." [8] Using that same definition, a later investigator, Robert J. Larner, undertook to examine whether management control within the 200 largest nonfinancial corporations had increased or diminished since 1929, the year to which the Berle and Means data applied. His conclusion was that as of 1963 management control had increased significantly. In 1929, 44 percent of the 200 corporations involved and 58 percent of their aggregate assets were management controlled. By 1963, almost 85 percent of the "200 largest" and 85 percent of total assets were subject to management control. [9]

To speak of management control is not to imply that the chief executive can do whatever he wishes with the corporation that he captains. What it does mean is that as long as things are going reasonably well he is substantially able to pick those men whom he wishes to sit on the board. His candidates are either already officers of the company (and therefore subordinate to him) or outsiders who are unable to spend the time necessary to review the activities of a giant enterprise, who do not have independent access to data even if they wished to spend the time, and who for the most part raise only broad (and usually friendly) questions to which they receive broad (and reassuring) answers. [10] These constitute a committee of individuals convened for a few hours at a time at infrequent intervals, rather than a cohesive body. Thus the chief executive of the typical large corporation today exercises a largely uninhibited initiative in the conduct of "his" corporation as long as he does not abuse his office. Normally he handpicks his successor, who generally is approved by the board he has chosen. It is primarily when a chief executive dies suddenly without having indicated his heir, or in times of corporate crisis, that the board comes to life and functions as a decision-making body.[11] Failure to do so at such times would subject its members to potential lawsuits from stockholders charging that the board had failed in its legal obligations to protect the interests of the shareholders.

This shift in the locus of actual control within the corporation means that stockholders are left without any effective way of evaluating the performance of the directors who nominally represent them, but in whose selection they have virtually nothing to say; nor can they objectively evaluate the performance of the management, who presides with substantial autonomy over the enterprise.

The Effect of Institutional Investors

In recent years substantial blocs of shares in particular corporations have been acquired by institutional investors—in particular investment trusts, pension funds, and mutual funds. Institutions as a class now own about one-fourth of the shares of all companies listed on the New York Stock Exchange. It has been suggested that this reconcentration of shares in the hands of relatively few holders may create a potential basis for influence over management authority. This potential has not yet been effectively realized, however. "The standard line of the institutional manager is: 'We vote with the management. If we don't like the management, we sell the stock.'"[12] This may not, however, tell the whole story. For one thing, some funds may hold enough shares of a stock that they can sell only at the risk of depressing the price. For another, institutional managers, simply by making inquiries about the performance of companies in the course of arriving at investment decisions, may exercise a cautionary influence whether or not they intend to. Thus the president of Bethlehem Steel testified before a Senate committee:

Well, most of these investment trusts, as you know, have a very expert staff studying the performance of the companies that they own stocks of and have in their portfolios, and they are perhaps as well posted on the affairs of the company as even an officer of the company.

They are almost, you might say, in continuous contact with our people, and they want to know details that the average stockholder perhaps is not particularly interested in. But we do get many requests from them for—well, they even come to the plants and they go through the plants. They like to inspect them to see what we are doing in connection with the facilities. They want to be sure that our maintenance is all right; and they are very careful, some of them, in their analysis of how we are doing.

So that we feel that those people carry a great deal of weight in our deliberations. . . .[13]

But even if one takes Homer's words at face value, and assumes that this is characteristic fund management, the picture of corporate control is not much altered, because the fund managers themselves are, like the companies they investigate, operating with substantial autonomy from the investors whose funds they manage. Thus at best one set of more or less independent managers looks over the shoulders of another set of independent managers, without legal authority to intervene and without legal responsibility to other stockholders. The radical shift in the placement of corporate control is not much lessened by the presence of institutional investors. They do constitute new concentration points of financial influence, but they are fully compatible and congenial with the concentrations of business authority with which they amicably deal.

The nonfinancial and nonprofit institutional holders of securities—foundations, universities, churches—are in a different category. We shall examine their role later. Suffice it to say at this point that they do not purport to evaluate the overall quality of corporate management, but judge its actions only with respect to certain social issues of concern to them. Their influence as a public critic is not to be disregarded, but it is something entirely different from that overall, objective review of managerial performance on behalf of stockholders that directors were originally intended, in law, to provide.

Criticisms of the Corporation

It is scarcely surprising that under these circumstances a number of proposals should have been forthcoming for reform of the corporate structure. The Berle and Means study and the Great Depression struck at almost the same time, the latter "demonstrating" (in those pre-Keynesian days) the "failure" of business, the former seeming to pinpoint responsibility for that failure. Government experimentation with a reformed industrial organization (in such legislation as the National Industrial Recovery Act, the Securities and Exchange Act, the National Labor Relations Act) was accompanied by plans and proposals for new forms of corporate organization, plans emanating from a number of quarters, from business itself no less than from critics of business.

The Government of the Corporation

The agitation of this period was ended by World War II, and the efficient wartime performance of business in the mobilization of industrial resources served to lull the earlier criticisms. The 1950s were characterized by self-confidence and satisfaction in corporate quarters. But with the civil rights movement of the 1960s, accompanied on the one hand by a youthful tendency towards antimaterialism and nonconformity and on the other by the public-defender following of Ralph Nader, who himself quickly assumed folk hero proportions, and all this shortly followed by the environmentalist movement in which business was cast as the arch-villain, there occurred a resurgence of demands for reform of corporate organization. The underlying issue was the extent to which the placement of private authority carried with it an enforceable social responsibility. The old criticisms and proposals of the 1930s blended with the fresh criticisms and recommendations of the 1960s and 1970s, making it pointless to distinguish the arguments of the two periods.

There were three grounds for dissatisfaction with the corporate role.
1. Some critics questioned the extent and legitimacy of management authority: what entitled the chief executive to his power, and what curbs were there on his power? As a vice president of one great corporation remarked in a private executive seminar: "I think what they [the critics] are reaching for really is a curb on the possibility of excessive power being granted to individual corporate executives, and I think they are distrustful that the present board setup gives them the checks and balances they want, especially when the management can itself perpetuate the board, and the board perpetuates itself and then perpetuates the management. They know in reality that the stockholders don't elect it. Nor in the main, in the typical case today, do the stockholders want to." [14]

2. A second criticism is that even if corporate government functioned as intended by law, with stockholders electing directors who directed, its performance would be judged only in terms of the benefit it brought to its stockholders. Such a narrow responsibility no longer suffices. This view had been voiced by numbers of business executives themselves in the soul-searching days of the Great Depression, and it is replayed today. Thus the president of Johns-Manville Corporation had written:

In this evolution of a complex industrial society the social responsibility of management has broadened correspondingly. . . . Today the executive head of every business is accountable not only to his stockholders, but to the members of his working organization, to his customers, and to the public. . . . The full implications which flow from this new concept of trusteeship have not been completely grasped by industry, and certainly not by workers and public. The traditional private status of industry has been supplanted, under changing social concepts and regulations, by a quasi-public status.[15]

This multiple-responsibility concept has found public acceptance in many executive suites. General Electric has repeatedly affirmed its objective of seeking "the balanced best interests of all." The difficulty is that just what constitutes such balance of interests is left to management's discretion to determine. Since the law remains as before, asserting that management responsibility runs only to the stockholders, "responsibility" to other groups or to society at large must be masked in the thesis that it is in the long-run interests of stockholders to be socially responsible. To say that the large corporation is quasi-public may describe a condition, but it does not prescribe conduct. To create other enforceable responsibilities against the corporation might endanger the very foundation of private property; if management decisions are to be judged by their impact on the public, how *much* weight must be given to public interests as against private property (that is, shareholder) interests?

3. It has been argued that the problems that have arisen in relations with customers and employees, the adverse effects inflicted on community and environment, could sometimes have been avoided if managements had been more aware of the consequences of their actions. Excessive concern with the efficiency aspects of business, in production and marketing, have made managers insensitive to undesirable accompanying effects that forethought might have mitigated or avoided. Like the impatient youngster who tramples the flower beds in his haste to get where he is going, managements have been so concerned with comparative advantage that they have neglected a civilized consideration of the welfare of others. What is needed is a new breed of managers with a wider and wiser view of their society, managers who are more sensitive to their social and physical surroundings, more conscious of how they relate to them.

In this view, corporate acts complained of may not have been taken callously, but simply unconcernedly. Managements should build into their organizations devices that ensure that explicit consideration is given to the social consequences of their undertakings.

Proposals for Reform: Voting

If these are the principal grounds for criticism of the large corporations —the legitimacy and extent of management's power, the singleness of its legal responsibility, and the narrowness of its operating concern—there have been numerous proposals for dealing with these. Some are directed to a single issue, others to all three.

Let us consider first the recommendations for dealing with the "usurpation" of authority by management. All these are intended to give the stockholders a more effective voice in the policies adopted by their company. Some concentrate on the small stockholders, often in the belief that their individual financial stake is sufficiently limited to make them more disposed to take a public-interest view of their company's actions.

Cumulative voting has been recommended, and occasionally adopted, as a means of giving representation on the board to minority stockholder interests. Under cumulative voting in a corporation with a board of fifteen directors, a shareholder would be entitled to fifteen votes, which he might distribute among the candidates as he saw fit, concentrating all fifteen votes on a single candidate if he so chose. Minority groups might thus combine their holdings to elect a representative of their interests. Management could be prevented from naming a board wholly favorable to its positions and thus would have to contend with one or more directors genuinely representative of at least certain stockholders. This arrangement is the corporation's closest parallel to proportional representation in civil governments.

Understandably, managements have been opposed to cumulative voting. Aside from their own self-interest however, there are at least two reasonable objections to this practice. One is that it might simply introduce on the board a factiousness that would prevent a unified course of action, subjecting every major decision to contentious argument rather than the reflective consideration that presumably is the objective. The other is that minority stockholder groups are likely to seek only their own advantage without giving any fuller expression to broader social concerns.

A more novel proposal, though one with historical precedent, is that the vote go with the shareholder rather than the share: thus, one shareholder, one vote, no matter how many shares he may hold. Such an arrangement would prevent a majority stockholder from receiving preferential treatment for himself at the expense of small shareholders (as in selling control of the company for an above-market price for his shares). The allocation of votes by number of shares is said to be no more logical than "making voting rights in school district elections proportional to the school taxes paid by the voters. . . ." [16] Under the proposed reform, any group—workers, consumers, dealers, environmentalists—that felt itself aggrieved by actions of the corporation could, with some prospect of success, mobilize its members to purchase shares in an effort to turn out the old management and institute its own. Of course, such a group might seek corporate control simply for its own benefit, but if the consequence were to disadvantage other interests, the latter in turn would mobilize their numbers to overturn the incumbents.

However democratic such a procedure may appear, the potential spoils attainable simply by organizing a coalition of holders of a single share that would be sufficient to obtain a majority over other such coalitions staggers the imagination. The result might be to democratize corporate raiding and, in the process, to submit the large corporation to perpetual political turmoil that would shatter its effective operation by any standards.

Another proposal to make shareholder representation more effective has been to divide shareholders into two groups, the short-term and long-term holders, and to limit the right to vote to the latter.[17] The presumption is that the former lot, who nip in and out of the organization, are concerned only with a gambler's rewards, while the latter have a commitment to the corporation that entitles them to a voice in its affairs. This interesting suggestion would seem worth consideration if its premise is valid, but my own guess is that many long-term holders of a corporation's securities have no more concern with its policies than the short-termers. Their durance may as well come from sentiment or apathy. In any event, their very persistence is likely to reflect satisfaction with management control rather than any penchant for involvement, if that is what is wanted.

Control of the Proxy Machinery

The one area of structural reform which has aroused greatest interest and the only significant one to have elicited legislative action has been the matter of control over the proxy machinery, that instrument by which hundreds of thousands of dispersed shareholders are asked by management to cede to it their vote, on behalf of directors who are named in the solicitation and sometimes in favor of certain propositions requiring stockholder approval under the charter or bylaws. The Securities and Exchange Commission (SEC) has been given powers to establish rules governing proxy solicitations. Modification of these rules over the years has extended to the individual stockholder the right to submit propositions relating to corporate affairs for inclusion in the proxy solicitation. If the proposal is one that management opposes, and whose rejection it therefore recommends, the initiating stockholder is entitled to support it with a 100-word statement.

The most important exceptions to this general rule are that a stock-holder proposal cannot be intended for purely personal advantage, nor can it be "primarily for the purpose of promoting general economic, political, racial, religious, social or similar causes." Moreover, because, as we earlier saw, common law, as well as the laws of most states, empowers the board of directors to act on behalf of the stockholders (in effect separating normal operating control of the business from the owners), a stockholder proposal is not eligible for inclusion in the proxy statement if it consists of "a recommendation or request that the management take action with respect to a matter relating to the conduct of the ordinary business operations" of the company.[18]

This rule, despite its limitations, has become the basis for efforts by public-interest groups holding shares in a company to win stockholder support for propositions restraining corporate actions viewed as objectionable or promoting certain corporate actions considered desirable. The importance of this new right of stockholder initiative was emphasized by Donald E. Schwartz in a letter to the SEC on behalf of a group of General Motors stockholders whose objective was to push the giant company toward a greater concern for its public impact. Schwartz argued that "Management's proxy statement is the only effective vehicle through which all of the shareholders can have an opportunity to express themselves, and even to hear any arguments on the questions involved." To say that dissident stockholders can circulate their own resolutions is in effect to deny them the opportunity to take their case to fellow stockholders, because the cost of such a solicitation would be virtually prohibitive.[19]

The SEC has been judicially nudged in the direction of cautious consideration of this position, notably in a case involving the Dow Chemical Company. In that case an organization known as the Medical Committee for Human Rights, which held shares in the company, requested inclusion in management's proxy statement of a proposition that "napalm shall not be sold to any buyer unless that buyer gives reasonable assurance that the substance will not be used on or against human beings." Its objection to such sale was based not only on "concerns for human life," but also on the adverse effect that the use of Dow's napalm in the Vietnamese war was having on the recruitment of able young men for company positions and on an unfavorable public reaction hurting the company's "global business." Dow management refused to include the proposition in the proxy solicitation, and the Medical Committee, as shareholder, appealed to the SEC, which sustained management's action. The Medical Committee thereupon appealed to the U.S. Court of Appeals for the District of Columbia, which on July 8, 1970, ruled that the SEC had stated a conclusion but had not supported it with a reasonable analysis that would permit judicial review. It directed that the SEC reconsider the matter.

At least as important as the court's decision was its supporting opinion. The issue turned on whether the Medical Committee's proposition was a "moral" matter, not clearly related to the company's normal business, in which case it would have been precluded by one exception to the general rule, or whether on the other hand it was so clearly a matter coming within the directors' normal discretionary authority that it fell under the ban of the second exception noted above because it constituted stockholder interference "with respect to a matter relating to the conduct of the ordinary business operations" of the company. If either of these conditions held, the stockholders' proposition would have been rendered ineligible.

The court noted in its opinion that these two exceptions are entirely consistent with the legislative purpose underlying the SEC's proxy rules: "for it seems fair to infer that Congress desired to make proxy solicitations a vehicle for *corporate* democracy rather than an all-purpose forum for malcontented shareholders to vent their spleen about irrelevant matters, and also realized that management cannot exercise its specialized talents effectively if corporate investors assert the power to dictate the minutiae of daily business decisions."

Thus neither the general rule concerning stockholder initiatives, nor the exceptions to it, were held in question by the court. What bothered the court was the application by the SEC of its own rules when it supported the Dow management in rejecting inclusion of the proposition in the official proxy solicitation. That application appeared to be inconsistent and partisan. It is apparent, the court noted, that the proxy rules "can be construed so as to permit the exclusion of practically any shareholder proposal on the grounds that it is either 'too general' or 'too specific.' " [20] In the present case the company had gone even farther by arguing both grounds. Thus on the one hand, the manufacture of napalm was held to be a simple business decision and hence immune from stockholder interference. But it was also argued that this was less a business decision than a patriotic one, which injected the issue of morality. On this latter basis, corporate management was in effect arrogating to itself the power of deciding *moral* issues confronting the company, not simply business issues, but denying to its stockholders the right to challenge the morality of its position.

Corporate law binds the board, and through it the management, to act only on behalf of stockholder interests. Traditionally it has been considered that stockholder interests are confined to a money return on their investment. But, the court in effect asserted, conceivably stockholders may not define their interests so narrowly.

In the court's words: "No reason has been advanced in the present proceedings which leads to the conclusion that management may properly place obstacles in the path of shareholders who wish to present to their co-owners, in accord with applicable state law, the question of whether they wish to have their assets used in a manner which they believe to be more socially responsible but possibly less profitable than that which is dictated by present company policy."

The court's opinion is worth quoting at length:

The management of Dow Chemical Company is repeatedly quoted in sources which include the company's own publications as proclaiming that the decision to continue manufacturing and marketing napalm was made not *because* of business considerations, but *in spite of* them; that management in essence decided to pursue a course of activity which generated little profit for the shareholders and actively impaired the company's public relations and recruitment activities because management considered this action morally and politically desirable. The proper political and social role of modern corporations is, of course, a matter of philosophical argument extending far beyond the scope of our present concern; the substantive wisdom or propriety of particular corporate political decisions is also completely irrelevant to the resolution of the present controversy. What *is* of immediate concern, however, is the question of whether the corporate proxy rules can be employed as a shield to isolate such managerial decisions from shareholder control. After all, it must be remembered that "the control of great corporations by a very few persons was the abuse at which Congress struck in enacting [stockholder access to the proxy statement]. We think that there is a clear and compelling distinction between management's legitimate need for freedom to apply its expertise in matters of day-to-day business judgment, and management's patently illegitimate claim of power to treat modern corporations with their vast resources as personal satrapies implementing personal political or moral predilections. It could scarcely be argued that management is more qualified or more entitled to make these kinds of decisions than the shareholders who are the true beneficial owners of the corporation; and it seems equally implausible that an application of the proxy rules which permitted such a result could be harmonized with the philosophy of corporate democracy which Congress embedded in . . . the Securities Exchange Act of 1934." [21]

The implication is clear that if corporate actions *are* taken on moral or social-interest grounds, the discretion of its directors is no longer necessarily privileged as involving only normal business considerations.

The Dow case was appealed by the SEC on a narrower issue of administrative law, but the Supreme Court denied review on the ground that because the company had included the Medical Committee's resolution in the proxy solicitation the following year, the matter had become moot. The specific issue thus remains in doubt, but the general drift is evident. Corporations are being increasingly urged on all sides to exercise social responsibility; many of them have responded affirmatively, a few enthusiastically. But in moving into these troubled waters of social controversy the corporation is clearly entering on matters of morality. Such discretion, because it is not privileged, may be challenged by more pecuniarily minded stockholders as not in their interest, or its exercise may be said to run counter to majority *stockholder* morality. Thus, willy-nilly, the corporation is being thrust into the thick of controversial social issues, their position on which they must publicly defend. If they fail to take action in matters of public interest, they run counter to the prevailing trend and may possibly subject themselves to stockholder initiatives via the proxy machinery. But if they do initiate social actions that are disapproved by other constituent groups, they face the same possibility of dissident stockholder action.

The public-interest reformers who are bringing pressures on management have no illusion that in fact they can capture a majority of stockholder votes. "For various reasons—inertia, economic disparity, and the like—it is highly unlikely that the dissidents can outpoll management." [22] "The shareholder did not become a shareholder in order to become a social reformer. The purpose of his investment was to make money. As such, his interest as a shareholder is antithetical to the public interest insofar as activity in the public interest involves any sacrifice on his part." [23] What the reformers are concerned with is creating a forum in which the issues of corporate conduct can be brought up for public debate. They cannot compel such discussions in the role of private citizen. If they can do so in the role of stockholder, the stockholder's meeting becomes the basis for requiring management to react openly to their proposals. "While management might argue privately that the proposal would hurt the corporation financially, it will not do so in a public-interest proxy contest since what is said to the shareholders will be overheard by nonshareholders. Therefore management must justify its opposition to the proposal in public interest terms lest the nonshareholder public react adversely to the corporation. . . . Hence . . .

shareholders and the public are brought within the process of corporate decision-making through the debate of issues in a public forum." [24]

One further reform in the proxy rules has been suggested, namely, that the shareholders should have the right to nominate directors for inclusion in the proxy solicitation, alongside management's candidates. At present they may nominate from the floor, but without the remotest chance of success.[25]

The Ethics of Institutional Stockholders

Pressures on corporate managements to recognize larger social responsibilities have been accompanied by pressures on institutional shareholders—usually nonprofit organizations such as churches, universities, foundations, and pensions funds, but including investment trusts and mutual funds as well—to take positions on the social conduct of the corporations in which they hold shares. Campaign GM, although relying on its proxy proposals to provide the ground for discussion at the annual meeting, believed that the 100-word supporting statement would not generate enough support for, or interest in, its position, and on its own initiative mailed a fifteen-page proxy statement to a select list of 5,000 institutions and brokers. This was followed, particularly in universities and churches, by direct pressure on, and persuasion addressed to, trustees and officers. A number of universities were induced to develop policies and procedures for determining how they would cast their proxies —whether on behalf of management or of reform groups—in any given situation.

Yale University undertook an especially elaborate investigation, subsequently published in book form,[26] the recommendations of which were adopted on an experimental basis. In brief, the "moral minimum" of the university is to take such action as it can to prevent or correct social injury by actions of any corporation in which it holds shares. An advisory committee of teachers and students, following guidelines, makes recommendations to the trustees, with whom final discretion lies. Recommendations are to be made only in cases where information is sufficient to support them, and commonly only with respect to the voting of proxies rather than any independent initiation of action by the university. The objective is not to champion social causes, but only to assume the responsibility of a part-owner in registering its views with respect to the desirable behavior of companies in which it has invested. As an "ethical investor," it eschews the easier path of simply selling securities of companies engaged in unsocial activity, but will endeavor to use its ownership influence to modify that activity. It will sell its holdings only as a last resort, when persuaded that its influence is without effect. Other universities have adopted roughly comparable policies.

The difficulties in such an approach are several. A large corporation is involved on many fronts. Its actions in some matters may be regarded as highly commendable, on others deplorable. Some overall assessment must be made; the weighting becomes a second-order matter of judgment. On campuses where interest groups are numerous and vocal, the decision as to whether trade relations with South Africa counterbalance forthright efforts at pollution control, or whether sale of missile launchers to Egypt should be condemned, but sale to Israel should not, may result in such strenuous efforts at "balancing" all such varied interests that campus turmoil would be fostered and the university's own primary purpose of education would be subverted. A second consideration is that the factual investigations that would be necessary to sustain recommended actions in good conscience would be both time-consuming and expensive. Given the diversified investments of a major university, the result could be a substantial diversion of energies and funds.

These objections are not necessarily fatal to Yale-type investment policies, but they do raise serious questions as to how institutions with diversified constituencies can effectively participate in the policy formulation of other institutions with diversified constituencies without creating a tangle of interests, precipitating more confusion than light. But in this instance, as in the case of government regulation of corporate activity, one may safely assume that the novelty of involvement will wear off and that routines will become established that will be far less interventionist than now appears.

Public Directors and Worker Directors

One proposal for corporate reform that was widely discussed during the 1930s and has surfaced again is that federal charters for major corporations replace state charters. This would presumably rule out the opportunity for companies to domicile themselves in whichever states are most permissive (Delaware is the most favored). Such a reform would seem to make sense only if the federal government was prepared to assert a more detailed and effective regulatory authority over national corporations, perhaps decentralizing some aspects of that authority to lesser political jurisdictions along the lines discussed in Chapter 6. The prospects for such a government "invasion" of corporate autonomy seem slim at best.

More significant is the proposal—again revived from the 1930s—that "public directors" serve on the boards of large corporations. Justice William O. Douglas, when chairman of the Securities and Exchange Commission, conceived the idea of a professional director who would devote his full time to the affairs of only a few corporations. Although elected by the stockholders, he would serve more as "a public director, representing not only the present but the potential stockholder, and representing the public as well." [27]

Robert Townsend has suggested a federal law requiring every corporation with assets of $1 billion or more to support the office of a public director to the tune of $1 million a year for staff. The manner of his appointment is not clear, but he "might be subject to approval by a Congressional committee," and once approved, "would be assigned to companies by lot and rotate by lot every four years." He could attend all board meetings; "all doors and files would be open to him," and he would call a press conference twice a year "to report on the state of the corporation and its effect on the public." [28] Somewhat more sweepingly, Ralph Nader has suggested that once a corporation passes a certain size or market share, a proportion—perhaps one-fourth—of its directors should be chosen by popular vote.[29]

A more revolutionary change in corporate government has been suggested by Professor Robert Dahl of Yale. He has concluded that only self-management, Yugoslav style, "can provide anything approaching genuine democratic authority in the American business firm."

> I do not see why a board of directors elected by the employees could not select managers as competent as those selected by a board of directors chosen by banks, insurance companies, or the managers themselves. The board of a self-governing firm might hire a management team on a term contract in the way that a board of directors of a mutual fund often does now—and also fire them if they are incompetent.[30]

The advantage would come in the added on-the-job satisfaction for workers who were in effect governing themselves. For the protection of interests other than those of the employees he would rely on government regulation.

Although I share a certain sympathy for the underlying philosophical premises of Dahl's position, and a certain admiration for the Yugoslav experiment, I am highly dubious that "self-management" would be anything but a label in organizations on the scale of large American corporations. It is one thing for workers to assume responsibility for the running of a plant employing 8,000; it is another thing to devise "industrial democracy" or "self-management"—call it what you will—in a corporation with a hundred or so plants in the United States, a score or more overseas, and three-quarters of a million employees. Somewhat less radically, Detlev Vagt has suggested following another foreign pattern, German codetermination, under which employee and public interests join with stockholder interests in being represented on the board.[31]

Size and Its Implications

When a country's population expands and includes a wider spectrum of special-interest groups, the need for a stronger central government increases. This was Rousseau's insight. As the economic functions of a growing society become more technologically complex and coherent, the need for governmental coordination becomes greater. This was Saint-Simon's insight. The representative function becomes more attenuated as a compact executive government, aided by experts, initiates more and more actions, subject only, if at all, to delay or veto by a less well informed and more cumbersome legislature.

Though this thesis has been applied primarily to civil governments, it applies as well to the corporations. It is no mere coincidence that Berle and Means could note that "The increase of management power has roughly paralleled the increasing size of corporate enterprise."[32] With organizations, no less than with public governments, growth brings the need for centralization of authority to coordinate the multiple interest groups and the multiple functional groups involved. Management assumes—to be effective, *must* assume—the reins of authority, subject to a readily conceded acquiescence on the part of the board of directors, who lack the inside knowledge and continuing contact and who are for the most part, in any event, management's own appointed.

And the representative function? With growth in the size of the corporation, it becomes increasingly difficult even to define its constituency, let alone represent it. The fact that management itself has come to speak of its obligations to a number of interests indicates the diffuseness and ambiguity of the representative function assigned to it. To continue to speak of the shareholders as the constituency is an historical lag. It provides only the necessary legal fiction, however illogical, for designating management and validating its authority.

For our large national corporations, the constituency can only be society at large. Not without reason have we referred to them as quasi-public. But unless we are prepared to concentrate control over them in the hands of the federal government, which is one alternative, it makes more sense to concede corporate control to management than to attempt any revival of "shareholder democracy," which would presume to make the corporation the servant of this special interest. For with management in control, and recognizing the obligation to balance the interests of "all" —whatever its interpretation of the words—management at least becomes the recognized focal point on which pressures can be brought for change of social policy or redress of public grievance.

Clearly the American people have no inclination, as of now, to socialize the large corporations. Even that most dedicated of reformers, Ralph Nader, professes as a theory of power "that if it's going to be responsible, it has to be insecure; it has to have something to lose. That is why putting all economic power in the state would be disastrous, because it would not be insecure. If General Motors is sensitive at all, right now, with the tremendous dominant position it has, it comes from fear of losing something it has." [33]

The insecurity that Nader wishes to build into management's position can perhaps best be achieved at the moment by increasing stockholder accessibility to the proxy statement—not because this would give substance to an illusory stockholder democracy, as Congress originally intended, but because it would provide the means for converting the annual meeting from ritual to public forum, as the public-interest reformers have been urging. In effect, the same legal fiction that gives corporate control to management would provide the public—or various publics—with the means for expressing its dissatisfaction and dissent.

The effect is not to challenge management's control but rather its judgment. Like labor unions, which do not attempt to unseat the management with which they bargain, but only to influence its decisions, so public-interest representatives (in stockholder guise) contest management's actions on socially sensitive fronts. Their bargaining power may be limited, but in the prevailing situation where management's control derives from so tenuous a legal base, their influence may not prove negligible.

How effective this restraint on managerial discretion may be depends in part on how many "public citizens," as Nader calls them, give of their time in organizing dissent, or whether an effective "common cause" (similar to the one that John Gardner has organized to bring pressure on public civil governments) can be directed to private corporate governments. Public directors may serve a useful function in collaborating with such public-interest representation, but by themselves I would expect that same absorption into the board, their co-optation by management, that occurs so often with government officials appointed to regulate industry.

If growth in the size of corporations has led to concentration of authority in the hands of management, and a consequent fuzziness of definition with respect to who constitutes the corporation's constituency, we should remind ourselves that corporate growth does not stop at the nation's boundaries. As we saw in the preceding chapter, the corporation has expanded globally. What then of its constituency? Whom does management of the multinational firm represent? If we regard public-interest shareholders and public directors as some conduit for channeling social grievances to management, what chance is there of shareholder proposals from disgruntled Canadians or Frenchmen, and even should such grievances find their way into the pipeline, what chance of winning American public opinion on their behalf? The restless corporation does not stay still long enough to allow for even tentative answers.

Continuity and Incremental Change

The "legitimacy" of power rests on the institutionalization of procedures for designating those who exercise it: what gives Jones, rather than Smith, the authority of the corporation presidency? The fact that management's power is presently legitimated by selection procedures that reverse those originally intended in law does not necessarily undermine it. All institutions change over time, but as long as the courts and the public at large accept the result, then the modified method of management selection has not lost its institutional validity.

To nurture that judicial and public acceptance may, however, require some reciprocal changes in management's own methods. In particular, the fact that our major corporations, by their expanded size, have vastly augmented the powers of management and the bureaucratic substructure of experts over which it presides virtually requires the improvisation of methods for giving voice to groups who feel themselves adversely affected by the exercise of those powers. Though many managements may not appreciate the fact, the readier access of stockholders to the proxy machinery and the rise of public-interest stockholders represent just such improvisations. In a sense, they legitimize management by the very fact that they address their grievances to it, within the existing institutional mechanisms. Management may feel indignant at being exposed to public criticism, but its indignation should be tempered by the realization that it is its exercise of discretion, not its authority, that is being questioned. To acquire a new skill of interacting reasonably and responsively with segments of the community, even with self-appointed community guardians, may be a painful experience for management, but it is a skill that its own organization has made necessary by its growth and the corollary centralization of authority.

To the extent that management accommodates itself to this new development, it probably need make only modest concessions to satisfy its critics. As the counsel for Campaign GM has himself said, the thrust of that campaign "was not war but an accommodation." [34] The stockholder dissidents were easily put down in the final vote count, by margins so lopsided as to appear ridiculous, but although they did not win their proposal for the appointment of three public directors to make the board more representative, GM soon afterward appointed its first black and female directors, and although they did not carry their proposal for a shareholders' committee on public responsibility, GM subsequently on its own formed a public policy committee of five directors to inquire into those phases of its operations which relate to matters of public policy, and then to recommend action to the full board.

Other corporations faced with stockholder protests over specific actions have adopted a similar policy of conciliation. Dow Chemical ceased the manufacture of napalm and established an environmental testing advisory board to study possible environmental effects of new products. Eastman Kodak, though refusing to honor dissident stockholder demands for minority quotas in hiring, then joined with the reformers in promoting new training and hiring policies.

The consequence of adding a public forum aspect to the annual meeting is to "open" the corporate system to the realities of a society that has altered markedly since the days when statutory and common law established the present legal form. In so doing it does not meet, but in fact turns back, demands for broader participatory roles; it requires no sharing of power. The government of the corporation remains firmly in place. All that has happened is that it has become more public in its operations, more attuned to those voices that it has tended to ignore in the past. Management retains its centralized control by making modest and incremental adjustments in its practices and procedures to palliate those who call for more sweeping change.

Even if the proxy machinery and the annual meeting prove inefficient vehicles for exposing management to its broader public constituencies, other improvisations consonant with its new political function will emerge. Of one thing we may be sure: The path away from present management control of the corporation does not lead back to some version of shareholder democracy. It lies over new terrain, with management seeking to legitimate its control by convincing its multiple constituencies that it is doing its best to act responsibly "in the public interest."

[10]

THE LIMITS OF

CORPORATE

RESPONSIBILITY

THE large corporations are dominant in American culture because they have won widespread acceptance for the values that they champion— the notion of a good life whose focus is material accumulation and consumption, the ideal of a constitutional order based more on private autonomy and freedom of action than on hierarchical order and government control, a conception of distributive justice that rests on equality of opportunity for all to make as much of, and for, themselves as their capabilities and motivation permit.

These values obviously conduce to the corporations' own advantage: the materialistic ideal generates support for their expansion and security; the extension to them of roughly the same autonomy accorded the individual gives them a philosophical basis for the greater power that in fact they possess relative to the individual; equality of opportunity maintains the egalitarian flavor, but continues to accord special advantage to those who start from a privileged position.

Because social values and corporate interests coalesce, each reinforces the other. Because the welfare of so many is anchored in corporate society, those who would radically alter that society are relatively few in number.

But the objective conditions of a society change over time, affecting some groups more than others, for better or for worse. Under these changing circumstances, it is inevitable that the large corporations become subject to criticism. Enmeshed as they are, at so many points, in the lives of the population, visible as they are as concentrations of economic authority, how can they escape a generalized if unfocused public belief that they are either the cause or accomplice of unwelcome change, or that their failure to use their "evident" power constructively is equivalent to willful preoccupation with self-interest, a kind of corporate delinquency?

But the fact is, as we have seen, that the power of any single corporation, however great in its own economic sphere, is limited indeed when it comes to taking effective action on any of our major social fronts. However much the conscience and desire of a corporate president might motivate him to enlist his organization in social causes, his first duty is to preserve and strengthen that organization. He is like the runner in a track meet: although he is one of the principals in the event, he is limited to competing according to the rules of the game.

But there is something more. Most corporation executives (like most runners) *prefer* the rules of the game. These embody values that are congenial to their thinking, that have contributed to their own prosperity, values that they genuinely identify with the welfare of their society. Of course not all business executives have identical value conceptions, forming a solid phalanx of true believers, any more than all Cardinals of the Church profess identical creeds. But the variations among them are matters of degree. Simply by virtue of having achieved their position within the organization, they have affirmed the faith.

In the face of this situation—social problems pressing for attention, corporations challenged to exercise social responsibility but having little capacity to do anything singly and captained by individuals who still believe deeply in the values of which their organizations are the chief carriers—what response can one expect? What else but a limited response? Modest concessions, within the realm of the corporation's limited discretion. Incremental changes in corporate policies and conduct, as long as these do not entail differential costs that jeopardize competitive performance. A public relations program designed to reassure uneasy segments of the public that their concerns are not being ignored.

The study group on business social responsibility sponsored by the Committee for Economic Development (CED) has expressed the essence of this limited responsibility approach very nicely.

Corporations are necessarily limited by various internal constraints on what and how much they can do to improve society. . . .

Cost-benefit considerations are a very important factor. No company of any size can willingly incur costs which would jeopardize its competitive position and threaten its survival. While companies may well be able to absorb modest costs or undertake some social activities on a break-even basis, any substantial expenditure must be justified in terms of the benefits, tangible and intangible, that are expected to be produced. Since major corporations have especially long planning horizons, they may be able to incur costs and forego profits in the short run for social improvements that are expected to enhance profits or improve the corporate environment in the long run. But the corporation that sacrifices too much in the way of earnings in the short run will soon find itself with no long run to worry about.

Thus, management must concern itself with realizing a level of profitability which its stockholders and the financial market consider to be reasonable under the circumstances. This means that substantial investments in social improvements will have to contribute to earnings, and the extent of such earnings will be a major factor in determining the mix of a company's commercial and social activities.[1]

The difficulty with this approach is that it continues to regard the large corporation as purely an economic institution. Following classical liberal thought, it accepts the notion that management's first objective is to produce a good product at a satisfactory price—this above all—and then, within whatever limits its profitability and its stockholders may permit, to "undertake some social activities on a break-even basis." But this view—adequate for an earlier period—no longer suffices. The corporation has become, by virtue of its size and scope, more of a public institution than a private one. Its management, as we have seen, exercises a political function no less than an economic one, responding to and coordinating contentious public-interest and special-interest groups. Even if its discretion is limited, even if it is constrained by the system of which it is a part, it now operates within a social context in which increasingly it can legitimate its authority only by assuring its numerous and often conflicting publics that it is doing its best to act responsively. After all, what politician does *not* have budgetary and system constraints?

The argument can thus be asserted, with increasing conviction, that management's political role is precedent to its economic function, rather than vice versa, as the CED report would have it. Or, at the least, that the political and economic functions are concomitant, each reinforcing— or undermining—the other.

This does not mean that the management of a corporation must be socially responsible in the sense of righting racial wrongs, investing in pollution controls beyond legal requirements, building extra quality into its products at no increase in cost to the consumer, underwriting community activities. It does mean that it must convince its numerous publics that, within the powers it exercises (however limited they may be), it has not ignored their interests (however outrageous they may seem to it). It cannot turn back a protest from minority groups discriminated against in employment by pointing to its good products, or satisfy an environmental group by proving that it sets prices competitively. Less and less it can rest its claim to power on a fictional stockholder election; more and more it is forced to seek legitimacy by demonstrating its responsiveness to its publics like a political officeholder.

In regarding management and the corporation in this light, we gain some insight into the elusive concept of corporate social responsibility, about which so much froth has been written. Social responsibility becomes political responsibility. There can be no universal creed or doctrine as to what business managers must do in order to be regarded as socially responsible, any more than there can be for a public officeholder. What is the social responsibility of the mayor of New York, or the governor of Missouri, or the president of the United States? It depends on the point of view of various segments of the public and the circumstances of the times. We can only expect that each of these officeholders will try to fill the functions of his office to the satisfaction of his multiple constituencies, some of which are more important than others. Similarly the "social" responsibility of a corporation executive runs to the numerous groups which he affects and with whom he interacts, some of which (the stockholders, perhaps) are more important than others, but all of which must be recognized. Not all corporations have identical constituencies nor face similar circumstances. Their social responsibilities cannot be subsumed under some common catalog of desirable behavior but measured only in terms of satisfactory political performance. The social responsibility of the president of General Motors is no more definable than the social responsibility of the mayor of Detroit. It is—at the moment—simply less accountable. The president of GM does not have to stand for re-election by a heterogeneous public, as a mayor does. But he cannot count on the persistence of that distinction unless he acts as though he *were* accountable.

There is more to the matter than this, however. As we have noted, the large corporations are the dominant carriers of social values which are shared, even if in varying degree, by most members of American society. When we refer to the United States as a business society, we are wrapping up those values—material advancement, individual autonomy, equal opportunity, competitive achievement—in a single word.

In labeling these *social* values, we really mean that they are the values commonly held by *individuals* in our society. They constitute articles of faith in which most Americans believe, just as in an earlier day most individuals in Western society affirmed a God-centered ethic prescribing and proscribing certain forms of personal conduct.

But there is a profound difference between the ethical standard governing personal conduct and the organizational imperative governing institutional conduct. Whatever the legal fiction which regards the corporation as a person, it is no more a person than is the Catholic church or Harvard University. Its leaders, in their private lives, subscribe to the same social values as their countrymen, but in their institutional roles they have larger responsibilities which at times must take precedence. If an institution's leaders believe that the kind of a society they prefer depends on the survival of that institution, they will develop a strategy for institutional survival which at times may—indeed, must —conflict with the individualistic (social) values they publicly affirm. The conflict cannot, however, be blatant, but must somehow be philosophically rationalized as compatible with—indeed, contributory to— those values.

Even the Catholic church has found it necessary to substitute for the Christian creed of self-sacrifice the institutional imperative of a continuing mission, regulating its conduct by quite different standards from those it preaches. The principle of individual self-sacrifice is retained symbolically—the bishop's washing of the beggar's feet—but Christian values cannot be allowed to conflict with institutional survival, since the latter is prerequisite to the former. Hence the Inquisition. Hence many other examples which history provides of the church's departure from the religious ethic it preaches. But hence, too, its survival.

Similarly a democracy is sometimes tyrannous in protecting itself from territorial dissolution despite the creed of autonomy and self-government which it affirms (as notably in the American Civil War). Similarly the modern university, while resting on a foundation of free inquiry, bars from its precincts those who do not possess credentials supplied by accepted schools of thought—how else protect its survival by separating the intellectual charlatan from the intellectually qualified? (Thus intuitive thinking and visual ideation have encountered a hostility not extended to rational and linear reasoning.) The same principle leads the corporation to recognize an imperative more binding on it, as an institution, than the individualistic social values in which its leaders also believe.

John Locke, Adam Smith, and their followers could endorse economic individualism as conducing to social advantage. After all, this was in a day when most businesses were small in size, usually extensions of households, and were constrained in their profit-seeking by the mores of the community. The ethic of individualism, encompassing private enterprise and competition, laid the basis for the rise of our large corporations. As the heirs and beneficiaries of that philosophy, but now operating under vastly altered objective conditions, they are its most ardent and effective advocates. Effective advocacy requires their own survival, but that in turn may dictate private acts difficult to defend, any longer, as contributing to social advantage—the closing down of a community plant which, while making a profit, is comparatively inefficient; the degrading of air or water, but within legal limits; economizing on the quality of a product, but in ways that do not jeopardize sales; converting work into jobs that are more productive, but devoid of inherent interest; encouraging economic growth, expansion of consumption and output, regardless of the impact on society.

The apparent contradiction between social value and institutional advantage (public and private good) must, however, be philosophically rationalized if the old values (and their beneficiaries) are to be preserved. With some modest modifications this can be done by reaffirming as the whole economic verity the partial (and diminishing) truth that profitability is the reward for individual merit, in open competition against all comers, in providing wanted goods and services to the community, that hence it is not only socially justifiable but socially advantageous. The harsh actions to which corporations are unfortunately *driven* in their struggle for efficiency and profit are thus, after all, only the sacrifice which *society* must make to preserve its own values. The real rationalization, however, is that these acts contribute to the strength and continuity of the *corporations*, which are the dominant support for the social values which make them dominant. The circle of faith must be kept closed.

It is just possible that under the pressure of changing objective circumstances, more people are now questioning the old philosophical rationalization of the coincidence between public and private welfare when the term "private" has been stretched to include the contemporary large corporation. If that should indeed be the case, the corporation's organizational imperative, which has been accepted because reinforcing widespread social values, would then become less acceptable. Dissident demands for greater corporate social responsibility (a new political relationship between the corporations and their multiple publics) would become more insistent. But the corporate sector would be *structurally* unable to meet such demands even if it listened to them.

This corporate weakness for undertaking joint political action may indeed drive it to the stratagem of *inviting* regulation or coordination of its activities by a government which could be counted on not to press for radical changes. The forms of government initiative could be bargained out in congressional committees, a process with which business representatives are not altogether unfamiliar. As the study group sponsored by the CED—an association representative of business interests —has noted: "Indeed, if corporations cannot deal individually with major social responsibilities such as pollution because of competitive cost disadvantages, and if they are unable to cooperate in resolving such difficulties, then they logically and ethically should propose and support rational governmental regulation which will remove the short-run impediments from actions that are wise in the long term." [2]

In this eventuality, "wisdom"—even long-term wisdom—need not be disruptive of corporate hegemony over American society. Government regulation of corporations in the public interest might continue to proceed by incremental changes of the type we have observed in the preceding chapters, changes to which corporate leaders—whatever their feelings of hurt—could adapt without significant loss of power and position.

Such modest, incremental changes by the corporations themselves and by government as corporate regulator may be enough to satisfy public criticisms—promising much but delivering Arpège. But even the most enlightened leadership of the corporate community and of government cannot guarantee that this will be sufficient. If social change is rapid, the alterations in its institutional strategy which business is willing to accept, even under pressure, may fail to satisfy the objective needs and political pressures of the times.

Former Secretary of the Interior Stewart Udall has posed such a possibility. Detroit automobile executives, he points out, have forecast 178 million registered vehicles in the United States by 1985. Aside from the contribution which this will make to pollution and congestion, Udall says that the oil companies will not be able to provide enough petroleum to fill the gas tanks of the 65 million additional cars that this figure represents. To him it is clear that to avoid having a transportation crisis thrust suddenly upon us, we must set limits on the numbers and use of the automobile, and move vigorously on other forms of transport. But neither government nor business shows signs of perturbation at what may lie in store.

. . . despite his expressed concern over energy shortage and air pollution, the President has chosen to shore up the economy by stimulating the production of automobiles. Too often the voice of government is the voice of industry.

For its part, the private sector has been dominated by oil and auto industries whose executives have been unable to contemplate production plateaus and low horsepower engines. When James Roche retired last December as chief executive of General Motors, he expressed the belief and the faith of Detroit by predicting the inevitability of the auto industry's growth. He then observed: "I think the average American today would give up about anything before he gives up his automobile." [3]

Is it possible that the major crisis in transport which Udall foresees may not only materialize, but may coincide with other pressures on the cities, on the environment, and on other fronts, to precipitate a situation with which incrementalism cannot cope? How can one say? But the possibility is there. History provides examples of situations that could not be dealt with by modest concessions and minor modifications.

If something of this sort should occur, it could result in a general deterioration of the social condition, or could invite a political figure to play a demagogue's role. Or a more formal collaboration may develop between government and business, perhaps along the lines of the French économie concertée—an economy more controlled and planned, but with business heavily involved in the controlling and planning, in effect, the social engineering approach on a national scale.

The CED's study group has foreseen this possibility even in the absence of any crisis or collapse.

The converging of two trends—the business thrust into social fields, and government's increasing use of market incentives to induce even greater business involvement—is gradually bringing these two powerful institutions into a constructive partnership for accelerating social progress. This emerging partnership is more than a contractual relationship between a buyer and seller of services. Fundamentally, it offers a new means for developing the innate capabilities of a political democracy and a private enterprise economy into a new politico-economic system capable of managing social and technological change in the interest of a better social order. It by no means will be an exclusive partnership, for other private institutions, especially universities, will also play very significant roles. Still, the government-business relationship is likely to be the central one in the last third of the twentieth century.[4]

This more formally structured government-business relationship would involve a more significant institutional realignment, with two consequences. The social values which guide the average citizen in some degree, molding his views of what is good and what is right, would be modified, perhaps not so dramatically as to undermine his sense of self but enough to redirect it. And the new dominant institutional forms would develop their own code of conduct, to justify their actions when these seem to deviate from the new social values of which they would be the chief support. They would have to rationalize their survival as necessary to the survival and greatness of the "new" society.

Every leadership group is in effect trapped by its own vision and values. Identified with, and believing in, a particular social order, it also develops its own institutional ethic, its organizational imperative, defending its survival as necessary to the survival of that order. In the face of social change, it is reluctant to tamper with and perhaps endanger its privileged and influential position. It is more inclined to temporize.

But at some point, in the face of cumulative, but unaccommodated, social pressures, temporizing may not be enough. If more radical change does not come from an insurgent group within the dominant class itself, it is likely to come from some new thrusting group outside that class, riding on a new social vision, asserting changed social values. If this occurs, we may be confident that in due course there will develop a quite separate ethic, not applicable to society at large but only to the new institution which presides over the new order. It will be based on that institution's survival needs, but rationalized as necessary to the preservation of the social order. It is this institutional imperative which embodies—as in corporate society today—the true limits of any institution's social responsibility.

[NOTES]

[1]
THE CORPORATE SYSTEM

1. Any dubious reader is referred to Edward R. Aranow and Herbert A. Einhorn, *Proxy Contests for Corporate Control*, 2nd ed. (New York: Columbia University Press, 1968).

2. T. V. Learson, "The Greening of American Business," *The Conference Board Record*, July 1971, p. 23 (adapted from remarks before the Western Region Conference of the Harvard Business School in San Francisco).

3. From an address at the Sixty-Ninth Annual Meeting of the New York State Welfare Conference, New York City, November 20, 1968.

4. The *Wall Street Journal* (December 9, 1971) surveyed some of these attempts. Its report on the Bank of America, one of the leading experimenters, is revealing:

> The bank set out originally to draw up a "social budget" comparable to its regular budget so it could get a clearer picture of just what it was investing in social causes. The first step, a spokesman says, was to inventory all outlays "likely to be classified as social or less than fully economic" in terms of their return to the bank.
>
> Before the inventory had gone very far, the bank discovered the cost figures were getting fuzzy. The dollar total of the bank's outright contributions was clear enough—but what about the "opportunity costs" of making a loan at less than full rate because a social benefit is involved? And if a bank executive worked on a social project, a portion of his salary could be chalked up to that project. But would that fully reflect the loss of the new business he might have brought in, had he followed his normal routine? Or, in special training for minority workers, how much does their productivity cut the "cost" to the bank?
>
> After pondering these matters, officials decided that adding up the dollar figures didn't really mean anything. Now the bank is taking a different tack, intensively examining specific activities to see if they throw off a social benefit.

[2]
CORPORATIONS AND CONSUMERS

1. S. E. Upton, vice president, Whirlpool Corporation, in an address before the American Marketing Association, Cleveland, Ohio, December 11, 1969.

2. October 21, 1970. The *Journal* was interested primarily in making the point that inflation subjected business to such cost pressures, and that Congress's more effective protection for consumers lay in controlling inflation rather than in passing regulatory legislation.

3. Paul Brodeur, "The Enigmatic Enzyme," *The New Yorker*, January 16, 1971, p. 74. From *Asbestos and Enzymes* (Ballantine Books) by Paul Brodeur. Originally in *The New Yorker*. Quoted with permission.

4. U.S. Chamber of Commerce, *Business and the Consumer—A Program for the Seventies* (Washington, D.C., 1970), p. 3.

5. Harper W. Boyd, Jr., and Henry J. Claycamp have discussed this matter at some length in "Industrial Self-Regulation and the Public Interest," *Michigan Law Review*, LXIV (1966), 1239–1254.

6. Federal Trade Commission, *Report of the Task Force on Appliance Warranties and Service* (Washington, D.C., 1968).

7. *The New York Times*, November 18, 1970.

8. *The New York Times*, March 11, 1972.

9. *Business Week*, July 10, 1971.

10. Robert L. Birmingham has collected some business responses to the proposed Fair Packaging and Labeling Act that reflect this attitude in "The Consumer as King: The Economics of Precarious Sovereignty," *Case Western Reserve Law Review*, XX (1968), p. 360.

11. An interesting account of business efforts to defeat the Hart Bill (which became the Fair Packaging and Labeling Act) is contained in Jeremy Main, "Industry Still Has Something to Learn About Congress," *Fortune*, February 1967, pp. 128–135.

12. Main (ibid.) quotes the president of the Grocery Manufacturers of America as boasting how he had obtained the help of national magazines: "We suggested to the publishers that the day was here when their editorial department and business department might better understand their interdependency relations as they affect the operating results of their company. . . . We invited them to consider publishing some favorable articles about the food industry instead of only singling out isolated cases of criticism."

In 1971 when Senator Philip Hart was conducting hearings on a fishing inspection bill, Castle & Cooke Co., producers of the Bumble Bee brand of tunafish, removed CBS television from its 1972 advertising schedule because it was dissatisfied with CBS's coverage of the hearings, claiming that the industry's rebuttal to critics had not been adequately presented. The president of the advertising agency handling the Bumble Bee account wrote to the president of the CBS Broadcasting Group: "Advertisers select television stations as hospitable vehicles for their messages. Our client, quite reasonably, feels that CBS has destroyed the hospitality of its affiliates for advertising from Bumble Bee, as well as all seafoods. We have been asked to transmit the hope that in the future, when presenting news, you will more objectively present both sides of an issue." *The New York Times*, March 7, 1972.

13. At the time that the possibly hazardous effects of enzyme detergents was under investigation, an FTC lawyer charged that the Soap and Detergent Association proposed to bring the National Academy of Sciences into the controversy—after previously accepting designation of the American Academy of Allergy as the appropriate body to study the matter—in "an attempt to retard a testing process already being developed" by the latter agency. Brodeur, "The Enigmatic Enzyme," p. 71.

14. *Business Week*, June 10, 1972.

15. Brodeur, "The Enigmatic Enzyme," p. 54. Quoted with permission. The issue of agency jurisdiction is discussed on pp. 54 and 61.

16. Robert J. Bazell, "Food and Drug Administration: Is Protecting Lives the Priority?" *Science*, April 2, 1971, pp. 41–43. The commissioner also emphasized that because Abbott was supplying 45 percent of intravenous feeding solutions, "We might have killed more people by banning the Abbott solutions than by allowing their use." Bazell points out, however, that the FDA did not check the availability of alternative supplies until several days after meetings with Abbott officials, when a tentative decision not to ban their products had been reached.

17. Main, "Industry Still Has Something to Learn About Congress."

18. *Business Week*, June 10, 1972.

19. FDA Commissioner Charles C. Edwards has argued that his agency *must* rely on voluntary compliance. He has said that "the FDA—no matter how much money, manpower, or legislative authority it had—would never be able to enforce compliance by many thousands of industries manufacturing hundreds of thousands of products." *Fortune*, March 1972, p. 140. Edwards's statement carries three possible interpretations—that regulation must be tempered to what industry is willing to comply with, or that standards must be set sufficiently low to make compliance a

normal practice, or that considerable violation of standards must be expected if standards are set where the more ardent advocates of consumer protection would set them.

20. Betty Furness, "The Time Is Now," *Trial Magazine,* August–September 1968, p. 17.

21. Professor Irving J. Selikoff, head of the Division of Environmental Medicine, Mount Sinai School of Medicine of the City University of New York, commented on the enzyme detergent controversy:

> What the manufacturers are saying, in effect, is that it is *not known* if there is a hazard associated with long-term low-level exposure to proteolytic enzymes. From there, however, it's a giant step to a statement such as "It is *known* that there is no such hazard." There is absolutely no way to take this step except to perform necessary studies of the consumer population. Such studies should be required *before* the introduction of a new substance like proteolytic enzymes, especially when it is known, as it has been since at least 1967, that human disease can occur with them. As things turned out, however, the detergent industry alone made the decision that studies to determine the long-range effects of their new product were unnecessary, and no one in the United States government was in any position to refute this judgment, or even to question it, until the investigations of Flindt and Pepys were published in the *Lancet.*

Quoted in Brodeur, "The Enigmatic Enzyme," pp. 67, 69, italics in the original. Quoted with permission. The *Lancet* is a respected English medical journal; Flindt and Pepys are British medical researchers.

22. Harry M. Philo, quoted in John Kolb, "The Price of Faulty Design Gets Steeper Every Day," *Products Engineering,* August 1, 1966, p. 35.

23. U.S. Chamber of Commerce, *Business and the Consumer—A Program for the Seventies* (Washington, D.C., 1970), p. 10.

24. Friedrich Kessler, "Products Liability," *Yale Law Journal,* LXXVI (1967), 900–901.

25. *Restatement (Second) of Torts,* paragraph 402A, comment *c* (1965), cited in Kessler, "Products Liability," pp. 925–926.

26. From the concurring opinion of Justice Traynor in *Escola* v. *Coca Cola Bottling Company,* 24 Cal. 2d 453, 462, 150 P.2d 436, 440–441 (1944), cited in Kessler, "Products Liability," p. 927.

27. That this is already occurring is nicely illustrated by the FTC's 1968 *Report of the Task Force on Appliance Warranties and Service,* which found that the "basic arrangements" of manufacturers for providing customer warranty service are through service centers managed and staffed by employees of the manufacturers, retailers, often franchised, who service as well as sell appliances, and factory-authorized independent service companies. Manufacturers used customer sampling, review of invoices, inspections, and related procedures to ascertain whether the service organizations were performing at the required level of efficiency. The orientation of these "basic arrangements" around the large manufacturing corporation is obvious.

28. Henry Ford II, chairman of the board, Ford Motor Company, in an address before the annual convention of Sigma Delta Chi, professional journalistic society, Chicago, Illinois, November 13, 1970.

29. David M. Potter, *People of Plenty* (Chicago: University of Chicago Press, 1954), pp. 176, 177.

30. Ibid., pp. 181–182. Potter wrote at a time when magazine circulation managers and advertisers operated on the principle of the more subscribers the better. His conclusions remain relevant even though there has since been a change in attitude, with circulation directed toward a more circumscribed, but still mass, audience whose average buying probability is considered higher.

When the FTC conducted hearings in 1971 to explore advertising practices, C. W. Cook, chairman of the General Foods Corporation, testified that "while some regulation is needed in the public interest, excessive restrictions on advertising will result in major damage to our economy and our society." Other industry witnesses held that advertising was vital to free enterprise, and likewise "the economic lifeblood of the free press." *The New York Times,* October 21, 1971.

31. The National Commission on Civil Disorders (1968) reported that in January 1967 over 88 percent of all Negro families had television sets. A 1961 study of 464 low-income families in New York City showed that 95 percent of these relatively poor families had TV sets.

32. David Caplovitz, *The Poor Pay More* (New York: Macmillan, 1963), pp. 29–30.

33. Nicholas Johnson, "Test Pattern for Living," *Saturday Review*, May 29, 1971, p. 14.

[3]

CORPORATIONS AND THE PHYSICAL ENVIRONMENT

1. Economic Research Division, Chase Manhattan Bank, "Improving the Quality of Life" (New York, 1972), p. 2.

2. *Economic Report of the President and Annual Report of the Council of Economic Advisers, 1971* (Washington, D.C.: Government Printing Office, 1971), p. 110. The table of per capita consumption expenditures appears on p. 215.

3. Jean Mayer, "Toward a Non-Malthusian Population Policy," *Columbia Forum*, XII (Summer 1969), 5.

4. "Improving the Quality of Life," pp. 6, 8.

5. Bruce Bliven, Jr., "Quiet Man," *The New Yorker*, June 17, 1972, p. 66.

6. Barry Commoner, "Economic Growth and Ecology—a Biologist's View," *Monthly Labor Review*, XCIV (November 1971), 6. His most extensive treatment of the subject is in *The Closing Circle* (New York: Alfred A. Knopf, 1971).

7. Commoner, "Economic Growth and Ecology," p. 12.

8. Barry Commoner, "The Closing Circle" *The New Yorker*, October 2, 1971, p. 46.

9. "Improving the Quality of Life," p. 2.

10. Juan Cameron, "The Trials of Mr. Clean," *Fortune*, April 1972, p. 130.

11. *Business Week*, February 5, 1972, p. 71. President Nixon's antipathy to "sweeping" control legislation was made evident not only by his veto of the Water Pollution Control Act of 1972 (a veto overridden by Congress), but also by his subsequent order to the EPA to withhold $6 billion of the funds appropriated by Congress for administration of that act during its first two years. The restriction, like the veto, was premised on a need for fiscal economy, but the underlying rationale was transparent.

12. *The New York Times*, June 4, 1972. Subsequently a Department of Commerce employee denied that any such figure had been released and suggested that the speaker had taken his statistic from a business-news syndicate that had misinterpreted a federal study.

13. *Business Week*, December 5, 1970.

14. Reynold C. MacDonald, "Steel and the Environment: Today," an address before the Steel Industry Seminar, University of Chicago, June 14, 1972.

15. John E. Kinney, "Economic Effects of Ecological Efforts," Earhart Foundation Lecture, University of Detroit, March 30, 1971.

16. Ibid.

17. *Natural History*, December 1971, p. 6.

18. From a series of advertisements, this one appearing in *Intellectual Digest*, June 1972, p. 48.

19. MacDonald, "Steel and the Environment: Today."

20. As I have delineated in *The Place of Business in America's Future: A Study in Social Values* (New York: Basic Books, 1973).

21. John C. Esposito, *Vanishing Air* (New York: Grossman Publishers, 1970), p. 275. This is the report of the Ralph Nader Task Force on Air Pollution.

22. The story is told in "A Corporate Polluter Learns the Hard Way," *Business Week*, February 6, 1971, pp. 52–56.

23. Gene Bylinsky, "The Mounting Bill for Pollution Control," *Fortune*, July 1971, p. 88.

24. MacDonald, "Steel and the Environment: Today."

Notes

25. "Improving the Quality of Life," p. 11.
26. Kinney, "Economic Effects of Ecological Efforts." Italics supplied.
27. "Improving the Quality of Life," p. 11.
28. Richard A. Hopkinson, *Corporate Organization for Pollution Control* (New York: The Conference Board, 1970).
29. "The Stormy Debate over 'Zero Discharge,'" *Business Week*, February 5, 1972, pp. 70–71.
30. *The New York Times*, June 4, 1972.
31. Bliven, "Quiet Man," p. 55.
32. Cameron, "The Trials of Mr. Clean," p. 103.
33. The characterization of Stans was made by Gladwin Hill in *The New York Times*, June 4, 1972. The account of his opposition to EPA is contained in "Nixon's Pollution Fighter Faces a Backlash," *Business Week*, August 21, 1971.
34. "A Backlash Against New-Car Standards," *Business Week*, March 25, 1972, p. 23. The article also reported "speculation in Washington that the Administration move was calculated to win friends in regulation-plagued Detroit during an election year."
35. Bylinsky, "The Mounting Bill for Pollution Control," p. 132.
36. Bylinsky, "The Mounting Bill for Pollution Control," p. 132; Cameron, "The Trials of Mr. Clean," p. 103. The official is William D. Ruckelshaus.
37. *Wall Street Journal*, June 6, 1972, from a news story by Charles Camp and Walter Mossberg, staff reporters.
38. *The New York Times*, February 14, 1973.
39. From a survey by Gladwin Hill, *The New York Times*, December 7, 1970. Among particular situations which Hill encountered were these: One Colorado state hearing on stream pollution by a brewery was presided over by the pollution control director of the brewer. For years a board member dealing with pollution of Los Angeles Harbor had been an executive of an oil company that was a major harbor polluter. The Governor of Indiana had to dismiss a state pollution board member because both he and his company were indicted as water polluters.
40. *Wall Street Journal*, May 18, 1972.
41. René Dubos, *Reason Awake* (New York: Columbia University Press, 1970), pp. 193–194.
42. *Wall Street Journal*, June 22, 1972. In most states there is nothing illegal about this operation; only automobile manufacturers and dealers are covered by federal law.
43. William D. Ruckelshaus, quoted in *Business Week*, August 21, 1971, p. 58.
44. *The New York Times*, April 23, 1972. Similarly, when the Secretary of the Interior was asked about the desirability of smaller cars and fewer neon signs, he replied that in the United States "the ethic has been growth. Historically, he added, national administrations 'have responded to the demands of the people.'"
45. James Spain, urban affairs director of Allied Chemical Corp. and president of the Association for the Integration of Management, quoted in "To Blacks, Ecology is Irrelevant," *Business Week*, November 14, 1970, p. 49.
46. *The New York Times*, June 19, 1972.
47. *Wall Street Journal*, November 19, 1971. Not all local union leaders have allowed fear of unemployment to blunt their demands for pollution control. As one example, Daniel Hannan, president of the U. S. Steel local at Clairton, Pennsylvania, has fought vigorously both in the Allegheny Air Pollution Board and in congressional hearings for strict enforcement of air-pollution standards, despite suggestions that this would lead to massive layoffs. Hannan has relied on independent studies to bolster his position, such as one by the National Institute of Health and University of Pittsburgh researchers, that coke workers positioned on top of the ovens had significantly higher death and lung cancer rates. *Business Week*, December 25, 1971.
48. Walter Sherman, vice president of the Flambeau Paper Co., quoted in the *Wall Street Journal*, November 19, 1971. Sherman praised the "very beneficial" support of Local 119 of the Pulp, Sulphite and Paper Mill Workers in seeking a delay in application of waste-treatment standards that, it was claimed, would require a partial shutdown of the mill and the loss of a hundred jobs.

49. William G. Magruder, quoted in *The New York Times,* May 23, 1972.

50. Robert J. Bazell, "Rapid Transit: A Real Alternative to the Auto for the Bay Area?" *Science* CLXXI (March 19, 1971), 1125, 1128.

51. Dubos, *Reason Awake,* p. 195.

52. Bylinsky, "The Mounting Bill for Pollution Control," p. 131.

53. Jane Jacobs, *The Economy of Cities* (New York: Random House, 1969), pp. 113–114.

54. Commoner, "Economic Growth and Ecology," p. 12.

55. Advertisement in *Business Week,* May 13, 1972, p. 78.

56. *Business Week,* February 5, 1972, p. 70.

57. "Improving the Quality of Life," p. 3.

58. *Economic Report of the President and Annual Report of the Council of Economic Advisers,* 1971, p. 117.

59. Biochemical oxygen demand is the measure of the dissolved oxygen in water required to degrade biologically the organic polluting matter.
A few communities have already experimented with the taxing principle. When Springfield, Missouri, imposed a waste-treatment charge of $1,400 a month on a meat packing plant, the latter altered its operations so that the charge was reduced to $225. Otsego, Michigan, initiated a charge on a large corporation that was overburdening the municipal sewage system, and the company very quickly cut its discharge from 1,500 pounds of BOD daily to 900 pounds, and to 500 pounds within another three months. *Business Week,* September 4, 1971.
A succinct statement of the pollution-tax idea is provided by Robert M. Solow, "The Economist's Approach to Pollution and Its Control," *Science,* CLXXIII (August 6, 1971), 498–503.

60. *Business Week,* May 19, 1973, p. 78.

61. René Dubos, *Man Adapting* (New Haven: Yale University Press, 1965), p. 224. Quoted with permission.

62. Merrill Eisenbud, professor of environmental medicine, New York University Medical Center, "Environmental Protection in the City of New York," *Science,* CLXX (November 13, 1970), 708. Similarly, Dubos comments that "knowledge concerning the medical significance of the pollution problem is still extremely scant. In most cases, knowledge hardly goes beyond the description of a few *immediate* pathological responses. Hardly anything is known of the *delayed* effects of pollutants on human life, even though they probably constitute the most important threats to health in the long run." *Man Adapting,* p. 220. Quoted with permission.

63. *The New York Times,* April 23, 1972.

64. Edward Hoagland, "Looking for Wilderness," *Atlantic Monthly,* August 1972, p. 41.

65. "Improving the Quality of Life," p. 12.

66. *Economic Report of the President and the Annual Report of the Council of Economic Advisers, 1971,* p. 114.

67. Ansley J. Coale, "Man and His Environment," *Science,* CLXX (October 9, 1970), 133.

68. Dubos, *Man Adapting,* p. 368. Quoted with permission.

69. *The Ecologist,* January 1972, pp. 14–17.

70. Thus, even Robert M. Solow, surely a reasonable economist, argues that however much the resulting system of prices might seem to impinge most harshly on the poor, that should not be allowed to muddy the economic principle involved, but instead should be provided for by a separate system of taxation that would redistribute income from the wealthy to the poor, enabling them to buy the necessities that effluent or materials-use charges had made expensive. Solow, "The Economists Approach to Pollution and Its Control."

71. When the Nixon Administration readied a bill that would have taxed the sulfur content of fuel, it originally proposed that the revenues should go into a special fund for pollution research. Opposition of the Treasury Department led to a revision that would channel revenues into the general treasury. *Business Week,* September 4, 1971, p. 78.

72. Solow, "The Economist's Approach to Pollution and Its Control," p. 500.

Notes

73. Walter Heller, "Economic Growth and Ecology—an Economist's View," *Monthly Labor Review*, XCIV (November 1971), 19–20. Solow makes the same point in the reference previously cited.

74. Ibid., p. 14.

75. William Ramsay and Claude Anderson, *Managing the Environment* (New York: Basic Books, 1972), p. 103.

76. Translated from Elie Halevy, *La Formation du Radicalisme Philosophe* (Paris: Germer Bailliere, 1901), vol. 1, p. 412.

77. Ramsay and Anderson, *Managing the Environment*, p. 105.

78. Ibid., pp. 113–115.

79. Commoner, *The Closing Circle*, pp. 197–198.

80. Carl H. Madden, "A New Knowledge Strategy," *Looking Ahead*, National Planning Association, May 1972, p. 2.

81. Dubos, *Man Adapting*, pp. 278–279. Quoted with permission.

82. Richard Gonzalez, "An Economist Talks about Zero Growth," *The Humble Way*, First Quarter 1972, p. 27. Though Gonzalez is a former Humble Oil official, his observations are quite compatible with general economic thought on pollution and depletion.

83. René Dubos, "Reports of the Death of New York Are Greatly . . ." *The American Scholar*, XLI, No. 2 (Spring 1972), 188.

84. Solow, "The Economist's Approach to Pollution and Its Control," p. 501.

85. Commoner, *Closing the Circle*, p. 300.

86. Dubos, *Reason Awake*, p. 198.

87. Heller, "Economic Growth and Ecology," p. 16.

88. The attitude of the Chinese representative to the United Nations conference on the environment, convened in Stockholm in 1972, is instructive and depressing in this respect. As reported by Nigel Hawkes in *Science*, CLXXVI (June 23, 1972), p. 1309, the Chinese vice-minister of fuel and chemical industries, Tang Ke, "expounded the view that the expansion of population was unimportant, that resources were inexhaustible, and that the pollution resulting from industrial expansion could always be cleaned up by more technology. Tang came out for uninhibited development and hang the consequences: 'One does not stop eating for fear of choking,' he remarked, a thought almost worthy of Chairman Mao himself."

89. Athelstan Spilhaus, "The Next Industrial Revolution," *The Conference Board Record*, February 1970, p. 39.

90. Henry Ford II, in an address before the annual convention of Sigma Delta Chi, professional journalistic society, Chicago, Illinois, November 13, 1970.

[4]
THE CORPORATION AND ITS INTERNAL COMMUNITY

1. A. A. Berle, *Twentieth-Century Capitalist Revolution* (London: Macmillan, 1955), chap. 3, presents a strong case for this position.

2. An interesting example of this transition is provided by Sam Bass Warner, Jr., in *The Private City* (Philadelphia: University of Pennsylvania Press, 1968), which contrasts that city in three different periods. In describing eighteenth-century Philadelphia, he writes (p. 6): ". . . this Philadelphia was a town of entrepreneurs. Artisans sewed shoes, made wagons, boiled soap, or laid bricks for customers who had already placed an order. Workers did not labor under the close price and time discipline of manufacture for large-scale inventories or big speculative wholesale markets. Most Philadelphians were either independent contractors hiring out on a job-by-job basis, or they were artisan shopkeepers retailing the products of their work." Then writing of the nineteenth-century city (pp. 63–64): ". . . specialization and rationalization of traditional tasks were the key elements in the first stage of industrialization."

3. *The New York Times*, January 23, 1972.

4. William Serrin, "The Assembly Line," *Atlantic Monthly*, October 1971, p. 63.

5. I raise a speculative question as to whether the lush bonus and stock-purchase plans that many top managements have engineered for themselves are not a subconscious effort to identify themselves with the balance sheet. Referred to as "incentive compensation," it may be more akin to conscience money, something to rationalize the otherwise irrational—their preoccupation with enriching an army of uninvolved stockholders.

6. *The New York Times.* January 23, 1972.

7. Serrin, "The Assembly Line," p. 68, quoting Kenneth Bannon of the UAW. Serrin adds that neither management *nor the UAW* have taken the proposal seriously. Workers at the GM Lordstown plant made similar suggestions, referring to Swedish experience, but this was pure daydreaming in a plant that was called the most modern and sophisticated in the world.

8. *The New York Times,* June 19, 1972.

9. *The New York Times,* January 23, 1972.

10. Richard Todd, "Notes on Corporate Man," *Atlantic Monthly,* October 1971, p. 93.

11. Harold M. F. Rush, *Job Design for Motivation* (New York: The Conference Board, 1971), p. 18. Quoted with permission.

12. Ibid., p. 21. Quoted with permission.

13. Ibid., p. 25. Quoted with permission.

14. Ibid., p. 19. Quoted with permission.

15. Todd, "Notes on Corporate Man," pp. 92–93.

16. Rush, "Job Design for Motivation," p. 10. Quoted with permission.

17. Alan Harrington has given a contemporary version of this in his *Life in the Crystal Palace* (New York: Alfred A. Knopf, 1959). Some readers will be reminded of Aldous Huxley's *Brave New World,* which for all its lack of literary merit continues to be widely read.

[5]
CORPORATIONS AND EDUCATION

1. Grant Venn, *Man, Education, and Work* (Washington: American Council on Education, 1964), p. 46.

2. Ibid., p. 46.

3. Marcia Freedman provides a good account of this phase of U.S. educational development in "Business and Education," in *The Business of America,* ed. Ivar Berg (New York: Harcourt, Brace & World, 1968), pp. 367–369.

4. E. Digby Baltzell, "The American Aristocrat and Other-Direction," in *Culture and Social Character,* ed. S. M. Lipset and Leo Lowenthal (New York: Free Press, 1961), p. 270.

5. Colin Greer, *The Great School Legend* (New York: Basic Books, 1972), pp. 74–75. Greer quotes Mann:

> Finally, in regard to those who possess the largest shares in the stock of worldly goods, could there, in your opinion, be any police so vigilant and effective, for the protection of all rights of person, property and character, as such a sound and comprehensive education and training as our system of common schools could be made to impart; and would not the payment of a sufficient tax to make such education and training universal, be the cheapest means of self-protection and insurance?

6. Venn, *Man, Education, and Work,* p. 48.

7. The first study was by F. W. Taussig and S. C. Joslyn, *American Business Leaders* (New York: Macmillan, 1932). The second was by W. Lloyd Warner and James C. Abegglen, *Occupational Mobility in American Business and Industry* (Minneapolis: University of Minnesota Press, 1955). Other less extensive studies have given generally comparable trend indications.

8. Among the best discussions of the role of the business school in the United States are Robert A. Gordon and James E. Howell, *Higher Education for Business* (New York: Columbia University Press, 1959); Frank Pierson, *The Education of*

American Businessmen (New York: McGraw-Hill, 1959); and Morrell Heald, *The Social Responsibility of Business* (Cleveland, Ohio: The Press of Case Western University, 1970), pp. 70–82.

9. *Report of the National Advisory Commission on Civil Disorders* (Washington, D.C.: Government Printing Office, 1968), p. 118.

10. Patricia Leavey Hodge and Philip M. Hauser, *The Challenge of America's Metropolitan Population Outlook—1960 to 1985*, Research Report No. 3, prepared for the National Commission on Urban Problems (Washington, D.C.: Government Printing Office, 1968), p. 58.

11. *Racial Isolation in the Public Schools*, Report of the U.S. Commission on Civil Rights, vol. 1 (Washington, D.C.: Government Printing Office, 1967), p. 199.

12. Thus from the National Advisory Commission on Civil Disorders: "New office buildings have risen in the downtowns of large cities, often near all-Negro areas. But the outflow of manufacturing and retailing facilities normally offsets this addition significantly—and in many cases has caused a net loss of jobs in central cities while the new white collar jobs are often not available to ghetto residents."

13. From Bettye K. Eidson, "Major Employers and their Manpower Policies," in "Between Black and White—the Faces of American Institutions in the Ghetto," by Peter Rossi and others, *Supplemental Studies for the National Advisory Commission on Civil Disorders* (Washington, D.C.: Government Printing Office, 1968), pp. 116–123.

14. U.S. Chamber of Commerce, *The Disadvantaged Poor: Education and Employment* (Washington, D.C., 1966).

15. Freedman, "Business and Education," p. 368.

16. Freedman remarks (ibid, p. 370): ". . . the structure of production, rather than any conscious assumption of role, has been responsible for the rejection by business of the school as the site for blue-collar training. For the most part the internal labor market of a large firm provides it with sufficient unskilled manpower."

17. From the annual report of the National Alliance of Businessmen, 1969, reprinted in *The Jobs Program*, a report prepared for the Subcommittee on Employment, Manpower, and Poverty of the Senate Committee on Labor and Public Welfare, 91st Cong., 2d sess. (1970), p. 8.

18. E. F. Shelley and Co., *Private Industry and the Disadvantaged Worker* (New York, 1969).

19. A useful survey of experience in some of these early programs has been provided by Elliot Carlson, "Education and Industry: Troubled Partnership," *Saturday Review*, August 15, 1970, pp. 45–47, 58–60.

20. Venn, *Man, Education, and Work*, p. 17.

21. Charles R. DeCarlo and Ormsbee W. Robinson, *Education in Business and Industry* (New York: The Center for Applied Research in Education, 1966), p. 80.

22. Baltzell, "The American Aristocrat and Other-Direction," p. 278.

23. Ibid., p. 279.

24. U.S. Equal Employment Opportunity Commission, *Help Wanted . . . Or Is It?*

25. Thus Athelstan Spilhaus: "We industrial revolutionaries must plan to move more and more into the fields of human service, and not abrogate this to the so-called public sector. . . . If private enterprise is not to dwindle, while the public sector grows to be an all-embracing octopus, then private enterprise must go into the human services field. Could not a corporation run a school system? It certainly could be no worse than the way some are being run today." Spilhaus, "The Next Industrial Revolution," *The Conference Board Record*, February 1970, p. 39.

[6]

CORPORATIONS AND THE CIVIC COMMUNITY

1. Percival Goodman, "The Concept of Community and the Size for a City," in *Urban America: Goals and Problems*, Materials Compiled and Prepared for the Sub-

committee on Urban Affairs of the Joint Economic Committee of Congress (Washington, D.C.: Government Printing Office, 1967), p. 59.

2. Sam Bass Warner, Jr., *The Private City* (Philadelphia: University of Pennsylvania Press, 1968), pp. 10–11. Quoted with permission.

3. Alexis de Tocqueville, *Democracy in America*, ed. Phillips Bradley (New York: Alfred A. Knopf, 1945), vol. I, p. 387. Indeed, Tocqueville believed that to free the slaves, but to continue to subject them to a degrading white superiority, would be intolerable. "One can understand slavery, but how allow several millions of *citizens* to exist under a load of eternal infamy and hereditary wretchedness?" (p. 388, italics added).

4. Warner, *The Private City*, p. 9. Quoted with permission.

5. Ibid., p. xi. Quoted with permission.

6. John R. Commons, "American Shoemakers, 1648–1895: A Sketch of Industrial Evolution," *Quarterly Journal of Economics*, November 1919, pp. 39–84.

7. Elting Morison writes of this period in *Men, Machines, and Modern Times* (Cambridge, Mass.: The MIT Press, 1966), chap. 7.

8. Warner, *The Private City*, pp. 68–71. Quoted with permission.

9. Ibid., pp. 82–85. Quoted with permission.

10. David Rogers and Melvin Zimet discuss this aspect in "The Corporation and the Community: Perspectives and Recent Developments," in *The Business of America*, ed. Ivar Berg (New York: Harcourt, Brace & World, 1968), pp. 44–45. William H. Whyte has developed the matter at greater length in his perceptive, if somewhat polemical, study, *Organization Man* (New York: Doubleday Anchor Books, 1956).

11. Richard J. Whalen, "A City Destroying Itself," *Fortune*, September 1964, pp. 116, 119, 121. Quoted by the courtesy of *Fortune*.

12. *The New York Times*, October 15, 1970.

13. Quoted in *The New York Times*, June 3, 1970.

14. Norton Long, *The Unwalled City* (New York: Basic Books, 1972), p. 127.

15. Edward N. Costikyan, "Who Runs the City Government?" *New York*, May 26, 1969, p. 40.

16. Long, *The Unwalled City*, p. 127.

17. Warner, *The Private City*, p. 173.

18. National Commission on the Causes and Prevention of Crime, excerpts from its statement on "Violent Crime," *The New York Times*, November 24, 1969.

19. "Corporations Make Politics Their Business," *Fortune*, December 1959, p. 223.

20. Ibid.

21. The story is told in S. Prakash Sethi, *Up Against the Corporate Wall* (Englewood Cliffs, N.J.: Prentice-Hall, 1971), pp. 107–128.

22. Judson Gooding, "Roadblocks Ahead for the Great Corporate Move-Out," *Fortune*, June 1972, p. 170.

23. Joseph W. McGuire and John B. Parrish, "Status Report on a Profound Revolution," *California Management Review*, XIII (Summer 1971), 79.

24. Homer C. Wadsworth, president, Kansas City Association of Trusts and Foundations, "Goals and Social Planning," *Urban America: Goals and Problems*, p. 55.

25. Milton Kottler, "Two Essays on the Neighborhood Corporation," *Urban America: Goals and Problems*, p. 179.

26. Robert B. Choate, "Responsibilities of the Private Sector," *Urban America: Goals and Problems*, pp. 299–300.

27. Long, *The Unwalled City*, p. 183.

28. *The New York Times*, November 10, 1970.

29. Quoted in McGuire and Parrish, "Status Report on a Profound Revolution," p. 86.

30. James Rouse, president, Urban America, Inc., "The Role of the Private Sector in Urban Problems," *Urban America: Goals and Problems*, pp. 284–285.

31. Daniel P. Moynihan, "A Symposium on Urban Problems," *The MBA*, February 1968, p. 43.

[7]
THE CORPORATION AND NATIONAL OBJECTIVES

1. John P. Davis, *Corporations* (New York: Capricorn Books, 1961), vol. II, p. 248. This study, completed in 1897, was first published in 1904. Davis, in classifying modern corporations, lists the political, eleemosynary, educational, scientific, religious, social-fraternal, and economic. In the economic category he distinguishes improvement, transportation, banking, insurance, trust and investment, and commercial companies. Under commercial companies he includes corporations for mining, agriculture, manufacturing, and trading, and comments: "The term 'private corporations' is commonly used to describe them. . . . A few of them are found in the history of the eighteenth century, but they were almost universally monopolistic in character, formed by individuals and sanctioned by the state for the purpose of protecting or promoting the use of improved processes or inventions, or to encourage the development of the natural resources of localities. With a few such exceptions, all of the class belong to the nineteenth and twentieth centuries and have multiplied most rapidly since 1850" (pp. 259–260).

2. Ibid., vol. II, p. 269.

3. James Willard Hurst, *The Legitimacy of the Business Corporation* (Charlottesville, Virginia: University Press of Virginia, 1970), p. 70.

4. Murray Weidenbaum, *The Modern Public Sector* (New York: Basic Books, 1969), p. 36. Weidenbaum served as assistant secretary of the treasury for economic policy in the Nixon Administration.

5. Ibid., p. 37.

6. Thus in opening bids for a "space shuttle orbiter," the government asked competing companies "to submit details on how many jobs that each estimates the contract would generate, with a geographic breakdown of where the jobs would be." *Business Week*, July 15, 1972, p. 32.

7. Weidenbaum, *The Modern Public Sector*, p. 33.

8. *Subsidy and Subsidy-Effect Programs of the U.S. Government*, materials prepared for the Joint Economic Committee of Congress (Washington, D.C.: Government Printing Office, 1965), p. 86.

9. Paul W. McCracken, quoted in *Business Week*, February 13, 1971, p. 22.

10. Henry Ford II, in an address before the Harvard Business School Public Affairs Forum, December 2, 1969.

11. Eli Goldston, "New Prospects for American Business," *Daedalus*, Winter 1969, p. 86.

12. Stephen S. Cohen, *Modern Capitalist Planning: The French Model* (Cambridge, Mass: Harvard University Press, 1969), p. 163.

13. Earl Cheit, ed., *The Business Establishment* (New York: John Wiley, 1964), p. 181.

14. Davis, *Corporations*, vol. II, pp. 279–280.

15. The speaker was Irwin Miller, chairman of the Cummins Engine Company, addressing the 73rd Congress of American industry, sponsored by the National Association of Manufacturers, December 5, 1968. It should be noted that Miller was speaking from humility rather than bravado. The paragraph of which the sentences quoted in the text constitute the introduction continues: "Will we remain content with our relatively pleasant position and concentrate our efforts on a holding operation? If we pursue *selfish* interest, there is no reason to suspect we will not meet the fate of all other power groups in history which pursued selfish interest. Or will we pursue *self*-interest? In clear recognition that we can flourish only in a thoroughly healthy society, will we place national interest above our own immediate advantage and lead the country in a wise, far-sighted attack upon its grave and critical weaknesses? Government, in all probability, will not step out and lead, and I am well aware that for a political candidate to propose seriously what we have just talked about might well be political death for him."

16. Thus Republican party strategists, preparing for the 1972 national elections, proposed that during the campaign "the Administration will deal forcefully with

both friends and foes to head off any economic developments that could slow its 1972 reelection drive. . . . Any major visible industry that seeks a price increase will get the same treatment that the auto industry got when the White House this week cracked down on auto prices and forced Detroit to scale back proposed price increases." *Business Week*, August 26, 1972, p. 17.

17. *Business Week*, December 25, 1971, pp. 36–39.

[8]
THE CORPORATION AND INTERNATIONAL RELATIONS

1. George W. Ball, "Cosmocorp: The Importance of Being Stateless," *Columbia Journal of World Business*, November–December 1967, p. 26.

2. Raymond Vernon, *Sovereignty at Bay* (New York: Basic Books, 1971), p. 61.

3. Frederic G. Donner, *The World-Wide Industrial Enterprise* (New York: McGraw-Hill, 1967), pp. 12–22.

4. Vernon, *Sovereignty at Bay*, p. 63, with tabular presentation on p. 64.

5. *Economic and Political Aspects of International Cartels*, a study made for the Subcommittee on War Mobilization, Committee on Military Affairs, United States Senate, 78th Cong., 2d sess. (Washington, D.C.: Government Printing Office, 1944), pp. 4–9.

6. Antonie T. Knoppers, "The Role of Science and Technology in Atlantic Economic Relationships," The Atlantic Institute, Boulogne-sur-Seine, 1967, pp. 8–12.

7. Raymond Vernon, *Fortune*, January 1972, p. 120.

8. "A Rougher Road for Multinationals," *Business Week*, December 19, 1970, p. 57.

9. Donner, *The World-Wide Industrial Enterprise*, pp. 35–36.

10. Allan W. Johnstone documents this with respect to home-office control over subsidiaries in France in *United States Direct Investment in France* (Cambridge, Mass.: The MIT Press, 1965), pp. 63–66. These strategic decisions may, indeed, so curb the discretion of companies in the first category, operating with more decentralized organizational structures, that this category can be, and has been, regarded as only an historical stage. In this view, multinational corporations will all wind up as "global scanners," with a centralized decision-making headquarters exercising the same planning controls over its foreign subsidiaries as it does over its domestic plants. This appears to be the view of Raymond Vernon, in *Sovereignty at Bay*, pp. 107–108. This may be true in degree, but I would impute a categorical difference to the operations of a Coca-Cola bottler in Uganda or Italy, on the one hand, and those of the assemblers and component makers of IBM electric typewriters in Europe or of GM cars in South Africa, on the other.

11. Tilford Gaines, "Economic Report: U.S. Business Abroad," Manufacturers Hanover Trust, March 1969, p. 2.

12. This and the other quotations in this paragraph are from Jack N. Behrman, a former Assistant Secretary of Commerce, "Multinational Corporations, Transnational Interests and National Sovereignty," *Columbia Journal of World Business*, March–April 1969, pp. 19–20. The quotation from *Le Monde*, cited in the same article, is from the issue of January 5, 1967.

13. *The New York Times*, April 19, 1972.

14. *Wall Street Journal*, April 24, 1972; also *The New York Times*, February 9, 1972.

15. William R. Hoskins, "The LDC and the MNC: Will They Develop Together?" *Columbia Journal of World Business*, September–October 1971, p. 64.

16. *Wall Street Journal*, April 24, 1972; *The New York Times*, April 19, 1972. It is not surprising that President Harold S. Geneen quoted Connally favorably at the annual meeting of the International Telephone and Telegraph Corporation, May 10, 1972. ITT had only shortly before been reported as seeking to influence U.S. foreign policy in Chile, with a view to undermining the position of Salvador Allende, an avowed Marxist, when he was seeking the presidency of Chile and was threatening expropriation of foreign interests, including ITT.

17. Behrman, "Multinational Corporations, Transnational Interests and National Sovereignty," p. 17.

18. Carl A. Gerstacker, at the White House Conference on the Industrial World Ahead, February 7, 1972, *The New York Times,* February 9 and February 13, 1972.

19. *The New York Times,* February 7, 1968.

20. When the Ford Motor Company acquired full control of its British operation it adopted the position: We are an American company, but we are run in Britain by Britons. To this the response has been given: "Detroit's 1960 guarantee to the British Government when it sought 100 percent of Ford U.K.—the promise that 'the majority' of Ford U.K.'s management would remain British—has not been broken. It was irrelevant. . . . Only four Americans are on the ruling Policy Board of 15, but they are the men with power." Kenneth Simmonds, "Multinational? Well, Not Quite!" *Columbia Journal of World Business,* Fall 1966, p. 121.

21. Rex Winsbury, "The Shape of America's Challenge," *Management Today,* February 1967, p. 48.

22. Omer Voss, quoted in Sanford Rose, "The Rewarding Strategies of Multinationalism," *Fortune,* September 15, 1968, p. 104.

23. Such charges were elaborated by Heribert Maier, head of the Economic, Social and Political Department of the International Confederation of Free Trade Unions before the Joint Economic Committee, United States Congress. *ICFTU Economic and Social Bulletin,* XVIII (August 1970).

24. India provides an example of this bargaining weakness on the part of a developing economy in the period following independence.

> Since, in the early stages of development, India required foreign investment and technology at any cost, foreign investment was welcomed almost without restrictions. The conditions imposed by foreign investors in retrospect appear rather stringent but were accepted because there were hardly any alternatives. Many foreign investors were allowed to stipulate conditions with regard to exports from India of the goods manufactured, sources of supply of raw materials, plant and machinery as well as the range of products that could be manufactured.
>
> Nearly half of the agreements which were implemented imposed one restriction or another. More than 45% required the foreign participant's permission for exports to third countries or allowed exports only to specified regions. Agreements with foreign firms thus became an obstacle to greater export effort, which was essential to repay debt obligations both on official and private accounts as well as to pay for the importation of essential raw materials and capital goods.
>
> About 15% of the agreements stipulated restrictions on the sources of supply of raw materials, plant and machinery. This obviously meant an increase in capital costs as well as operating expenditures. Thus, although foreign participation assisted India's development effort by supplying technology and capital, there were also factors that tended to reduce its effectiveness. Besides, there was a large outflow of foreign exchange through remittances of dividends, royalties and technical fees.

Bharat Ram, "India Sets the Guidelines for Foreign Investment," *Columbia Journal of World Business,* July–August 1970, p. 24.

25. Ball, "Cosmocorp: The Importance of Being Stateless," p. 27.

26. Winsbury, "The Shape of America's Challenge," p. 54.

27. Sanford Rose, "The Rewarding Strategies of Multinationalism," p. 104.

28. As one example of the employment effect, Professor John H. Dunning of Reading University concludes that in "the less prosperous areas of Wales, Scotland and North East England" U.S. firms "are currently providing jobs for about 125,000 people." Dunning, "U.S. Direct Investment in the United Kingdom and National Economic Objectives," *Banco Nazionale del Lavoro Quarterly Review,* March 1971, p. 51.

29. Donner, *The World-Wide Industrial Enterprise,* p. 95.

30. Vernon comments on these points in *Sovereignty at Bay,* pp. 244–245.

31. Behrman, "Multinational Corporations, Transnational Interests and National Sovereignty," p. 18.

32. Winsbury, "The Shape of America's Challenge," p. 54.

33. Vernon, *Sovereignty at Bay*, p. 247.

34. Gaines, "Economic Report: U.S. Business Abroad," p. 3.

35. From "Declaration of the IMF World Auto Company Councils, London, March 23–25, 1971," *ICFTU Economic and Social Bulletin*, XIX (May–June, 1971), p. 7. The same declaration comments:

> Operating on the basis of centralized decisions made in complete disregard of national loyalties and social responsibilities, they play a divide and rule game calculated to pit each national group of workers against the others to the mutual harm of all and to involve governments in demeaning competition for their favors. To intimidate workers and governments they use without inhibitions the threat to move investments and jobs elsewhere, unless they obtain submission to their dictates concerning wages, working conditions, legislation, regulations, taxation or government subsidies.

36. Gus Tyler, assistant president of the International Ladies' Garment Workers' Union, "Multinationals: A Global Menace," *AFL-CIO American Federationist*, July 1972, p. 1.

37. "The Unions Move Against the Multinationals," *Business Week*, July 24, 1971, p. 49.

Although Vernon (*Sovereignty at Bay*) appears skeptical of the unions' claims (p. 189), he concedes: "The multinational corporation is strong and supple. When confronted as an adversary, it seems to have options that U.S. labor does not, such as the option to move its production abroad. From labor's viewpoint, the hand of management is strengthened by the existence of the options, whether or not they are exercised." (p. 190).

38. These are the conclusions of Professor Robert Stobaugh of the Harvard Graduate School of Business Administration, for example. *Fortune*, February 1972, pp. 62–63.

39. This point has been nicely argued by Robert d'A. Shaw, "Foreign Investment and Global Labor," *Columbia Journal of World Business*, July–August 1971, pp. 52–62. "The transfer of the most modern technology can now be done with almost no time lag, so that a corporation can almost immediately send production facilities involving sophisticated technology abroad and train workers there to manufacture products with lower unit labor costs. Ford-Philco, for example, developed a new series of minicircuits and initiated production in Taiwan. . . . Bendix transferred the assembly of some aircraft components from Pennsylvania to Matamoros in Mexico; recently the Mexican plant has begun to machine the components as well."

40. Gaines, "Economic Report: U.S. Business Abroad," p. 2. Italics supplied.

41. Frederic G. Donner, "The World-wide Corporation in a Modern Economy," address before the 8th International Congress of Accountants, New York, September 27, 1962, p. 17.

42. Carl A. Gerstacker, at the White House Conference on the Industrial World Ahead, February 7, 1972, reported in *The New York Times*, February 9 and February 13, 1972.

43. Frank Tannenbaum, "The Survival of the Fittest," *Columbia Journal of World Business*, March–April 1968, pp. 18–19.

44. Charles Stewart, "Business and American Foreign Relations," in *The Business of America*, ed. Ivar Berg (New York: Harcourt, Brace & World, 1968), p. 122.

45. Knoppers, "The Role of Science and Technology in Atlantic Economic Relationships," p. 20.

46. Sidney E. Rolfe, quoted in "A Rougher Road for Multinationals," *Business Week*, December 19, 1970, p. 59.

47. Tannenbaum, "The Survival of the Fittest," pp. 19–20. By speaking of corporate bodies instead of multinational corporations, Tannenbaum obviously intended to keep open the door for other than business loyalties. But in the context of his article, he clearly is writing of industrial corporate bodies, and I would presume he used the broader term primarily to permit the inclusion of multinational labor unions, because he himself came out of a labor-oriented background.

Presumably the halfway stage to this supersession of national loyalties by corporate loyalties is where the two compete for primacy within the individual—the situation experienced today by many a foreign executive of a multinational subsidiary, and humorously illustrated in a story retold by Vernon (*Sovereignty at Bay*, pp. 149–150): "According to one tale, the victorious leader of a company of Nazi tanks, whose peacetime job had been the direction of the National Cash Register subsidiary in Berlin, marked his entry into Paris by pledging his unbounded cooperation to the crushed and defeated French manager of the Paris office of the company."

48. Quoted by Henry H. Fowler, "National Interests and Multinational Business," in *Multinational Corporate Planning*, ed. George A. Steiner and Warren M. Cannon (New York: Macmillan, 1966), p. 125.

49. Arnold Toynbee, "How Did We Get This Way—and Where Are We Going?" in *Management's Mission in a New Society*, ed. Dan H. Fenn (New York: McGraw-Hill, 1959), p. 16.

50. Roy A. Matthews, "The International Economy and the Nation State," *Columbia Journal of World Business*, November–December 1971, p. 60. Matthews continues: "Thus the multinational corporation, while having the potential to play a most useful role in the restructuring of our political order, must gear its own evolution to the momentum and direction of other forces. While the ramifications of technique are certainly transcending national boundaries, they have in no way obscured the industrial nation state as the focus for political action."

51. Editorial, *Business Week*, December 19, 1970, p. 146.

52. Ball, "Cosmocorp: The Importance of Being Stateless," p. 29.

53. Heribert Maier, in the *ICFTU Economic and Social Bulletin*, XVIII (August 1970), 4.

54. Raymond Vernon, while skeptical of any imminent movement in this direction, nevertheless concludes: "The basic asymmetry between multinational enterprises and national governments may be tolerable up to a point, but beyond that point there is a need to reestablish balance. When this occurs, the response is bound to have some of the elements of the world corporation concept: accountability to some body, charged with weighing the activities of the multinational enterprise against a set of social yardsticks that are multinational in scope." Vernon, *Sovereignty at Bay*, p. 284.

[9]
THE GOVERNMENT OF THE CORPORATION

1. *Manice v. Powell*, 201 N.Y. 194, 201 (1911).

2. Abram Chayes, "The Modern Corporation and the Rule of Law," in *The Corporation in Modern Society*, ed. Edward S. Mason (Cambridge, Mass.: Harvard University Press, 1959), p. 39.

3. Ibid.

4. Adolf A. Berle, Jr., and Gardiner C. Means, *The Modern Corporation and Private Property* (New York: Macmillan, 1932).

5. Theoretically, directors can be nominated from the floor at stockholder meetings, but practically this is an exercise in futility. The 1970 General Motors annual meeting, which attracted national attention because reform groups were attempting to initiate changes in the form of corporate government, was attended by only 700 of the company's more than 1,350,000 shareholders. For nominations made from the floor, the highest number of votes recorded was 850. For management's candidates, the lowest vote tallied was 237 million—most by proxies.

6. Courtney C. Brown and E. Everett Smith, *The Director Looks at His Job* (New York: Columbia University Press, 1957), p. 17.

7. Adolf A. Berle, Jr., and Gardiner C. Means, "Corporation," in *Encyclopedia of the Social Sciences* (New York: Macmillan, 1944), vol. IV, p. 421.

8. Ibid., p. 418.

9. Robert J. Larner, "Ownership and Control of the 200 Largest Nonfinancial Corporations, 1929 and 1963," *American Economic Review*, LVI (September 1966), 777–787.

10. Robert Townsend, a former chief executive of Avis Corporation, in reviewing a book on the Penn Central failure, commented:

> The P. C. [Penn Central] directors were fairly typical as I look over the list: decent, well-meaning people of average intelligence. But they were precluded by the force of custom from doing their jobs. It is considered rude to ask and pursue answers to questions that might embarrass the chief executive. It is bad form—out of bounds—simply not done, old man. A director who joined the P. C. board in December 1969, too late to have much effect, is quoted as saying:
> "They sat up there on the 18th floor in those big chairs with the [brass name-] plates on them and they were a bunch of, well, I'd better not say it. . . . They took their fees and they didn't do anything. Over a period of years, people just sat there. That poor man from the University of Pennsylvania [Gaylord P. Harnwell], he never opened his mouth. They didn't know the factual picture and they didn't try to find out." Book review, *The New York Times*, December 12, 1971, pp. 40–41.

A more recent general study confirming this picture has been provided by Myles L. Mace, *Directors: Myth and Reality* (Boston, Mass.: Harvard Graduate School of Business Administration, 1971).

11. Melvin T. Copeland and Andrew R. Towl have made this point in *The Board of Directors and Business Management* (Boston, Mass.: Harvard Graduate School of Business Administration, 1947), especially pp. 33–36, 43, 52–57, 65–66, and 71–72.

12. David L. Ratner, "The Government of Business Corporations: Critical Reflections on the Rule of 'One Share, One Vote,'" *Cornell Law Review*, LVI (November 1970), 26.

13. A. B. Homer, president of Bethlehem Steel, in *Administered Prices*, hearings before the Subcommittee on Antitrust and Monopoly of the Committee on the Judiciary, U.S. Senate, 85th Cong., 1st sess. (Washington, D.C.: Government Printing Office, 1958), part 2, p. 593.

14. Quoted in Brown and Smith, *The Director Looks at His Job*, pp. 103–104.

15. Lewis H. Brown, "New Objectives of Management," in *The New Outlook in Business*, ed. Bronson Batchelor (New York: 1940), pp. 95–96.

16. Ratner, "The Government of Business Corporations," p. 19.

17. François Bloch-Lainé, *Pour une Reforme de l'Entreprise* (Paris: Editions du Sueil, 1963), pp. 118–119.

18. The present rule covering stockholder proposals is known as Rule 14a-8, issued by the SEC in 1969. Its first formulation goes back to 1942.

19. Donald E. Schwartz, "The Public-Interest Proxy Contest: Reflections on Campaign GM," *Michigan Law Review*, LXIX (January 1971), 452.

20. This and the previous quotation from the court's opinion come from *Medical Committee for Human Rights* v. *Securities and Exchange Commission*, U.S. Court of Appeals for the District of Columbia, No. 23, 105 (Fall 1970), pp. 19–20.

21. Ibid., pp. 24–25.

22. Schwartz, "The Public-Interest Proxy Contest: Reflections on Campaign GM," p. 530. Donald Schwartz was counsel to Campaign GM in its effort to secure certain structural innovations and reforms.

23. Ibid., p. 480.

24. Ibid., p. 481. Schwartz himself harbors the interesting view that the private and public interests of shareholders are likely to become increasingly *less* antithetical. "The great majority of shareholders are affected by corporate decisions more as citizens than as shareholders. With their mounting numbers, the shareholders increasingly represent a cross-section of our society, and if they view their interest as aligned with the general public, then they might serve as surrogate for the community as a whole." Ibid., p. 480. I find this expectation somewhat dubious, partly because it is doubtful whether there is such a thing as "the public interest," but rather a number of interests, and partly because even "little" shareholders, however large their numbers, are often as pecuniarily minded as their bigger brothers. Unions, for example, have not been as celebrated for their social consciousness as for their self-interest.

25. That assiduous counsel for the public-interest reformers, Donald E. Schwartz,

has discussed this in "Corporate Responsibility in the Age of Aquarius," *Business Lawyer*, XXVI (November 1970), 513–526, especially 517.

26. John G. Simon, Charles W. Powers, and Jon P. Gunnemann, *The Ethical Investor: Universities and Corporate Responsibility* (New Haven, Conn.: Yale University Press, 1972).

27. William O. Douglas, *Democracy and Finance* (New Haven, Conn.: Yale University Press, 1940), p. 53.

28. Robert Townsend, book review, *The New York Times Book Review*, December 12, 1971, p. 40.

29. Eileen Shanahan, "Reformer: Urging Business Change," *The New York Times*, January 24, 1971, p. 9.

30. Robert Dahl, "Power to the Workers?" *New York Review of Books*, November 9, 1970, pp. 21, 24.

31. Detlev Vagt, "Reforming the 'Modern' Corporation: Perspectives from the German," *Harvard Law Review*, LXXX (November 1966), 23–89, especially p. 85.

32. Berle and Means, "Corporation," p. 418.

33. Shanahan, "Reformer: Urging Business Change," p. 9.

34. Schwartz, "The Public-Interest Proxy Contest: Reflections on Campaign GM," p. 530.

[10]
THE LIMITS OF CORPORATE RESPONSIBILITY

1. Committee for Economic Development, *Social Responsibilities of Business Corporations* (New York, 1971), pp. 32–33.

2. Ibid., p. 46.

3. Stewart Udall, "The Last Traffic Jam," *Atlantic Monthly*, October 1972, pp. 72–76.

4. *Social Responsibilities of Business Corporations*, p. 59.

[INDEX]

A

Abbott Laboratories, 19
Abegglen, James C., 104, 218
Abrams, Frank W., 111
Adams, Sherman, 6
advertising:
    as institution, 28
    restrictions on, 16–18, 20
affluence:
    effects on pollution, 34–35
Air Quality Act of 1967, 38, 43–44
alienation:
    worker, 82–86
American Bar Association, 18
American creed, 10
American Federation of Labor, 101
American Metal Climax Co., 53
Anderson, Claude, 69–73
Aranow, Edward R., 211
Army Corps of Engineers, 47
Atlantic Richfield Co., 9, 42
automobile pollution, 49, 54

B

balance of payments, 161
Baldwin, Matthias, 123
Ball, George, 154, 164, 176, 225
Baltzell, E. Digby, 102, 111
Bannon, Kenneth, 86, 218
bargaining:
    on regulatory legislation, 44–45
Bay Area Rapid Transit, 57
Bazell, Robert J., 212, 216
Behrman, Jack N., 159, 160, 167, 222, 223

Bentham, Jeremy, 69
Berle, A. A., 181 ,182, 196, 217
Bethlehem Steel Co., 88–89, 183–184
Birmingham, Robert L., 212
blacks:
    attitude toward environmentalism, 55
    employment discrimination, 107
    population shifts, 105–107
Bliven, Bruce Jr., 214, 215
Bloch-Lainé, François, 226
Blough, Roger, 175–176
Boyd, Harper W., 212
Brodeur, Paul, 15, 212, 213
Brown, Lewis H., 185–186, 226
business education, 104
business values, 97
    See also social values
Business Week, 49, 60, 152, 170, 176, 214, 215, 225
Bylinsky, Gene, 214, 216

C

Cameron, Juan, 214, 215
Camp, Charles, 215
Campaign GM, 193, 199
Campbell Soup Co., 12
Caplovitz, David, 29
Carlson, Elliot, 219
Castle & Cooke Co., 212
Catholic church, 205
Chamber of Commerce (U.S.), 15, 22
Chase Manhattan Bank, 35, 38, 45, 65
Chayes, Abram, 180–181
Cheit, Earl, 149
Choate, Robert B., 134, 220

U

Udall, Stewart, 207–208
Union Carbide Corp., 44
unionization:
  cause of, 119
Upton, S. E., 211
Urban Coalition, 109
urban environment:
  corporate influence on, 126–128
  See also cities
USM Corp., 164–165

V

Vagt, Detlev, 196
valuation problems:
  in pollution control, 69–74
values:
  See social values
Venn, Grant, 99, 111, 218, 219
Vernon, Raymond, 155, 157, 165,
  168, 222–225
vocational education, 98–101
  business attitudes toward, 108
Voss, Omer, 163, 223

W

Wadsworth, Homer C., 133–134, 220
Wall Street Journal, 14, 51–52
Warner, Sam Bass Jr., 116–124, 217
Warner, W. Lloyd, 104, 218
Water and Environmental Quality Enforcement Act of 1970, 39

Water Pollution Control Act of 1972, 52, 60
Water Pollution Control Act of 1965, 39
Webster, Daniel, 103
Weidenbaum, Murray, 142–145
welfare, 152–153
  relation to consumption orientation, 29
Western Electric Co., 134–135
Whalen, Richard J., 127, 128
Wharton, Joseph, 105
Wheeler-Lea Act, 12, 18
Whyte, William H., 220
Winsbury, Rex, 163, 164, 167–168, 223
Woodcock, Leonard, 56
Wool Labeling Act, 12
work:
  alienation from, 82–86
  attitudes toward, 94
worker directors, 195–196

X

Xerox, 3, 95, 109

Y

Yale University, 193–194
Yugoslavia, 195

Z

zero discharge, 40, 46, 60
Zimet, Melvin, 220